TWENTIETH CENTURY VIEWS

The aim of this series is to present the best in contemporary critical opinion on major authors, providing a twentieth century perspective on their changing status in an era of profound revaluation.

Maynard Mack, *Series Editor*
Yale University

EDWIN ARLINGTON ROBINSON

A COLLECTION OF CRITICAL ESSAYS

Edited by
Francis Murphy

Prentice-Hall, Inc. A SPECTRUM BOOK *Englewood Cliffs, N. J.*

Quotations from the poetry of Edwin Arlington Robinson used by permission of The Macmillan Company, Charles Scribner's Sons, and the Harvard University Press.

C-13-782011-9; P-13-782003-8. *Library of Congress Catalog Card Number 70-104853*. Printed in the United States of America.

Current printing (last number):
10 9 8 7 6 5 4 3 2 1

PRENTICE-HALL INTERNATIONAL, INC. (*London*)
PRENTICE-HALL OF AUSTRALIA, PTY. LTD. (*Sydney*)
PRENTICE-HALL OF CANADA, LTD. (*Toronto*)
PRENTICE-HALL OF INDIA PRIVATE LIMITED (*New Delhi*)
PRENTICE-HALL OF JAPAN, INC. (*Tokyo*)

Contents

Introduction

by Francis Murphy

Looking at American poetry written between 1865 and 1914, George Santayana complained that for the "average human genteel person, with a heart, a morality, and a religion," there was "no poetry to give him pleasure or to do him honor." Before the Civil War our literature was at least humane, Protestant, "grandmotherly in that sedate spectacled wonder with which it gazed at this terrible world and said how beautiful and how interesting it all was"; after the war there was only Walt Whitman or the aesthetic school, and Whitman was losing ground:

> the genteel manner having become obsolete, and the manner of the great mystical tramp not having taken root, the poetic mind of America suffered a certain dispersion. It was solicited in turn by the seductive aesthetic school, by the influence of Browning, with his historico-dramatic obsessions, by symbolism, by the desperate determination to be expressive even with nothing to express, and by the resolve to write poetry which is not verse, so as to be sure of not writing verse which is not poetry. The spontaneous me has certainly been beaten in the first round by the artistic ego.[1]

Santayana would have found no satisfactory alternative to the aesthetic school in the early work of Edwin Arlington Robinson ("Oh for a poet—for a beacon bright/To rift this changeless glimmer of dead gray . . ."), but almost alone among American poets (E. R. Sill is a distinguished exception), Robinson was working his way out of pre-Raphaelite mellifluousness and discarding the rich adjectives employed by the triple-decker lady poets like Louise Chandler Moulton, Louise Imogen Guiney, and Lizette Woodworth Reese for the more insistent measures and the plainer

[1] George Santayana, "Genteel American Poetry," *New Republic,* III, No. 30 (May 29, 1915), 94–95. Reprinted in Douglas L. Wilson, ed., *The Genteel Tradition* (Cambridge: Harvard University Press, 1967), pp. 72–76.

beauties of the moral style. Santayana, like most American critics, ignored Robinson's *Children of the Night* (1897), *Captain Craig* (1902), and *The Town Down the River* (1910), accomplishments which already showed Robinson as one poet who addressed himself to something other than the heart's needle. In the midst of America's most "inflated" cultural period, Robinson was a nosayer of the first order, a realist, as Morton Zabel once put it, "not only in conscience but in style and diction; in *milieu* as much as in imagery; and this gave him the license to explore the problems of abstract casuistry and moral contradiction which he filed down into that style of attenuated rumination, impassioned hair-splitting, and bleak aphorism which will always remain unmistakably his own." [2]

If life in declining Gardiner, Maine, did not make the boy skeptical of the "bitch-goddess success," life in the Robinson family did. There is little to tell of the external events of Robinson's life, but the internal differences—"where the meanings are"—are only now coming to light. I do not know when Robinson first heard the story of how he was named, but he surely must have learned that his parents, in their disappointment that their third child was a boy, waited six months and finally allowed his name to be pulled from a hat by a visitor from Arlington, Massachusetts. The fact that he was less wanted, however, did not weaken his affection for his two older brothers. Like his father, who retired early to watch his sons grow up, Robinson idolized his brothers, particularly the elder, Dean. What he watched was not their triumph, but their failure: the slow disintegration of one by drugs, the other by alcohol. He wrote to Amy Lowell that "when I was a small child . . . I used to rock myself in a chair many sizes too large for me and wonder why the deuce I should ever have been born. I was indignant about it for several years, but I've got over all that now. . . ."

Robinson was enough of a Puritan to think of poetry as his "calling" and enough of a Yankee to feel guilty all his life that he had been called to a vocation that would have so little value in the eyes of the world. Like Frost, he felt a determination to write that was fierce and uncompromising. The feelings of guilt that he was bound to have must have been most intense in the years after his return to Gardiner from Harvard (where he was enrolled as a special student from 1891 to 1893), when he had to watch the

[2] Morton Dauwen Zabel, "Robinson in America," *Poetry*, XLVI, No. 3 (June, 1935), 157–62. Reprinted in this collection.

deterioration of the whole family and could do nothing about it. Robinson found some consolation in the society of his friends and in the small circle of literary types (a local physician, the local bluestockings) that a town the size of Gardiner in the late 1890s might collect, but he was always to consider himself slightly freakish. To his other family problems must be aded the fact that he fell hopelessly in love with his brother Herman's wife, making the tension at home unbearable. If the facts were not so grim, Robinson's letters to his friend Harry Smith might well be thought to verge on self-pity ("How long do you think a man can live in hell?"); as it is, they show a remarkable degree of self-control. Robinson never played the village parson (or the village atheist) during these years; he wrote, as Frost put it, "of griefs, not grievances," though these sad events made their mark on his spirit as well as his art. Robinson gave up so much for poetry that he seems to have thought of poetry itself as a renunciation, with the result that there is a certain unyielding joylessness in his work, even granting moments of wit and occasional notes of muted wonder.

Robinson left Gardiner in 1897 after an open break with Herman. For a time he was employed at Harvard as a clerk to President Eliot, but he hated the position. After Dean's death in the fall of 1899, he moved to New York. The financial collapse of the family estate left him penniless, dependent almost entirely upon the generosity of his friends. In Theodore Roosevelt he found a sympathetic admirer who came to his aid when he was destitute. Roosevelt's son had introduced his father to *The Children of the Night*. The President became so enthusiastic that he wrote a review of the book to let the public know that in this "glimmer of dead gray" he had found some light.[3] The president did not understand "Luke Havergal," but was "entirely sure" he liked it, and he admired "The House on the Hill" and "Richard Cory." "The Wilderness" was his favorite poem in the volume; it was written, he said, "by a man into whose heart there had entered deep the very spirit of the vast and melancholy northern forests," an observation which tells the reader more about Roosevelt than Robinson, for "The Wilderness" is a poem with greater affinity to early Yeats than to Cooper. But what the review lacked in literary awareness, it made up for in generosity of spirit. Through Roosevelt's efforts,

[3] Theodore Roosevelt, "The Children of the Night," *The Outlook*, LXXX (August 12, 1905), 913–14.

Scribner's reprinted *The Children of the Night* (it was originally published in a small vanity press edition). Scribner's also published Robinson's first commercially distributed volume, *The Town Down the River,* but the sales were so poor that they never published his poetry again. In 1905 Roosevelt provided Robinson with a job in the New York Customs House, where he was free to come and go as he pleased. Robinson stayed on into the change of administrations in 1909, when it seemed advisable to leave.

Until 1921, when Robinson received the Pulitzer Prize for *Collected Poems,* the pattern of his life remained essentially the same. Not that his financial independence changed his routine—until the very end he spent winters in New York and summers in New Hampshire at the MacDowell Colony—but it did allow him to indulge himself in the stock market and to play, however half-heartedly, the role of the man of the world (something his brother Herman had failed at). After years of poverty, no one could begrudge Robinson that. Unfortunately, Robinson's fame made it too easy to publish, year after year, the endless procession of psychological narratives that flowed from his pen. Although they may have seemed, in their sheer bulk, worthy of a Pulitzer Prize winner, they are, by any frank assessment, almost unreadable. Unlike Frost, Robinson never thought of himself as a teacher; he never gave a reading, never delivered a public lecture. There was only the poetry he felt born to write. "To think of oneself as a poet," J. V. Cunningham warns, "has serious consequences. . . . The professed poet must keep writing . . . the role is vatic; the poet must intuit and communicate a meaning in the universe. So Robinson kept asking the inadmissible question, What is it all about? especially considering the pain. That it was unanswerable he thought guaranteed the question." [4] The incredible thing was that the poetry became popular. *Tristram* sold 58,000 copies the first year (1927) and, before Robinson died, well over 100,000. I suspect that the Americans who bought him so eagerly read him for his respectability, not his verse: in contrast to Eliot and Pound he looked substantial enough to trust (*Collected Poems* ultimately ran to fifteen-hundred pages) and sober and difficult enough to seem worthwhile. The praise in his later years could not, however, dissipate the ef-

[4] J. V. Cunningham, "Edwin Arlington Robinson: A Brief Biography," *The University of Denver Quarterly,* III, No. 1 (Spring, 1968), 28–31.

fects of the silence which had surrounded his earlier ones. "The solitary worker," Henry James remarks, "loses the profit of example and discussion; he is apt to make awkward experiments; he is in the nature of the case more or less an empiric. The empiric may, as I say, be treated by the world as an expert; but the drawbacks and discomforts of empiricism remain to him and are in fact increased by the suspicion that is mingled with his gratitude, of a want in the public taste, of a sense of the proportion of things." [5] Like Hawthorne and Faulkner, Robinson went his way alone. And in his isolation lay his weakness as well as his strength.

It was Robinson's peculiar misfortune that he no sooner made his voice heard than his younger readers tired of it. Eliot dismissed him as "negligible"; William Carlos Williams thought the versification "pure stucco": "it loosens nothing for thought, for feeling, for inclusion of a variety of understanding." If he was acknowledged for a period in the twenties as the "best" of American poets, this praise was, as Conrad Aiken notes, "more tacit than express." It is to Aiken's credit that he could cut through the cant of his contemporaries and look at a narrative poetry closer to the fiction of Hawthorne and James than to the poetry of Donne, and admire it just the same. The truth is, Robinson wrote too much for too long. The generation of American critics (so far as I can tell Robinson had and still has no reputation in England)—Blackmur, Tate, Ransom, Wilson—who wrote so well about Yeats and Eliot, sighed a note of despair when assigned to reviewing Robinson. Robinson was such a decent sort, and his reputation so hard won, that it seemed necessary to apologize for a quality of verse that now could be admired only because it offended so little. "The custom has staled," Blackmur wrote, "the variety seems less infinite than academic, and in short, we cannot accept verse which demands even less of our sensibilities than it forces upon them. . . . 'Verse that is too easy is like the tail of a roasted horse.' " Even more surprising than Allen Tate's reference to Robinson as the "most *famous* of living American poets," [6] is his appeal at the end of his review of *Talifer* (1933) for a more honest critical treatment. The fact that "Mr. Robinson is unable to write badly," Tate concludes, "will not excuse us to

[5] Henry James, *Hawthorne* (1879: reprint ed., Ithaca, New York: Cornell University Press, 1956), p. 25.

[6] Italics mine.

posterity."[7] For most of us who went to college after World War II, Tate's remark seemed to have been taken to heart. It would be hard to find a critic who was willing to say Robinson wrote well. Despite the claims of the Literary Guild, Robinson has not been acknowledged as our greatest poet, and the fact that he was writing his weakest poetry at the very time that the most exaggerated claims for his reputation were being publicized has not made his position in modern letters secure.

The one major critic whose admiration of Robinson never seems to have faltered is Yvor Winters. Beginning with his remarkable review of *Collected Poems* (written when he was twenty-one) through *Forms of Discovery* (1968), Winters continued to praise Robinson for the very things that made his work so alien to younger readers: rational progression of thought, absence of sensual imagery, clarity of meaning, and "polished stoniness" of mind. In addition to Winters' early review, I have included a chapter from his book on Robinson (1946). Winters not only sorted out the essential Robinson, but was also enough attracted and repelled by New England piety (first the Congregational and later the Transcendental variety) to remain one of its best critics.

Robinson has been the subject of a number of personal reminiscences and biographical-critical studies. Chard Powers Smith's *Where the Light Falls* seems to me to be the best of these, and no serious student of Robinson will omit looking at Estelle Kaplan's *Philosophy in the Poetry of Edwin Arlington Robinson.* But Robinson is no philosopher, and the fact that he wrote about tragic humanity does not make him a great poet, though I must admit to a strong personal liking for his subjects. As Winters puts it, "Mr. Robinson's greatness lies not in the people of whom he has written, but in the perfect balance, the infallible precision, with which he has stated their cases." We must first be convinced that Robinson is worth reading. I suggest that the reader begin this collection with the essays by Yvor Winters, Louis Coxe, and James Dickey. Without minimizing Robinson's weaknesses, these critics present a convincing case for seeing in him a realistic poet with "a complex symbolic technique," a poet under whose "apparently calm surface many forms are in motion."

If we are to do justice to Robinson's "particularity," J. C. Leven-

[7] Allen Tate, "Edwin Arlington Robinson," *Collected Essays* (Denver: Allen Swallow, 1959), pp. 358–64.

son remarks, "we would do well to understand what he made of the literary conventions and philosophical conceptions that came to him for ready use. Like every major artist, he changed in using them the methods and ideas which were a part of his culture, and at this distance in time, we should be able to discern his originality as well as his traditionalism." Edwin Fussell tests Robinson's ability to "mold the forms he found into a fresh way of saying," with particular reference to the sonnet; Josephine Miles surveys Robinson's diction with an eye to the combination of old and new in his vocabulary; and Warner Berthoff looks at not only Robinson's "verbal resourcefulness" but also the syntax of argument, Robinson's "predicative style." In the essays which conclude this volume, W. R. Robinson, Hyatt Waggoner, and J. C. Levenson explore Robinson's "speculative education," his response to popular culture and the intellectual tradition (with special reference to William James and Josiah Royce) out of which he divined his own modern faith, accommodating old forms of poetry to new forms of thought.

The prevailing tone of Robinson criticism is defensive and slightly apologetic. A taste for Robinson has to be justified. But there are signs of a change. In literature, at least, it is now possible to admire old-fashioned ways of being new. The student will find in Robinson no "gargoyles of memorable phrase," no "startling juxtaposition" of images. Robinson became an acknowledged master of the conventional forms—the sonnet, the dramatic monologue in blank verse, the lyric in the moral style—and they served his purpose well. He had no interest in orchestrating the modern spirit of dissolution. Though he ponders lives spent in uncertainty and doubt, his tightly controlled and deliberately paced lines seem to affirm a final order of experience. "The plain style, the rational statement, the psychological insight, the subdued irony, the high seriousness, and the stubborn persistence," Winters was quick to observe, are Robinson's special virtues. In creating "a body of major poetry" contrary to the manner but not the spirit of the age, Robinson, as James Dickey suggests, "has done what good poets have always done . . . he has forced us to reexamine and finally to define what poetry is . . . and so has enabled poetry itself to include more, to *be* more, than it was before he wrote."

A Cool Master

by Yvor Winters

Near the middle of the last century, Ralph Waldo Emerson, a sentimental philosopher with a genius for a sudden twisted hardness of words, wrote lines like:

> Daughters of Time, the hypocritic days,
> Muffled and dumb like barefoot dervishes,
> And marching single in an endless file,
> Bring diadems and fagots in their hands.

And it was with Emerson that American poetry may be said to have begun. He was slight enough, but at his best a master, and above all a master of sound. And he began a tradition that still exists.

He was followed shortly by Emily Dickinson, a master of a certain dowdy but undeniably effective mannerism, a spinster who may have written her poems to keep time with her broom. A terrible woman, who annihilated God as if He were her neighbor, and her neighbor as if he were God—all with a leaf or a sunbeam that chanced to fall within her sight as she looked out the window or the door during a pause in her sweeping:

> And we, we placed the hair,
> And drew the head erect;
> And then an awful leisure was,
> Our faith to regulate.

The woman at her most terrible had the majesty of an erect corpse, a prophet of unspeakable doom; and she spoke through sealed lips. She was greater than Emerson, was one of the greatest

"A Cool Master" by Yvor Winters. (A review of *Collected Poems of Edwin Arlington Robinson.*) From *Poetry,* XIX, number 5 (1922), 277–88.

poets of our language, but was more or less in the tradition that Emerson began. She and Emerson were probably the only poets of any permanently great importance who occurred in this country during their period.

The tradition of New England hardness has been carried on by Mr. Robinson, in many ways may be said to have reached its pinnacle in Mr. Robinson. This poet, with a wider culture than his predecessors, has linked a suavity of manner to an even greater desperation than that of Dickinson's *The Last Night*—his hardness has become a polished stoniness of vision, of mind.

This man has the culture to know that to those to whom philosophy is comprehensible it is not a matter of the first importance; and he knows that these people are not greatly impressed by a ballyhoo statement of the principles of social or spiritual salvation. A few times he has given his opinion, but quietly and intelligently, and has then passed on to other things. A man's philosophical belief or attitude is certain to be an important part of his milieu, and as a part of his milieu may give rise to perceptions, images. His philosophy becomes a part of his life as does the country in which he was born, and will tinge his vision of the country in which he was born as that country may affect his philosophy. So long as he gives us his own perceptions as they arise in this milieu, he remains an artist. When he becomes more interested in the possible effects of his beliefs upon others, and expounds or persuades, he begins to deal with generalities, concepts (see Croce), and becomes a philosopher, or more than likely a preacher, a mere peddler. This was the fallacy of Whitman and many of the English Victorians, and this is what invalidates nearly all of Whitman's work. Such men forget that it is only the particular, the perception, that is perpetually startling. The generality, or concept, can be pigeon-holed, absorbed, and forgotten. And a ballyhoo statement of a concept is seldom a concise one—it is neither fish nor flesh. That is why Whitman is doomed to an eventual dull vacuum that the intricately delicate mind of Plato will never know.

Much praise has fallen to Mr. Robinson because he deals with people, "humanity"; and this is a fallacy of inaccurate brains. Humanity is simply Mr. Robinson's physical milieu; the thing, the compound of the things, he sees. It is not the material that makes a poem great, but the perception and organization of that material. A pigeon's wing may make as great an image as a man's tragedy, and in the poetry of Mr. Wallace Stevens has done so. Mr. Robinson's greatness lies not in the people of whom he has written, but in the perfect balance, the infallible precision, with which he has stated their cases.

Mr. Robinson's work may be classified roughly in two groups—his blank verse, and his more closely rhymed poems, including the sonnets. Of his blank verse, the *Octaves* in *The Children of the Night* fall curiously into a group by themselves, and will be considered elsewhere in this review. The other poems in blank verse may be called sketches—some of people the poet may have known, some of historical figures, some of legendary—and they have all the evanescence, brittleness, of sketches. However, there are passages in many of these poems that anticipate Robert Frost, who in at least one poem, *An Old Man's Winter Night,* has used this method with greater effect than its innovator, and has created a great poem. Mr. Frost, of course, leaves more of the bark on his rhythms, achieves a sort of implied colloquialism which has already been too much discussed. But with Frost in mind, consider this passage from *Isaac and Archibald:*

> A journey that I made one afternoon
> With Isaac to find out what Archibald
> Was doing with his oats. It was high time
> Those oats were cut, said Isaac; and he feared
> That Archibald—well, he could never feel
> Quite sure of Archibald. Accordingly
> The good old man invited me—that is,
> Permitted me—to go along with him;
> And I, with a small boy's adhesiveness
> To competent old age, got up and went.

The similarity to Frost is marked, as is also the pleasing but not profound quality of the verse. It has a distinction, however, that many contemporaries—French as well as English and American—could acquire to good advantage.

Ben Jonson Entertains a Man from Stratford, a much praised poem, seems largely garrulous, occasionally brilliant, and always brittle; and one can go on making very similar comments on the other poems in this form, until one comes to those alternately praised and lamented poems, *Merlin* and *Lancelot.* Remembering Tennyson, one's first inclination is to name these poems great, and certainly they are not inconsiderable. But there are long passages of purely literary frittering, and passages that, while they may possess a certain clean distinction of manner, are dry and unremunerative enough. But there are passages in these poems which are finer than any other blank verse Mr. Robinson has written—dark, massive lines that rise out of the poem and leave one bitter and empty:

> On Dagonet the silent hand of Merlin
> Weighed now as living iron that held him down
> With a primeval power. Doubt, wonderment,
> Impatience, and a self-accusing sorrow
> Born of an ancient love, possessed and held him
> Until his love was more than he could name,
> And he was Merlin's fool, not Arthur's now:
> "Say what you will, I say that I'm the fool
> Of Merlin, King of Nowhere; which is Here.
> With you for king and me for court, what else
> Have we to sigh for but a place to sleep?"

But passing on from this less important side of Mr. Robinson's work to his rhymed poems, one finds at least a large number of perfectly executed poems of a sensitive and feline approach. What effect rhyme, or the intention of rhyme, has upon an artist's product, is a difficult thing to estimate. The question verges almost upon the metaphysical. The artist, creating, lives at a point of intensity, and whether the material is consciously digested before that point is reached, and is simply organized and set down at the time of creation; or whether the point of intensity is first reached and the material then drawn out of the subconscious, doubtless depends a good deal on the individual poet, perhaps on the individual poem. The latter method presupposes a great deal of previous absorption of sense impressions, and is probably the more valid, or at least the more generally effective, method. For the rhythm and the "matter," as they come into being simultaneously and interdependent, will be perfectly fused and without loose ends. The man who comes to a form with a definitely outlined matter, will, more than likely, have to cram or fill before he has finished, and the result is broken. The second method does not, of course, presuppose rhyme, but it seems that rhyme, as an obstacle, will force the issue.

The best of Mr. Robinson's poems appear to have come into being very much in this second fashion. He has spun his images out of a world of sense and thought that have been a part of him so long that he seems to have forgot their beginning—has spun these images out as the movement of his lines, the recurrence of his rhymes, have demanded them. A basic philosophy and emotional viewpoint have provided the necessary unity.

This method inevitably focuses the artist's mind upon the object of the instant, makes it one with that object, and eliminates practically all individual "personality" or self-consciousness. The so-called personal touch is reduced to a minimum of technical habit that is bound to accrue in time to any poet who studies his medium with an eye to his individual needs. The man of some intelligence who cannot, or can seldom, achieve this condition of fusion with his object, is driven back to his ingenuity; and this man, if he have sufficient intelligence or ingenuity, becomes one of the "vigorous personalities" of poetry; and he misses poetry exactly in so far as his personality is vigorous. Browning, on two or three occasions one of the greatest of all poets, is, for the most part, simply the greatest of ingenious versifiers. He was so curious of the quirks with which he could approach an object, that he forgot the object in admiring, and expecting admiration for, himself. And it is for this reason that Mr. Robinson, working in more or less the same field as Browning, is the superior of Browning at almost every turn.

And it is for this reason also that Mr. Robinson's *Ben Jonson* is a failure. For the poet, while in no wise concerned with his own personality, is so intent upon the personality of Jonson, his speaker, that, for the sake of Jonson's vigor, he becomes talkative and eager of identifying mannerism; and the result is, that Shakespeare, about whom the poem is written, comes to the surface only here and there, and any actual image almost never.

The following stanza is an example of Mr. Robinson's work at its best:

And like a giant harp that hums
On always, and is always blending
The coming of what never comes
With what has past and had an ending,
The City trembles, throbs, and pounds
Outside, and through a thousand sounds
The small intolerable drums
Of Time are like slow drops descending.

And there is the compact, intensely contemplated statement of *Eros Turannos,* a poem that is, in forty-eight lines, as complete as a Lawrence novel. And the nimble trickery of *Miniver Cheevey,* as finished a piece of burlesque as one can find in English. A few of us have feared, in the last few years, that Mr. Robinson was deteriorating; but going through this book one is reassured. If there is nothing in *The Three Taverns* to equal *Eros Turannos,* there are at least two or three poems as great as any save that one Mr. Robinson has written; and there is nothing in these last poems to preclude the possibility of another *Eros Turannos.*

Mr. Robinson, as probably the highest point in his tradition, has been followed by Frost, a more specialized, and generally softer artist. And there is Gould, who, if he belongs to the tradition at all, is a mere breaking-up of the tradition, a fusion with Whitman. But in considering the work of a man of so varied a genius as Mr. Robinson, it is interesting, if not over-important, to observe the modes of expression that he has anticipated if not actually influenced; even where he has not chosen, or has not been able to develop, these modes.

The resemblance in matter and manner, save for Mr. Robinson's greater suavity, of certain poems, especially the sonnets, in *The Children of the Night,* to the epitaphs in *The Spoon River Anthology,* has been noted by other writers; and I believe it has been said that Mr. Masters was ignorant of the existence of these poems until after the *Anthology* was written. There is little to be said about such a poem as Mr. Robinson's *Luke Havergal:*

No, there is not a dawn in eastern skies
To rift the fiery night that's in your eyes;
But there, where western glooms are gathering,
The dark will end the dark, if anything:
God slays Himself with every leaf that flies,
And hell is more than half of paradise.
No, there is not a dawn in eastern skies—
In eastern skies.

Out of a grave I come to tell you this,
Out of a grave I come to quench the kiss
That flames upon your forehead with a glow
That blinds you to the way that you must go.

And Mr. Masters' satire has been forestalled and outdone in these early sonnets.

But a more curious and interesting resemblance to a later poet is found in the *Octaves* in the same volume:

To me the groaning of world-worshippers
Rings like a lonely music played in hell
By one with art enough to cleave the walls
Of heaven with his cadence, but without
The wisdom or the will to comprehend
The strangeness of his own perversity,
And all without the courage to deny
The profit and the pride of his defeat.

If the actual thought of this passage is not that of Wallace Stevens, nevertheless the quality of the thought, the manner of thinking, as well as the style, quite definitely is. To what extent Mr. Robinson may have influenced this greatest of living and of American poets, one cannot say, but in at least three of the *Octaves,* one phase of Mr. Stevens' later work—that of *Le Monocle de Mon Oncle* and other recent and shorter poems—is certainly foreshadowed. Mr. Robinson's sound is inevitably the less rich, the less masterly.

In another of the *Octaves* there are a few lines that suggest the earlier poems of Mr. T. S. Eliot, but the resemblance is fleeting and apparently accidental.

If the tradition of New England seems to be reaching an end in the work of Mr. Frost, Mr. Robinson has at least helped greatly in the founding of a tradition of culture and clean workmanship that such poets as Messrs. Stevens, Eliot, and Pound, as H. D. and Marianne Moore, are carrying on. Mr. Robinson was, when he began, as much a pioneer as Mr. Pound or Mr. Yeats, and he has certainly achieved as great poetry. While the tradition begun, more or less, by Whitman, has deteriorated, in the later work of Mr. Carl Sandburg, into a sort of plasmodial delirium; and while the school of mellifluous and almost ominous stage-trappings, as exemplified by Poe, has melted into a sort of post-Celtic twilight, and has nearly vanished in the work of Mr. Aiken; the work of these writers and a few others stands out clear and hard in the half-light of our culture. I cannot forget that they exist, even in the face of the desert.

Three Reviews

by Conrad Aiken

I

Of his story, *The Altar of the Dead,* Henry James observed that it was on a theme which had been bothering him for years, but of which the artistic legitimacy was suspect; he had to write it, but he knew it to be pitched in a richly sentimental key which, under the hands of another, he might have condemned. His story, *The Turn of the Screw,* surely one of the finest ghost stories in any language, he frankly derided as a potboiler, making no reservations for its brilliance. He was, of course, right in both of these opinions: he was a better judge of Henry James than any other critic has been, he knew his parerga when he saw them, he could afford to wave them blandly aside. We should think, perhaps, a little less of him, as we are tempted to do of any artist, if he had taken his parerga too seriously—if he had appeared to see only dimly, or not at all, any distinction between these things, which were carved from stones flawed at the outset, and those others, which no flaw rebukes.

Thus, toward Mr. Edwin Arlington Robinson, whom we are accustomed to think of as the most unfailing artist among our contemporary poets, one looks with the barest shade of suspicion after reading his latest book, *Avon's Harvest.* One has, of course, with the critic's habitual baseless arrogance, no hesitation in placing it—it fits, in Mr. Robinson's list, in so far as it fits at all, very much as *The Turn of the Screw* fits in the completed monument of Henry James. One is not disposed, that is, to take it with

"Three Reviews" (original title: "Three Essays on Robinson") by Conrad Aiken. From *A Reviewer's ABC* (New York: Meridian Books, Inc., 1958), pp. 333–46. Reprinted in *The Collected Criticism of Conrad Aiken* (New York: Oxford University Press, 1968). Reprinted by permission of Brandt & Brandt.

too great a seriousness. More precisely, the degree of our seriousness will depend on the degree of Mr. Robinson's seriousness; if we had any reason to suppose that Mr. Robinson regards *Avon's Harvest* as he regards *Merlin* or *Lancelot* or *The Man Against the Sky,* then we should accept it with concern. For, clearly, it is not as good as these, and the most cursory inquiry into the reasons for its comparative unimportance will disclose its defects as not merely those of technique but, more gravely, those of material—as in the case of *The Altar of the Dead.* We must grant, at this point, that to every artist come moments when he delights in abandoning for an interim the plane of high seriousness, to allow play to lesser and lighter motives: when Keats dons the "Cap and Bells," the critic, smiling, doffs robe and wig. This is both legitimate and desirable. By all means let the poet have his *scherzo!* We shall be the richer for it, we shall have, as audience, a scrap the more of the poet's singular soliloquy. But it is imperative that the poet, if his *scherzo* be abruptly introduced, and amid the graver echo of graver music, should accompany it with an appropriate twinkle of eye. Otherwise his audience may do him the dishonor of supposing that he has nothing more to say.

We prefer to believe, then, that Mr. Robinson does not himself intend *Avon's Harvest* as weightily as many of his other things. It is a ghost story, and a fairly good one. That Mr. Robinson should deal with an out-and-out ghost is not surprising, for ghosts have figured in his work from the very outset—ghosts, that is, as the symbols of human fears or loves, ghosts as the plausible and tangible personifications of those varieties of self-tyranny which nowadays we call psychotic. For this sort of ghost there need be no justification, no more than for the ghost of Banquo. If Mr. Robinson had been content with this, if his ghost in *Avon's Harvest* had been simply this—as it might well have been—we should have less cause to quarrel with him. As it is, we are bound to observe that he has *not* been content with this, that he has yielded to the temptation, which an unfailing realist would have resisted, of heightening the effect of the supernatural for its own sake. The knife, with which in a fulminous nightmare the ghost assails Avon, must later be re-introduced by Avon as a knife of ponderable enough reality, which the ghost, in evaporating, left behind. The actuality of the knife's presence there, after the admirable nightmare, might indeed have been explained by another mechanism than that of the supernatural;

but no such explanation is hinted at, or, for that matter, can be hinted at, since Avon is himself the narrator. This is a grave defect; but a graver one is that which again calls to mind *The Altar of the Dead* as a fine thing made of flawed material—the psychological weakness with which the theme is conceived. If Mr. Robinson wished to give us, in Avon, a case of incipient insanity, with a pronounced persecutional mania, then he should have given us, for this aspect, a better lighting. Either we should have been made, therefore, before Avon uttered the first word of his story, more dubious of the man's soundness of mind; or else there should have been, in the story itself, more light upon Avon's character as a thing easily shaken and destroyed—ready, in short, for the very insignificant provocation which was to turn out as sufficient to make a ruin of it. But we are assisted in neither of these ways, and in consequence the provocative action can not help striking us as disproportionately and incredibly slight: we accept it, as necessary to the story, very much as we often accept a ridiculous element in the plot of a photo-play—accept because acceptance conditions pleasure, not because we believe. We waive our incredulity for the moment; but it returns upon us at the end with the greater weight.

One wonders, in this light, whether it would be unjust, after our provisos for the artist's right to the *scherzo,* to see in *Avon's Harvest,* as one often sees in an artist's less successful work, a clearer indication of Mr. Robinson's faults and virtues than might elsewhere be palpable. The poem is extravagantly characteristic of its author—there is perhaps no other poet, with the exception of Mr. Thomas Hardy, who so persistently and recognizably saturates every poem with his personality. We have again, as so many times before, the story told by the retrospective friend of the protagonist—apologetic, humorous, tartly sympathetic, maintaining from beginning to end a note about midway between the elegiac and the ironic. This is the angle of approach which has been made familiar to us in how many of the short ballad-like narratives of Mr. Robinson, of which the characteristics were almost as definite and mature in the first volume as in the last: "John Evereldown," "Richard Cory," "Luke Havergal," "Reuben Bright," in that volume, and after them a crowd of others; and then, with the same approach again, but in long form, "Captain Craig," and "Ben Jonson Entertains a Man from Sratford," and "Isaac and Archibald." What we see here, in short, is an instinctive and strong preference for that approach which will most enable the poet to adopt, toward his *personae,* an informal and colloquial tone, a tone which easily permits, even invites, that happy postulation of intimacy which at the very outset carries to the reader a conviction that the particular *persona* under dissection is a person seen and known. The note, we should keep in mind, is the ballad note—best when it is swiftest and most concise. If, as we observed above, the elegiac also figures, it is as a contrapuntal device (by "device" one does not mean to suggest, however, a thing deliberated upon), with a clear enough melodic line of its own. To narrative speed much else is ruthlessly sacrificed. Should we admit also, in our effort to place this very individual note, an element suggestive of the rapid lyrical summary, cryptically explanatory, a little subdued and brooding, as under a giant shadow—of the choruses in the tragedies of Aeschylus and Sophocles? In one respect Mr. Robinson's briefer narratives appear closer to these than to the English ballad—the action is so consistently a thing known rather than a thing seen. The action is indeed, in the vast majority of cases, an off-stage affair, the precise shape and speed of which we are permitted only to know in dark hints and sinister gleams.

The dark hint and sinister gleam have by many critics been considered the chief characteristics of this poet's style; and it is useful to keep them in mind as we consider, in a workshop light, his technique and mode of thought. Technique, for our purpose, we cannot regard as a mere matter of iambics and caesuras; it is perhaps merely a more inquisitive term for "style," by which, again, I suppose we mean the explicit manifestation of an individual mode of thought. At all events, technique and mode of thought are inseparable, are two aspects of one thing, and it is impossible to discuss any artist's technique without being insensibly and inevitably led into a discussion of his mode of thought. Thus it is permissible, in the matter of the dark hint and the sinister gleam, to isolate them either as tricks of technique or as characteristics of a particular way of thinking: and it does not greatly matter which way we choose.

If we examine Mr. Robinson's early work, in *The Children of the Night* or *The Town Down the River,* in search of the prototype of the "hint" and "gleam" which he has made—or found—so characteristic of himself, we discover them as already conspicuous enough. But it is interesting to observe that at this stage of his growth as an artist this characteristic revealed itself as a technical neatness more precisely than as a neatness of thought, and might thus have been considered as giving warning of a slow increase in subservience of thought to form. The "subtlety"—inevitable term in discussing the gleaming terseness of this style—was not infrequently to be suspected of speciousness. In "Atherton's Gambit," and other poems, we cannot help feeling that the gleam is rather one of manner than of matter: what we suspect is that a poet of immense technical dexterity, dexterity of a dry, laconic kind, is altering and directing his theme, even inviting it, to suit his convictions in regard to style. Shall we presume to term this padding? Padding of a sort it certainly is; but Mr. Robinson's padding was peculiar to himself, and it is remarkable that precisely out of this peculiar method of padding was to grow a most characteristic excellence of his mature manner. For this padding (the word is far too severe) took shape at the outset as the employment, when rhyme-pattern or stanza dictated, of the "vague phrase," the phrase which gave, to the idea conveyed, an odd and somewhat pleasing abstractness. Here began Mr. Robinson's preference, at such moments, for the Latin as against the English word, since the Latin, with its roots in a remoter tongue, and its original tactilism therefore less apparent, permits a larger and looser comprehensiveness; and for such English words as have, for us, the dimmest of contacts with sensory reality. However, it must be remarked that, for the most part, in the first three volumes, the terse "comprehensiveness" thus repeatedly indulged in was often more apparent than real: one suspects that behind the veil of dimness, thus again and again flourished before us by the engaging magician, there is comparatively little for analysis to fasten upon. The round and unctuous neatness of the poems in these volumes has about it just that superfluity which inevitably suggests the hollow. This is not to imply that there are not exceptions, and brilliant ones—"Isaac and Archibald" is a wholly satisfying piece of portraiture, and "Captain Craig" has surely its fine moments. But for the development of this characteristic into something definitely good one must turn to the volume called *The Man Against the Sky* and to the others that followed it. Here we see the employment of the "vague phrase" made, indeed, the keynote of the style—the "vague phrase," no longer specious, but genuinely suggestive, and accurately indicative of a background left dim not because the author is only dimly aware of it, but because dimness serves to make it seem the more gigantic. That, if true of the background, a strange, bare, stark world, flowerless, odorless, and colorless, perpetually under a threat of storm, is no less true of the protagonists. These, if their world is colorless, are themselves bodiless: we see them again and again as nothing on earth but haunted souls, stripped, as it were, of everything but one most characteristic gesture. If they are shadowy they seem larger for it, since what shadow they have is of the right shape to "lead" the eye; if their habiliments of flesh, gesture and facial expression are few, we see them the more clearly for it and remember them the better. This is the style at its best, but if we move on once more to the last volume, *The Three Taverns,* and *Avon's Harvest,* even perhaps to some things in *Lancelot* (though here there are other inimical factors to be considered), we shall see a deterioration of this style, and in a way which, had we been intelligent, we might have expected. For here the "vague phrase" has become a habitual gesture, otiose precisely in proportion as it has become habitual. The "vague phrase" has lost its fine precision of vagueness, the background has lost its reality in a dimness which is the dimness, too often, of the author's conception, and the one gesture of the protagonist is apt to be inconsiderable and unconvincing. We savor here a barren technical neatness. The conjuror more than ever cultivates a fine air of mystery; but nothing answers the too-determined wand.

In connection with this characteristic vague phrase, with its freight of hint and gleam, it is useful to notice, as an additional source of light, Mr. Robinson's vocabulary. We can not move in it for long without feeling that it indicates either a comparative poverty of "sensibility" or something closely akin to it; either a lack of sensibility, in the tactile sense, or a fear of surrendering to it. We have already noted, in another guise, the lack of color; we must note also the lack of sense of texture, sense of shape. As concerns his meter these lacks manifest themselves in a tendency to monotony of rhythm, to a "tumbling" sort of verse frequently out of key with the thought. It is an iron world that Mr. Robinson provides for us: if roses are offered they are singularly the abstractions of roses, not at all the sort of thing for the senses to grow drunk on. He gives us not things, but the ideas of things. We must be careful not to impute to him a total lack of sensory responsiveness, for, as we shall see in *The Man Against the Sky* and *Merlin,* this element in his style reaches its proportional maximum and betrays a latent Mr. Robinson, a romanticist, who, if he uses color sparingly, uses it with exquisite effect.

In general, however, Mr. Robinson's eye is rather that of the dramatist than of the poet—it is perceptive not so much of the beautiful as of significant actions; and the beautiful, when it figures here at all, figures merely as something appropriate to the action. In this regard he is more akin to Browning than any other modern poet has been, if we except Mr. Thomas Hardy. Like Browning, he is a comparative failure when he is an out-and-out playwright; but he is at his most characteristic best when he has, for his poetic framework, a "situation" to present, a situation out of which, from moment to moment, the specifically poetic may flower. This flowering, we are inclined to think, is more conspicuous and more fragrant in *The Man Against the Sky* and *Merlin* than elsewhere, most fragrant of all in *Merlin.* Differences there are to be noted—"Ben Jonson Entertains a Man from Stratford" represents the perfection of Mr. Robinson's sense of scene and portraiture, sees and renders the actual, the human, with extraordinary richness. In *Merlin,* however, where Mr. Robinson's romantic *alter ego,* so long frustrated, at last speaks out, we cannot for long doubt that he reaches his zenith as a poet. The sense of scene and portraiture are as acute here, certainly, but the fine actuality with which they are rendered is, as in the best poetry, synonymous with the beautiful; and the poem, though long, is admirably, and beyond any other American narrative poem, sustained. The "vague phrase" here swims with color, or yields to the precise; the irony (Mr. Robinson's habitual mode of "heightening," so characteristically by means of ornate understatement) is in tone elusively lyrical. Merlin and Vivien move before us exquisitely known and seen, as none of the people whom Tennyson took from Malory ever did. It is one of the finest love stories in English verse.

It is not easy to explain why Mr. Robinson should thus so superlatively succeed once, and not again. Shall we say that, if intellectually and ironically acute, he nevertheless lacks "energy"? There is no Chaucerian or Shakespearean breadth here; it is the closer and narrower view in which Mr. Robinson excels, and it may well be this, and the lack of energy (aspects of one thing?) which have in the main led him to a modern modification of the ballad form, in which simplification and the "hint and gleam" may take the place of the richly extensive. These are not the virtues on which to build in long form: they are stumbling-blocks in a long narrative poem, since if they are allowed free rein they must render it fragmentary and episodic. These stumbling-blocks Mr. Robinson amazingly surmounted in *Merlin,* thanks largely, as we have said, to the fact that here at last a long-suppressed lyric romanticist found his opportunity for unintermittent beauty. But in *Lancelot,* fine as much of it is, failure may be noted almost exactly in proportion as Mr. Robinson's theme has compelled him to "broaden" his narrative stream. Of the soliloquy he can be a master, and even, as in *Merlin,* of the duet; but when the stage fills and the necessity is for a franker, larger, more robustious and changeable complex of action, as in *Lancelot,* poetic energy fails him, he resorts to the factitious, and is often merely melodramatic or strained. We grant the nobility of theme, the austerity of treatment, and, of the latter half especially, the beauty. But the poem as a unit is not a success.

When we have considered *Merlin* and *The Man Against the Sky,* it becomes unjust to consider again *The Three Taverns* or *Avon's Harvest.* We feel a technical and temperamental slackening in these, a cyclic return to the comparatively illusory "depth" of the earlier work. They are parerga which we must hope do not indicate an end.

(1921)

II

The usual succession of best-seller novels, diagnostic novels, and volumes of spicy or grisly short stories—each of them attended in turn by the fatuous illiterate little clamor which, in America, ascends on these occasions as if it were the essential voice of criticism—cannot conceal the fact that the most important book published during the winter was the *Collected Poems* of Mr. Edwin Arlington Robinson. No great clamor went up, as far as I am aware, over this: if Mr. Robinson has for some time been accepted as the "best" of contemporary American poets, the acceptance has been more tacit than express, and, when confessed, more remarkable for a vague bright generosity (pitched in a lower key than the usual generosity of American criticism—one supposes because American criticism has lost that part of its apparatus which deals with the fine as opposed to the large) than for a sure perceptiveness. It is difficult to imagine Mr. Mencken, for example, dealing at length and subtly with Mr. Robinson—Mr. Robinson would be for Mr. Mencken, one feels, merely the most provokingly fugitive and impalpable of ghosts. Nor, on the other hand, has there been much unanimity among the craftsman-critics. The poets of the Poetry Society applaud Mr. Robinson, but their applause is largely manual, and almost wholly unintelligent: what they applaud is something they vaguely think is Mr. Robinson's aesthetic orthodoxy. The poets outside the Poetry Society seldom applaud him at all. By some few of these latter he is contemptuously referred to as a kind of American Georgian. But there is none like him among the Georgians.

Nor is it particularly easy to find anywhere, in English or American poetry, clear affinities for Mr. Robinson, or obvious prototypes. Crabbe, Wordsworth, and Browning have all, for this purpose, been invoked, but without much success. Traces, yes: Mr. Robinson has written a few brilliant dramatic monologues, notably *Ben Jonson Entertains a Man from Stratford;* a few meditative poems which might claim relationship with *Intimations of Immortality*—*The Man Against the Sky,* perhaps; and a good many small concise narrative portraits which suggest comparison with the carved oak of Crabbe. But beyond that, nothing—nothing, that is, unless we abandon the search for precursive signals in the poetry of the past, and look rather for Mr. Robinson's blood-relations among contemporary novelists. It is natural to think of Mr. Hardy's poetry as somewhat akin to Mr. Robinson's—Mr. Robinson has the same predilection for the narrative lyric, the stringent compression of the actual, the ballad tone, the sharp dramatic gesture. But if Mr. Robinson shares these predilections with Mr. Hardy, he shares them only partially, and he shares as much, or more, with Henry James. It is, in fact, impossible to read the poetry of Mr. Robinson without thinking of Henry James. If, more than Henry James, Mr. Robinson chooses the succinct, and if his narrative, whether short or long, is less complex, it springs, none the less, from the same sources, reveals a temperament strikingly analogous. It is, like the narrative of Henry James, an affair pre-eminently of relations: a narrative, it would be more exact to say, of relations and contacts (between character and character) always extraordinarily *conscious.* If it is permissible to conceive the individual human being as standing, like a lighthouse, at the center of his small bright circle of consciousness; and if we think of another such individual as coming so near to the first that at one point the two bright circles overlap, sharing a small segment in common; and if we then conceive our two individuals as staring, fascinated, at that small segment, with its double light, and as approaching each other, or withdrawing from each other, to watch, in that segment, the permutations of shape and light—living, so to speak, almost wholly in their awareness of the consciousness shared, and having little awareness apart from that; in some such manner we may conceive how it is that Henry James regarded his *dramatis personae,* and moved them, and was moved by them. His interest, like theirs, lay in the varyingly luminous contact, and in the influences thus shed; in the alteration or corruption of character by character. And something of the sort is true of Mr. Robinson. His *Merlin* and his *Lancelot* give us a Malory as Henry James might have rewritten and enlarged it, had Henry James been a poet. I am not sure that the *Lancelot* is altogether successful—in so far as it calls for breadth of narrative stream, for a crowded and noisy stage, Mr. Robinson, clearly, has not the necessary vigor. In the "crowded" scenes of the first parts, one feels a thinness, a straining, a hint of hollow melodrama; but the instant that the poem becomes a dialogue, with none but Lancelot and Guinevere on the stage, Mr. Robinson makes a clear beauty of it. And of his *Merlin* what is it possible to say but that it is one of the most exquisite love stories ever told in verse? Merlin and Vivien have here all the dim subtleties and delicate mutual awarenesses of the people, let us say, in *The Wings of the Dove.* The story, the poetry, is precisely in these hoverings and perturbations, these pauses and approaches and flights. Everything is hint and gleam. Flat, outrageous statement is nowhere. The express is at a minimum, the implications are vast. The batlike flittings and pipistrelline sensitiveness are, of course, Mr. Robinson's own, as they might have been Henry James's. The thought, seen to be moving in gleams and hints, and the language and prosody, reticent and dimly suggestive, are one indivisible thing. There is nothing showy or ornate, no splashing in purple: the language verges often on the coldly abstract, betraying only the most attenuated of tactilisms; the verse is often monotonous, seldom rich, and achieves its effect with a spare simplicity that is classic.

In all this one traces the affinity between Mr. Robinson and Henry James—in either case one may hazard that the fastidiousness, the love of the veiled, the luxuriation in half-lights, constitute a sort of defense mechanism, the protective cunning of souls whom Mr. Shaw would describe as "on the shrink." This, certainly, should serve as an indication of the "texture" of Mr. Robinson's poetry. We san see it, if we like, as we can see the subtle texture of Henry James, or of Hawthorne, as a product peculiarly American—the over-sensitiveness of the sensitive soul in an environment where sensitiveness is rare. But this need not blind us to the fact that Mr. Robinson can be dramatic, or mordantly ironical, or exquisitely lyrical, or even, on occasion (as in the Shakespeare poem), robust. His range is sufficient, his thought is richly and bitterly his own. It amounts pretty nearly to a disgrace that in England he still remains unpublished, almost unknown; and that he can be referred to, as he was referred to the other day in an English weekly, as "one of the dullest poets" now alive. If the notion needs refuting, I quote one of the smallest of Mr. Robinson's lyrics as refutation. It is called "For a Dead Lady" and appeared in 1910 in the volume entitled *The Town Down the River.*

No more with overflowing light
Shall fill the eyes that now are faded,
Nor shall another's fringe with night
Their woman-hidden world as they did.
No more shall quiver down the days
The flowing wonder of her ways,
Whereof no language may requite
The shifting and the many-shaded.

The grace, divine, definitive,
Clings only as a faint forestalling;
The laugh that love could not forgive
Is hushed, and answers to no calling;
The forehead and the little ears
Have gone where Saturn keeps the years;
The breast where roses could not live
Has done with rising and with falling.

The beauty, shattered by the laws
That have creation in their keeping,
No longer trembles at applause,
Or over children that are sleeping;

And we who delve in beauty's lore
Know all that we have known before
Of what inexorable cause
Makes Time so vicious in his reaping.

(1922)

III

To his two preceding poems dealing with themes from the Arthurian cycle, Mr. Robinson now adds a third, this time courageously venturing on a new treatment of the Tristram and Isolt story: courageously, because more than any other tale from Malory has this been drawn upon by poets. Wagner, Swinburne, and Arthur Symons have all had their turn at it; and it is to Mr. Robinson's credit that, despite the crystallization, or conventionalization, of the theme, which has inevitably resulted from this repeated handling, he has again, as in *Merlin* and *Lancelot,* made the thing remarkably his own. Whatever his merits or defects as a narrative poet, Mr. Robinson never fails to saturate his theme with his own character. Like Miss T., of whom Mr. De la Mare writes that "whatever Miss T. eats turns into Miss T.," Mr. Robinson turns his Arthurian heroes and heroines and brooding villains into such figures as could not conceivably exist anywhere else. They are as signally and idiosyncratically stamped, as invariably and unalterably Robinsonian, as the characters of Henry James are Jamesian. These Merlins and Tristrams and Isolts and Lancelots are modern and highly self- conscious folk; they move in a world of moral and emotional subtlety which is decidedly more redolent of the age of Proust than of the age of Malory; they take on a psychological reality and intensity which would have astonished, and might have shocked, either Tennyson or William Morris—whose aim, in dealing with the same material, was so largely decorative.

Mr. Robinson's method lies halfway between the tapestry effect of Morris and the melodrama of Wagner. Its chief excellence is an excellence of portraiture. And, again like James—of whom he is in many respects curiously a poetic counterpart—he particularly excels in his portraits of women. Merlin was not so good as Vivien, nor Lancelot as Guinevere; and in *Tristram* it is again true that the heroines are much more sharply and sympathetically realized than the hero. For the full-length portraits of the two Isolts—Isolt of Ireland and Isolt of the White Hands—one can have only the highest praise; both of them are as admirable and subtle as they can be; and in Isolt of the White Hands especially, Mr. Robinson has created a figure of extraordinary loveliness and pathos, as deeply moving, in its way, as the figure of Milly Theale.

To realize, beside these, the comparative failure of Mr. Robinson with his *Tristram,* is to realize also his chief weakness as a narrative poet; and, in particular, his weakness as an adapter of Malory. For he is curiously unable to deal with a hero as "man of action." Mr. Robinson's heroes think and feel—they think and feel almost inordinately; but they do not act. Every one of them is a kind of helpless introspective Hamlet; and not only that, but a Hamlet shorn of all masculine force. One cannot much respect this melancholy Tristram—one even feels that he is rather a namby-pamby creature; and without a forceful hero, how can one possibly have an altogether forceful poem? Mr. Robinson avoids "action" as he would avoid the plague. Such action as takes place in the present poem at all takes place offstage, soundlessly and briefly. This contributes to one's feeling that the poem is too long—perhaps twice as long as it needed to be; but there are other factors as well. One cannot safely, in a poem two hundred-odd pages long, restrict oneself wholly to analytic dialogue and romantic description, with interlardings of lyricism. The lyricism is sometimes very beautiful, though perhaps not as beautiful as certain passages in *Merlin;* the analytic dialogue is often acute; but there is a great deal too much of both.

With this diffuseness in the narrative itself goes a corresponding diffuseness in the verse. Mr. Robinson's habit of ironic elaboration has grown upon him. An excellence in the short poems, where it was kept within bounds, it has now become, or is at any rate becoming, a dangerous mannerism. In the dialogue, especially, Mr. Robinson too often gives himself up to a sort of overwrought verbalistic *playing* with an idea: as if he were bent on saying the same thing three times over, each time more complicatedly and abstractedly and involutely than before. Sometimes these tortuous passages conceal a subtlety worth the pain of extraction—and sometimes they do not. On at least one occasion, Mr. Robinson becomes so involved in his own involutions that he forgets to finish his sentence—losing himself, as now and then Henry James did, in a maze of inversions and parentheses. This elaborate obscurity, with its accompanying absence of tactile qualities in the language and of ruggedness in the blank verse, too frequently makes these pages hard and unrewarding reading. It is the more regrettable as Mr. Robinson has given to his poem great beauty of design. And that it contains many pages of extraordinary loveliness and tragic force goes without saying.

(1927)

Robinson in America

by Morton Dauwen Zabel

Robinson's outward indifference both to his early hardship and to his later success was, first of all, his way of being a poet; he left no other record of his genius, in prose or action. But it was something more. It was his way of defining and surviving a point of view that belongs peculiarly to the half-century of American history that shaped his mature thought and his twenty books of verse. Born in 1869, he reached his twenties by the time the United States entered its full era of pride and commercial splendor; he was approaching fifty when the bursting prowess of 1917 announced the country in its new rôle of world-savior; death overtook him on April 5th when the outlook of both hemispheres—already darkened by the doubts of economic and political desperation—had reached a new crisis of profound pessimism. Robinson had learned how to offer resistance both to the fulsome glitter of material progress and to the fatalism of defeated hopes. His early struggles as a poet were largely ignored by an age of inflated "culture" that respected few men of sober judgment; it was an age which, at best, stopped its fears with the messianic eloquence of yea-sayers and prophets of utopian prosperity. He could in turn afford to ignore the fame that arrived so profusely during his last twenty years. Except for the dangerous ease with which it permitted him to publish his frequent long poems of the past decade, he committed no act of conventional folly in acknowledging the respect of a public at last dutiful in its homage.

The vantage-point Robinson occupied was maintained by the help of a diffident personality, but this was bred by two factors that reach beyond the limits of temperament. One was his inheritance of the taciturn rigors of New England empiricism—a legacy whose

"Robinson in America" by Morton Dauwen Zabel. From *Poetry,* XLVI, number 3 (June, 1935), 157–62.

sterility he could recognize even though he affirmed it in some of his last poems; the other was his dogged resistance to any form of illusion in his thought. The first of these factors is hard to dissociate from his Maine birth and childhood; the other is difficult to credit to anything but his revulsion from the gilded pretensions surrounding his manhood. He had the good fortune to resist any temptation toward public oratory even in pre-War years when that method was the one guaranty of success for an American writer. The retreat drove him toward a discipline of infinitely greater advantage to him as a poet: the discipline of facts and of critical thought—of facts judged at close hand instead of approached through abstract theory, of ideas scanned and appraised, instead of felt by means of the deceptive emotional apparatus in vogue in the 'nineties. Robinson possessed at the outset the grip on reality which a poet like Yeats has come into only after many years of struggle and intellectual exploration; his work shows none of the phenomena of growth that makes Yeats' career so dramatic; and if he never achieved what Yeats has finally mastered in the way of personal eloquence and symbolic richness of style, it is because, by an initial impulse, he rejected the pathways of sensation, trance, and illusion that may lead, by chance or accident, to a clear and final resolution about man and his destiny.

Robinson's Maine days provided him—out of an environment as unpromising as any section of America could offer—with more than a natural and involuntary grip on human ordeal: with characters to illustrate failure and obscure victory in that struggle. These are the men of his native American drama—Captain Craig, Luke Havergal, Aaron Stark, Bewick Finzer, Richard Cory, Flammonde, Miniver Cheevy, John Gorham, Fernando Nash, Roman Bartholow—a gallery in whom are embodied the puritan tradition in its dark days of spiritual dispossession, and a skeptical courage which saw no substitute for that tradition in the coming age of commercial optimism. Misers and profiteers like Finzer and Stark lean toward the shadow as fatally as glittering husks of popular heroism like Richard Cory. The blighting touch of moral presumption is on all of them, while madmen, imbeciles, and hermits alone appear to have worked out a saving irony. But Robinson is saved from the dogged fatalism of *Spoon River* by the same force that deprived him of the subtle spiritual victories granted to Henry James. His faith was stoic; he was unprepared for more exacting demands on man's intellectual responsibility; but his was a stoicism that came at an hour of bewildered confidences and betrayed trusts, an hour that needed (and perhaps permitted) only that kind of critical reaction which remains sealed and safe in the private integrity of the individual. It was the hour of "skeptical faith," and faith that shatters as soon as it becomes public. Outward shows were the surest ways of losing even such strength as a disillusioned stoicism affords. But Robinson's long line of defeated men are testimony to the fact that he hoped his inward discipline would prepare a new kind of leadership. When he turned away from the typical American life of "Tilbury Town" or from its analogies in Arthurian legend, he could seize on a hardier and more active kind of doctrine. He saw the need of a more vigorous corrective to the facile casuistry of popular rationalism. He celebrated the "sure strength" of George Crabbe's consecrated "flicker"; "the racked and shrieking hideousness of Truth" in Zola; the Shakespeare who knew "too much of what the world had hushed in others"; Rembrandt, who scorned "the taste of death in life"; the sense of "undeceiving fate" in Lincoln. Robinson did not make these men into *personae* of himself; they remain as objective as the duties which he employed them to illustrate. By that acceptance of the "Titan" with the quietist, the "Forger" with the "Watcher," he saves his irony from irresponsibility, and his grim detachment from the grief of suicide.

Robinson's art, at its best, derives from his sense of the plainest use of speech. Even his lyrics are written in a taciturn English that lies between the purely logical and the obviously colloquial style. His lyric perceptions, like his human values, are rooted in the known and the possible—the capacities of man which survive even in his sorriest condition of stultification and confusion. He never allowed his tragic sense to carry him toward the impotent Promethean rhetoric of Jeffers. It is these firm roots, not only in experience but in language, that bind Robinson so certainly to his moment in modern history—to its economic and social conditions, its moral conflict, its political crisis and immense human claims. He is a realist not only in conscience but in style and diction; in *milieu* as much as in imagery; and this gives him his license to explore the problems of abstract casuistry and moral contradiction which he filed down into that style of attenuated rumination, impassioned hair-splitting, and bleak aphorism which always remain unmistakably his own. He wrote searching judgments not only on tragedies of love, jealousy, and envy, but on the crimes of imperialism, the folly of the Eighteenth Amendment, and the toppling recklessness of industrial inflation. The grey monotone of his collected works is deceptive, for within it may be discovered both the sweep and anger of righteous denunciation, and the suddenly lavish beauty of such lines as the endings of *Eros Turannos* and *The Sheaves*.

He was a poet without school or cenacle; he was fundamentally as inimitable as unapproachable; and his bleaker or more repetitious volumes might almost be interpreted as warning to the public to expect from him none of the innovation or sensationalism that makes literary creeds, movements, and manifestoes. For this he was scorned by youthful insurgents, and apparently by most of the greater names that rival his in recent literature. His influence was more subtle. He brought form and toughness of language into modern verse long before most of his contemporaries, and he corrected by modest example a slow drift toward slovenly habits and facile impressionism in poetic thought. His equipment, technical and verbal, needed only the enriching substance of a more positive and committal belief; like Conrad's, his strength and brilliance are darkened by the touch of negation. But of him, as of Conrad, it may be said that whatever his contemporaries have achieved in art, either by novelty of means or by insurrection of ideas, has been done better because of his cleansing influence, and his model of honesty that no experimental or revolutionary activity can ignore. This was the particular and limited honor of Robinson and the courageous men of his generation. In this satisfaction he ended his work, and left American literature richer for a quality it had never known before in a form so complete or in an art so firm.

Introduction to *King Jasper*

by Robert Frost

It may come to the notice of posterity (and then again it may not) that this, our age, ran wild in the quest of new ways to be new. The one old way to be new no longer served. Science put it into our heads that there must be new ways to be new. Those tried were largely by subtraction—elimination. Poetry, for example, was tried without punctuation. It was tried without capital letters. It was tried without metric frame on which to measure the rhythm. It was tried without any images but those to the eye; and a loud general intoning had to be kept up to cover the total loss of specific images to the ear, those dramatic tones of voice which had hitherto constituted the better half of poetry. It was tried without content under the trade name of poesie pure. It was tried without phrase, epigram, coherence, logic and consistency. It was tried without ability. I took the confession of one who had had deliberately to unlearn what he knew. He made a back-pedalling movement of his hands to illustrate the process. It was tried premature like the delicacy of unborn calf in Asia. It was tried without feeling or sentiment like murder for small pay in the underworld. These many things was it tried without, and what had we left? Still something. The limits of poetry had been sorely strained, but the hope was that the idea had been somewhat brought out.

Robinson stayed content with the old-fashioned way to be new. I remember bringing the subject up with him. How does a man come on his difference, and how does he feel about it when he first finds it out? At first it may well frighten him, as his difference with the Church frightened Martin Luther. There is such a thing as being too willing to be different. And what shall we say to people

From "Introduction" by Robert Frost to *King Jasper* by Edwin Arlington Robinson (New York: The Macmillan Company, 1935), pp. v-xv.

who are not only willing but anxious? What assurance have they that their difference is not insane, eccentric, abortive, unintelligible? Two fears should follow us through life. There is the fear that we shan't prove worthy in the eyes of someone who knows us at least as well as we know ourselves. That is the fear of God. And there is the fear of Man—the fear that man won't understand us and we shall be cut off from them.

We began in infancy by establishing correspondence of eyes with eyes. We recognized that they were the same feature and we could do the same things with them. We went on to the visible motion of the lips—smile answered smile; then cautiously, by trial and error, to compare the invisible muscles of the mouth and throat. They were the same and could make the same sounds. We were still together. So far, so good. From here on the wonder grows. It has been said that recognition in art is all. Better say correspondence is all. Mind must convince mind that it can uncurl and wave the same filaments of subtlety, soul convince soul that it can give off the same shimmers of eternity. At no point would anyone but a brute fool want to break off this correspondence. It is all there is to satisfaction; and it is salutary to live in the fear of its being broken off.

The latest proposed experiment of the experimentalists is to use poetry as a vehicle of grievances against the un-Utopian state. As I say, most of their experiments have been by subtraction. This would be by addition of an ingredient that latter-day poetry has lacked. A distinction must be made between griefs and grievances. Grievances are probably more useful than griefs. I read in a sort of Sunday-school leaflet from Moscow, that the grievances of Chekhov against the sordidness and dullness of his home-town society have done away with the sordidness and dullness of home-town society all over Russia. They were celebrating the event. The grievances of the great Russians of the last century have given Russia a revolution. The grievances of their great followers in America may well give us, if not a revolution, at least some palliative pensions. We must suffer them to put life at its ugliest and forbid them not, as we value our reputation for liberality.

I had it from one of the youngest lately: "Whereas we once thought literature should be without content, we now know it should be charged full of propaganda." Wrong twice, I told him. Wrong twice and of theory prepense. But he returned to his position after a moment out for reassembly: "Surely art can be considered good only as it prompts to action." How soon, I asked him. But there is danger of undue levity in teasing the young. The experiment is evidently started. Grievances are certainly a power and are going to be turned on. We must be very tender of our dreamers. They may seem like picketers or members of the committee on rules for the moment. We shan't mind what they seem, if only they produce real poems.

But for me, I don't like grievances. I find I gently let them alone wherever published. What I like is griefs and I like them Robinsonianly profound. I suppose there is no use in asking, but I should think we might be indulged to the extent of having grievances restricted to prose if prose will accept the imposition, and leaving poetry free to go its way in tears.

Robinson was a prince of heartachers amid countless achers of another part. The sincerity he wrought in was all sad. He asserted the sacred right of poetry to lean its breast to a thorn and sing its dolefullest. Let weasels suck eggs. I know better where to look for melancholy. A few superficial irritable grievances, perhaps, as was only human, but these are forgotten in the depth of griefs to which he plunged us.

Grievances are a form of impatience. Griefs are a form of patience. We may be required by law to throw away patience as we have been required to surrender gold; since by throwing away patience and joining the impatient in one last rush on the citadel of evil, the hope is we may end the need of patience. There will be nothing left to be patient about. The day of perfection waits on unanimous social action. Two or three more good national elections should do the business. It has been similarly urged on us to give up courage, make cowardice a virtue, and see if that won't end war, and the need of courage. Desert religion for science, clean out the holes and corners of the residual unknown, and there will be no more need of religion. (Religion is merely consolation for what we don't know.) But suppose there was some mistake, and the evil stood siege, the war didn't end, and something remained unknowable. Our having disarmed would make our case worse than it had ever been before. Nothing in the latest advices from Wall Street, the League of Nations, or the Vatican incline me to give up my holdings in patient grief.

There were Robinson and I, it was years ago, and the place

(near Boston Common) was the Place, as we liked afterward to call it, of Bitters, because it was with bitters, though without bitterness, we could sit there and look out on the welter of dissatisfaction and experiment in the world around us. It was too long ago to remember who said what, but the sense of the meeting was, we didn't care how arrant a reformer or experimentalist a man was if he gave us real poems. For ourselves, we should hate to be read for any theory upon which we might be supposed to write. We doubted any poem could persist for any theory upon which it might have been written. Take the theory that poetry in our language could be treated as quantitative, for example. Poems had been written in spite of it. And poems are all that matter. The utmost of ambition is to lodge a few poems where they will be hard to get rid of, to lodge a few irreducible bits where Robinson lodged more than his share.

For forty years it was phrase on phrase on phrase with Robinson, and every one the closest delineation of something that *is* something. Any poet, to resemble him in the least, would have to resemble him in that grazing closeness to the spiritual realities. If books of verse were to be indexed by lines first in importance instead of lines first in position, many of Robinson's poems would be represented several times over. This should be seen to. The only possible objection is that it could not be done by any mere hireling of the moment, but would have to be the work of someone who had taken his impressions freely before he had any notion of their use. A particular poem's being represented several times would only increase the chance of its being located.

The first poet I ever sat down with to talk about poetry was Ezra Pound. It was in London in 1913. The first poet we talked about, to the best of my recollection, was Edwin Arlington Robinson. I was fresh from America and from having read *The Town Down the River*. Beginning at that book, I have slowly spread my reading of Robinson twenty years backward and forward, about equally in both directions.

I remember the pleasure with which Pound and I laughed over the fourth "thought" in

> Miniver thought, and thought, and thought,
> And thought about it.

Three "thoughts" would have been "adequate" as the critical

praise-word then was. There would have been nothing to complain of, if it had been left at three. The fourth made the intolerable touch of poetry. With the fourth, the fun began. I was taken out on the strength of our community of opinion here, to be rewarded with an introduction to Miss May Sinclair, who had qualified as the patron authority on young and new poets by the sympathy she had shown them in *The Divine Fire.*

There is more to it than the number of "thoughts." There is the way the last one turns up by surprise round the corner, the way the shape of the stanza is played with, the easy way the obstacle of verse is turned to advantage. The mischief is in it.

> One pauses half afraid
> To say for certain that he played—

a man as sorrowful as Robinson. His death was sad to those who knew him, but nowhere near as sad as the lifetime of poetry to which he attuned our ears. Nevertheless, I say his much-admired restraint lies wholly in his never having let grief go further than it could in play. So far shall grief go, so far shall philosophy go, so far shall confidences go, and no further. Taste may set the limit. Humor is a surer dependence.

> And once a man was there all night,
> Expecting something every minute.

I know what the man wanted of Old King Cole. He wanted the heart out of his mystery. He was the friend who stands at the end of a poem ready in waiting to catch you by both hands with enthusiasm and drag you off your balance over the last punctuation mark into more than you meant to say. "I understand the poem all right, but please tell me what is behind it?" Such presumption needs to be twinkled at and baffled. The answer must be, "If I had wanted you to know, I should have told you in the poem."

We early have Robinson's word for it:

> The games we play
> To fill the frittered minutes of a day
> Good glasses are to read the spirit through.

He speaks somewhere of Crabbe's stubborn skill. His own was a happy skill. His theme was unhappiness itself, but his skill was as happy as it was playful. There is that comforting thought for those who suffered to see him suffer. Let it be said at the risk of offending the humorless in poetry's train (for there are a few such): his art was more than playful; it was humorous.

The style is the man. Rather say the style is the way the man takes himself; and to be at all charming or even bearable, the way is almost rigidly prescribed. If it is with outer seriousness, it must be with inner humor. If it is with outer humor, it must be with inner seriousness. Neither one alone without the other under it will do. Robinson was thinking as much in his sonnet on Tom Hood. One ordeal of Mark Twain was the constant fear that his occluded seriousness would be overlooked. That betrayed him into his two or three books of out-and-out seriousness.

Miniver Cheevy was long ago. The glint I mean has kept coming to the surface of the fabric all down the years. Yesterday in conversation, I was using "The Mill." Robinson could make lyric talk like drama. What imagination for speech in "John Gorham"! He is at his height between quotation marks.

> The miller's wife had waited long,
>   The tea was cold, the fire was dead;
> And there might yet be nothing wrong
>   In how he went and what he said:
> "There are no millers any more,"
>   Was all that she had heard him say.

"There are no millers any more." It might be an edict of some power against industrialism. But no, it is of wider application. It is a sinister jest at the expense of all investors of life or capital. The market shifts and leaves them with a car-barn full of dead trolley cars. At twenty I commit myself to a life of religion. Now, if religion should go out of fashion in twenty-five years, there would I be, forty-five years old, unfitted for anything else and too old to learn anything else. It seems immoral to have to bet on such high things as lives of art, business, or the church. But in effect, we have no alternative. None but an all-wise and all-powerful government could take the responsibility of keeping us out of the gamble or of insuring us against loss once we were in.

The guarded pathos of "Mr. Flood's Party" is what makes it merciless. We are to bear in mind the number of moons listening. Two, as on the planet Mars. No less. No more ("No more, sir; that will do"). One moon (albeit a moon, no sun) would have laid grief too bare. More than two would have dissipated grief entirely and would have amounted to dissipation. The emotion had to be held at a point.

> He set the jug down slowly at his feet
> With trembling care, knowing that most things break;
> And only when assured that on firm earth
> It stood, as the uncertain lives of men
> Assuredly did not . . .

There twice it gleams. Nor is it lost even where it is perhaps lost sight of in the dazzle of all those golden girls at the end of "The Sheaves." Granted a few fair days in a world where not all days are fair.

> "Well, Mr. Flood, we have the harvest moon
> Again, and we may not have many more;
> The bird is on the wing, the poet says,
> And you and I have said it here before.
> Drink to the bird."

Poetry transcends itself in the playfulness of the toast.

Robinson has gone to his place in American literature and left his human place among us vacant. We mourn, but with the qualification that, after all, his life was a revel in the felicities of language. And not just to no purpose. None has deplored.

> The inscrutable profusion of the Lord
> Who shaped as one of us a thing

so sad and at the same time so happy in achievement. Not for me to search his sadness to its source. He knew how to forbid encroachment. And there is solid satisfaction in a sadness that is not just a fishing for ministration and consolation. Give us immedicable woes—woes that nothing can be done for—woes flat and final. And then to play. The play's the thing. Play's the thing. All virtue in "as if."

> As if the last of days
> Were fading and all wars were done.

As if they were. As if, as if!

The Shorter Poems

by Yvor Winters

I

In dealing with the shorter poems, I still employ a loose scheme of classification designed to illustrate the aspects of Robinson's thought; it is only in respect to the thought that any particular classification seems necessary. Robinson was not a systematic thinker, and his thought shows conflicting tendencies. I believe that Robinson is essentially a counter-romantic, and yet he resembles other great counter-romantics of the nineteenth and twentieth centuries in the uncritical fashion with which he adopts a few current notions of a romantic nature as if they were axiomatic. One can find such writers as Henry James, Matthew Arnold and Robert Bridges doing much the same thing. There is not any change in Robinson's thinking from the beginning to the end of his work; and if there is any change of emphasis, it is indistinctly perceptible.

II

The evidence of a counter-romantic tendency in Robinson's thinking is to be found easily and repeatedly in his best poems, of which one of the most imposing is "Hillcrest," from *The Man Against the Sky*. (See "Hillcrest," pages 15–17 in *Collected Poems* of Robinson.)[1] The setting of the poem, which is dedicated to Mrs. Edward MacDowell, is the MacDowell farmhouse at the Peterborough

"The Shorter Poems" by Yvor Winters. From *Edwin Arlington Robinson* (New York: New Directions Publishing Corporation, 1946), pp. 29–60.

[1] [Page references in this essay are to *Collected Poems of Edwin Arlington Robinson* (New York: Macmillan, 1937).]

colony. The place is praised for its isolation and because it is conducive to contemplation. We are told in the first six stanzas that in such a place one may discount one's gains and losses, that one may acquire sufficient humility not to indulge one's own graceful accomplishments or to offer easy consolation to others, and that by contemplation one may learn that one's plans and ideas are often less sound than they sometimes at first appear. The next three stanzas deal with one of Robinson's favorite themes, that of stoical endurance and of the certain necessity for it. In these stanzas and those following, Robinson's style is at something near its greatest; in the second of these three stanzas the visual image, and in the third the abstract statement of the last two lines, are equally impressive. The tenth stanza states the necessity for great wisdom amid the trials of life, and the danger of a little; and the last three stanzas state the illusory nature of a childlike, or romantic, triumph and of the easy assumption of spiritual peace. The phrase "as far as dreams have gone" is perhaps not of the strongest, but the writing in these last stanzas has great strength, and the sensory image of the final stanza has not only extraordinary descriptive beauty but great power of summary. The first six stanzas show less strength than the last seven, but they seem largely successful, both in themselves and as a preparation for what follows. In two lines one sees an indication of one of Robinson's characteristic weaknesses, to which I have alluded in the preceding chapter and to which I shall have to allude more than once again, a tendency to a facile and superficial intellectualism, an intellectualism which is clever rather than perceptive, and which reduces his dry rhythm to the jingling parlor verse which I have described in connection with Praed. In fact, so far as these two lines are concerned, they are too facile not only to be good Robinson but even to be moderately good Praed. (See "Hillcrest," lines 13–14, on page 16 of *Collected Poems* of Robinson.) This kind of thing intrudes, or almost intrudes, too often in Robinson's best work. As a statement of principles, the poem represents a pretty explicit negation of the essential ideas of the romantic movement, especially as that movement has been represented by the Emersonian tradition: it tells us that life is a very trying experience, to be endured only with pain and to be understood only with difficulty; that easy solutions are misleading; that all solutions must be scrutinized; and that understanding is necessary. It is a poem on the tragedy of human life and on the value of contemplation; it expresses neither despair nor triumph, but rather recognition and evaluation.

There are many poems of which the subject is the endurance of suffering, endurance unlightened with hope of anything better. These poems commonly deal with the lives of persons other than the poet, and the subjects offer material for the intellectual examination recommended in "Hillcrest," for the moral curiosity of the heir of the Puritans. Such a poem as "Eros Turannos," for example, puts into practice the principles stated in "Hillcrest"; like "Hillcrest," it is one of Robinson's greatest poems. (See "Eros Turannos," pages 32–33 of *Collected Poems* of Robinson.) This is a universal tragedy in a Maine setting. In the first three stanzas there is an exact definition of the personal motives of the actors and an implication of the social motives; in the fourth stanza the tragic outcome; and in the last two stanzas the generalized commentary. In such a poem we can see to an extraordinary degree the generalizing power of the poetic method; for this piece has the substance of a short novel or of a tragic drama, yet its brevity has resulted in no poverty—its brevity has resulted, rather, in a concentration of meaning and power. In spite of this success, the poem shows in the fifth stanza Robinson's weakness for a kind of provincial cleverness; the paraphrasable substance of the stanza is necessary to the poem, but the statement is undistinguished. Two phrases are especially unfortunate—"tapping on our brows" and "no kindly veil"—but the entire stanza is commonplace. Elsewhere the writing seems to me beyond praise; although it is worth while to call attention especially to the hard and subdued irony of the last lines of the second and third stanzas and to the fact that this irony can enter through the sharp style and metrical form without seeming to intrude into surroundings foreign to it.

I think it worth while to mention a few other poems dealing largely with the theme of endurance, though most of them are less dramatic than "Eros Turannos." Those which I think of first are "Veteran Sirens," "The Poor Relation," "Luke Havergal," "For a Dead Lady" and "Mr. Flood's Party." I could easily add other titles, but these will suffice to illustrate what I have in mind, and they are all among the best poems.

"Veteran Sirens" is an expression of pity for old prostitutes who must continue as best they are able at their trade. It calls to mind Baudelaire's great poem *"Le Jeu,"* but although it is quite as successfully written as Baudelaire's poem, it is far simpler. Baudelaire sees his prostitutes and his gamblers as souls lost through a surrender that has led to automatism, but as having the one surviving virtue of clinging passionately to what life, or, to use the more explicit and theological term, to what being, is left them; and he sees himself as having sunk to a lower level of sin in that he has lost his desire for being. His poem is not a mere lament over suffering and the approach of death, but is a judgment of sin, guided by traditional and theological concepts; it is a judgment upon that way of life which attenuates and diminishes and ultimately abandons what we variously call life, being, or intelligence, instead of augmenting it. Robinson's poem is a simple expression of pity at evident suffering, but is stated in the most admirable language. (See "Veteran Sirens," lines 9–12 and 17–20 on page 40 of *Collected Poems* of Robinson.) "The Poor Relation" describes an old woman, presumably of good family, living in loneliness and in poverty. The first seven stanzas of this poem give the effect of some redundancy; what they have to say is simple and could be said in less space. Furthermore, a fair number of lines are saved from sentimentality, if indeed they are saved, only by the clipped intricacy of the stanza and the hardness of the meter. (See "The Poor Relation," lines 7–8 on page 45 and lines 9–10 and 21–22 on page 46 of *Collected Poems* of Robinson.) In the eighth stanza, however, the poem is drawn together by the old woman's vision of the city, in one of the greatest triumphs of Robinson's rhetoric. (See "The Poor Relation," lines 1–8 on page 47 of *Collected Poems* of Robinson.) The simile of the last two lines of this stanza is one of the few successful comparisons in literature between the visual and the auditory, the success being made possible by the fact that the two items have a common ground for comparison in the *rhythm* of their movements. The secondary levels of the Imagist movement, the work of Amy Lowell and of J. G. Fletcher, for example, abounded in comparisons of sounds with colors, comparisons which in their nature are arbitrary and meaningless; but Robinson's comparison has life because it is founded in reality. The last stanza, which is admirable throughout, contains two lines which seem to me finer, perhaps, than anything else in the poem. (See "The Poor Relation," lines 11–12 on page 47 of *Collected Poems* of Robinson.) This bare statement of perfect tragedy seems to me beyond improvement. It is not Emersonian, nor is it the work of an Emersonian.

"Luke Havergal" is less simple in its subject than are the last two poems which I have mentioned, and it illustrates less purely the theme of simple endurance. The poem is an address to Luke Havergal, spoken, apparently, by the woman whom he had loved, from beyond the grave; or at any rate such is his illusion. He is told that he may find her through suicide. It might be said, I presume, that the poem seems to display a faith in life after death; but if one considers the intense desolation of the tone, it becomes rather an expression of longing for death, of inability to endure more. (See "Luke Havergal," lines 9–16 on page 74 of *Collected Poems* of Robinson.) "For a Dead Lady" is an elegy unlightened by any mitigating idea or feeling; it is purely a lament for the dead. Robinson suggests no way of dealing with the experience except that we understand it and endure it. (See "For a Dead Lady," lines 17–24 on page 355 of *Collected Poems* of Robinson.) "Mr. Flood's Party" is less compact than most of these poems, and it is written with a kind of compassionate humor, but the same theme of irremediable tragedy governs it.

"The Wandering Jew" is a few years later than any poem I have thus far mentioned except the last. It is certainly one of the greatest of Robinson's short poems, perhaps the greatest; it comes closer to complete success than most. It is an interesting poem for certain incidental reasons as well. Although most of Robinson's great poems contain very little sensory imagery, this poem contains less than most; it is almost purely a poetry of ideas. Yet the ideas arise from the consideration of the particular case; the case is not used to illustrate the ideas. That is, the poem is not what we would call a didactic or philosophic poem. Except in "Hillcrest," Robinson probably never succeeds very brilliantly with the didactic or philosophical, whereas he often succeeds brilliantly with the poem of the particular case. It is curious to see a poet handle "abstract" language so brilliantly as in this poem and in "Eros Turannos" and so ineptly as in "The Man Against the Sky" and certain other poems which I shall discuss later in this chapter. He *thinks* well here; he does other things well likewise—but he thinks well and intricately; in "The Man Against the Sky" he thinks badly. But what I want to point out above all is this: that in a period which is convinced that thought and poetry are mutually destructive, that rational structure is a defect in a poem rather than a virtue, that genuine poetry must be confused to express a confused period, that poetry is primarily sensory and depends for its strength upon large quantities of sensory imagery, Robinson has written a poem (to mention only this one) which is rational in general structure, packed with thought in its detail, perfectly clear in its meaning and development, and nearly free from sensory imagery, and that this poem is one of the great poems not only of our time but of our language. (See "The Wandering Jew," pages 456–459 in *Collected Poems* of Robinson.) It is interesting to observe here the complete transmutation of the method of Praed's poem "The Vicar" and of Robinson's "Old King Cole" into something deeply serious. The feminine rimes of those poems, with their excessive emphasis on neatness, have been abandoned; in fact the number of rimes has been reduced to half, with the result that the precision of statement, though it is undiminished, is muted and unobtrusive. The same method of extremely careful definition of shades of meaning is employed; but in those poems the meanings were slight to the point of triviality, and the care resulted in cleverness; in this poem the meanings are profound, and the care results in a power which has seldom been equaled. I can only recommend a careful study of this poem, a study concentrated especially upon the last five stanzas, in which the force of the statement begins to accumulate. To cite excerpts is perhaps foolish, for the language is quiet and its effectiveness depends upon its place in the context; nevertheless, the isolation of a few passages may help the reader to observe the quality which I have in mind. The last two lines of the third stanza are a remarkably fine statement of an acute though limited insight. The last two lines of the fourth stanza have a similar virtue. But it is the later stanzas, in which the central theme is developed, which offer the most powerful passages. (See "The Wandering Jew," lines 12–17 and 24–25 on page 458 of *Collected Poems* of Robinson.) This is very great poetry, perhaps as great as one can easily find. I do not wish to labor the point unnecessarily, but there is a common inability in our time to distinguish between poetry written in plain and generalized diction and poetry which is dull or even trite; it is essential that the distinction be made.

The poem should not be construed, I think, as an attempt to evaluate Jewish character, if such an entity may be said to exist; it is rather an attempt to examine a spiritual vice which may occur in any group at a fairly high intellectual and spiritual level. The vice is the vice of pride in one's own identity, a pride which will not allow one to accept a greater wisdom from without even when one recognizes that the wisdom is there and is greater than one's own; the result is spiritual sickness. The Wandering Jew is simply a mythological figure who embodies this vice in a useable form. This meaning is pointed repeatedly and sharply in the last stanzas, and finally in the last two lines of the poem.

Three of Robinson's later sonnets seem to me among the greatest of his works: "Lost Anchors," "Many Are Called," and "The Sheaves." In fact if one adds to these sonnets and "The Wandering Jew" two or three of the blank verse monologues—"The Three Taverns," "Rembrandt to Rembrandt," and perhaps "John Brown" —one probably has Robinson at his greatest.

"Lost Anchors" is a commentary on the conversation of an old sailor; the sailor is not of great importance in himself, but he is made a symbol of the immeasurable antiquity of the sea and of its ruins. (See "Lost Anchors" on pages 577–578 of *Collected Poems* of Robinson.) The poem is wholly admirable, but the skill with which the sailor's illegitimate birth, mentioned, as it is, at the very end, is made to imply the amoral and archaic nature of the sea, is something which can scarcely be too long pondered or too greatly admired.

"Many Are Called" is a sonnet on the rarity of poetic genius and the loneliness of its reward. (See "Many Are Called" on pages 581–582 of *Collected Poems* of Robinson.) The second half of the octave displays a characteristic form of Robinson's irony, and the sixth line follows in a measure a familiar Victorian formula which the Fowlers have described,[2] of which the procedure is to relate disparate elements in a parallel construction, with the intention of startling. Robinson's line is a curious variant, however. The word *vain* in English is in almost every expression an adjective, coming

[2] H. W. and F. G. Fowler, *The King's English* [Oxford: Clarendon Press, 1906], p. 182, in the chapter entitled "Airs and Graces." Among the examples listed are: ". . . they return together in triumph and a motor-car" (*Times*); "Miss Nipper . . . shook her head and a tin-cannister" (Dickens).

from the Latin *vanus,* so that we feel vaguely in using this expression, *in vain,* that a subsequent noun is somehow understood; or perhaps the fixed form of the expression gives us the sense of a single adverb instead of the sense of an adverbial phrase; and to the extent that we have either feeling, we get the impression that the phrase *in vain* is not parallel grammatically with the two phrases preceding, but is parallel only in superficial appearance. Since the word *vain* in this expression is derived from the substantive *vanum,* however, the three phrases are actually parallel in construction, and any such feeling which one may have is delusive, yet I suspect that Robinson desired to invoke such a feeling. The real divergence from parallelism is not in the grammar but in the sense, for the first two phrases relate to states of mind, and the third to an end. In the passages cited by the Fowlers, the humor resides in a descent from the heroic to the prosaic, or in a shift from the natural to the ridiculous. But the irony in this case is spiritual; Robinson means each one of his items seriously, and the irony is the tragic irony of frustration. The risk involved in the use of any such formula is great, but the passage appears successful. And such rhetorical device, no matter how stereotyped, may be used successfully if it is used deliberately and with adequate motive by a poet of ability, as a study of the puns and other plays upon words in the English poets of the Renaissance will fully demonstrate.[3] The irony is quiet, and to some extent the formulary statement of it keeps it quiet; and the quietness permits the poem to return easily to the high seriousness of the sestet and even to return with a certain intensification of that seriousness. These four lines might easily have slipped into the superficial cleverness of which Robinson is so often guilty; they represent a successful handling of what he apparently tries and fails to do in other passages to which I have already called attention.

"The Sheaves" employs a descriptive technique to symbolize the

[3] See for example "A Farewell," one of the greatest sonnets by Sidney, with its tireless play upon *part, depart* and *impart;* Shakespeare's "Golden lads and girls all must/ As chimney-sweepers, come to dust"; and Donne's "Thy Grace may wing me to prevent his art/ And Thou, like adamant, draw mine iron heart." One can find innumerable other puns and plays upon words in the period, and even in Shakespeare, which are very bad; but they are bad because the formula is badly managed or badly inspired, not because the formula is employed.

impenetrable mystery of the physical universe as seen at any moment and the mystery of the fact of change. (See "The Sheaves" on pages 870–71 of *Collected Poems* of Robinson.)

III

There is another aspect of Robinson which I must discuss briefly —his obscurity. Much of Robinson was found obscure by his earlier readers, and for the most part as a result of their own indolence or ignorance, and the term "mysticism" was frequently employed to describe the obscurity; I take it that the word was used as a polite form of disapproval and was not intended seriously, for whatever there is or is not in Robinson's verse, there is no mysticism.[4] There has been a great deal of obscurity in modern verse, and where it has not been due merely to incompetent writing, it has been mainly of two kinds. Sometimes the poet endeavors to be perfectly lucid, but he thinks so badly that he makes statements which are without his realizing it incomprehensible. Such statements in modern American verse belong most frequently to the tradition of Emerson and Whitman, and there are a few mild examples of this kind of obscurity in Robinson, examples to which I shall eventually refer. When Emerson, in "The Problem," tells us that the artist produces art unconsciously, functioning as a divinely controlled automaton, we cannot understand him, because we can imagine an automaton only as a madman; the statement is unbelievable and unimaginable. When Hart Crane, in "The Dance," describes under veils of metaphor the apotheosis of Maquokeeta as union with the American soil, we are similarly baffled, for a man cannot be imagined as

[4] The mystic, traditionally considered, is one who experiences occasionally and briefly a direct communion with God, a communion which is supra-rational and incommensurate with normal human experience, so that it cannot properly be described in language. The discipline of the mystic is a religious and moral discipline which prepares him for this experience. Mystical poetry deals either with the experience itself, but imperfectly and by way of some human analogy, or with the discipline. According to the Catholic doctrine, the mystical experience is granted to very few persons and is not a necessary part of the religious life. Calvinistic and related Protestant doctrine, however, tends to identify the mystical experience with the operation of Grace and to make it a necessary part of the religious life, and to identify both with "conscience," which thus becomes an inexplicable feeling instead of right reason, with which Catholic doctrine identifies conscience. Emerson, with his pantheistic doctrine, identified God with his creation, impulse with conscience, and surrender to impulse with the mystical experience.

both keeping and losing his personal identity. Sometimes, however, the poet may be fully conscious that he is obscure; he may follow the example of the later Mallarmé and suppress the rational element in his poems in the mistaken idea that he is thus strengthening the emotional; or he may write as it would seem that Rimbaud frequently wrote, more or less automatically, in a state more or less approximating hallucination, with the mistaken idea (one which Emerson shared without putting it into practice) that the automatic is of necessity divinely inspired, thus achieving fantastic symbols with the empty semblance only of significance, symbols arranged in a meaningless sequence.[5] Reference to strange bits of erudition, such as we get in Pound, may cause temporary obscurity, but only till an appropriate doctoral dissertation may be written; and this is true likewise of reference to a private set of symbols, such as we get in Blake. The method of progression by revery, or random association, which we get in Pound's *Cantos,* may seem to result in obscurity, but only if one fails to recognize the method and is expecting to disentangle something which was never there.[6]

Robinson's commonest form of obscurity, I should judge, has no relationship to any of these varieties. His esthetic is not Mallarméan, his philosophy is a matter of relatively simple common sense, and the themes of such of his obscure poems as I have been able to understand are anything but profound. But there is a kind of New Englander, of which Robinson is a belated and somewhat attenuated example, in which ingenuity has become a form of eccentricity; when you encounter a gentleman of this breed, you cannot avoid feeling that he may at any moment sit down on the rug and begin inventing a watch or a conundrum. Franklin and the first O. W. Holmes were specimens of the ingenious Yankee at his best; Henry Adams with his theory of history is in part a specimen of the ingenious Yankee gone wrong; and Robinson in a few of his poems is a specimen of the ingenious Yankee become whimsical.

The method of the obscure poems is best introduced by a poem which does not quite succeed in becoming obscure and in which

[5] This describes most of Rimbaud's poems in prose and some but not all of those in verse. There is much else that one could say of Rimbaud, a good deal of it in his favor, but this is his chief defect, and heaven knows it is sufficiently serious.

[6] These matters are discussed in a good deal of detail in my book entitled *Primitivism and Decadence,* Arrow Editions, New York, 1937.

one can therefore see plainly how the method works. The poem is "The Mill" from *The Three Taverns.* (See "The Mill" on pages 460–61 of *Collected Poems* of Robinson.) We learn in the first stanza that the miller's wife has forebodings because her husband has left her with an expression of discouragement at the disappearance of his trade; in the second stanza that her husband has hanged himself; and in the third stanza that she drowns herself in the millstream; yet all this is stated with a certain amount of indirectness, though not with enough to obscure the meaning. In the poem "The Whip," the method results in more difficulty. I suggest that the reader examine it carefully at least two or three times, before proceeding to my comment, to see if he can deduce the meaning. (See "The Whip" on pages 338–39 of *Collected Poems* of Robinson.) The indirection of statement, aided by what one might call a more or less metaphysical tone, results in pretty successful obscurity; one suspects a concealed symbolism, dealing with a more or less general theme—or at least I did so for a number of years, although my obtuseness now strikes me as somewhat curious.[7] The poem actually deals with a brutal melodrama, of a kind of which Robinson was especially fond,[8] and of which "The Mill" is a rather mild specimen. We are given a man and wife and the wife's lover. The husband had long suspected his wife's fidelity, but had fought the suspicion. The three are in some fashion tipped out from a boat in a river, perhaps from the same boat, perhaps, as the fifth line of the fourth stanza suggests, from two boats, or at any rate with the husband in some way in pursuit of the two others. As the three are about to emerge to safety, the wife turns and strikes her husband across the face; and recognizing the certainty of what he had before suspected, he chooses to sink rather than save himself and face his tragedy. All of the necessary information is given us in pretty clear statements; but it is given fragmentarily, and interspersed with comments which are likely to be misleading, and in a tone which is misleading. As a conclusion to this topic, I wish to cite a sonnet for which I am unable to offer an explanation but which I suspect to be a highly successful experiment in the same kind of procedure. It is called "En Passant." (See "En Passant" on pages 886–87 of *Collected Poems* of Robinson.)

[7] For my paraphrase of this poem I am indebted to Mr. Don Stanford.

[8] See, for example, "Aaron Stark," "Reuben Bright," "The Tavern" and "Haunted House"; and among the longer poems *Cavender's House.*

IV

There are a good many poems which deal with the subject of God and immortality, but they are not remarkably clear. The most ambitious of these is "The Man Against the Sky," a fairly long contemplative poem, of which the versification is generally similar to that of "Dover Beach." The poem opens with a description of a solitary man crossing a hilltop into the sunset. This man is symbolic of man in general approaching death. Robinson says that his symbolic man may have progressed through great anguish to a triumphant death; or that he may have proceeded easily in the light of an uncritical faith; or that he may have been disillusioned, a stoical artist or philosopher, passing indifferently to extinction; or that he may have been disappointed in life and fearfully unreconciled to death; or that he may have been a mechanistic philosopher, proud of an intellectual construction which gave him no personal hope; but in any event that he represents all of us in that he approaches death alone, to face it as he is able. Robinson asks, then, whether we may not have some expectation of a future life, even if we doubt the existence of Heaven and Hell; and why, if we believe in Oblivion, we are guilty of perpetuating the race. He replies that we know, "if we know anything," the existence of a Deity, a Word, which we perceive fragmentarily and imperfectly, and that this knowledge is our sole justification for not ending ourselves and our kind. (See "The Man Against the Sky," lines 26–32 on page 66 of *Collected Poems* of Robinson.) The nature of this Deity, and the nature of our knowledge, are not defined further than this; the crux of the poem is thus offered briefly and vaguely in a few lines; and the greater part of the concluding section is devoted to describing the desolation which we should experience without this knowledge. Philosophically, the poem is unimpressive; stylistically, it is all quite as weak as the lines referred to above; and structurally, it seems to defeat its purpose—for while it purports to be an expression of faith, it is devoted in all save these same few lines to the expression of despair.

"Credo," from *Children of the Night,* perhaps expresses a similar concept and in an equally unsatisfactory manner, but the connective *for* which introduces the second half of the sestet is confusing. (See "Credo" on page 94 of *Collected Poems* of Robinson.) In a

"Sonnet," from the same collection, there is a statement of belief in God based on the evidence of human love and the beauty of nature; this, as far as it goes, might be Christian or Emersonian or neither. (See "Sonnet" on page 96 of *Collected Poems* of Robinson.) I do not mention these poems for their poetic virtue, for they have little; the language is vague and trite, the fifth line of the poem just noted is rhythmically very flat and is guilty of a needless and clumsy use of the progressive form of the verb, and Belshazzar's wall is a curious place on which to read the glory of eternal partnership. But the poems are characteristic expressions of this phase of Robinson's thought; they are characteristic, in fact, of his efforts to express generalized thought of any variety; and they may perhaps serve as some justification of my failure to come to definite conclusions with regard to the precise form of Robinson's theology.

In the "Octaves," from the same collection, we have a sequence of poems for the most part on the experiential evidence for a belief in God; the evidence is defined very vaguely, in spite of the effort to achieve a gnomic style, but the writing in certain lines achieves a strength greater than any in the three poems which I have just been discussing. The ninth of these is clearer than most; it deals with the disappointment which we feel when a person of high character displays weakness, and the disappointment is offered as evidence of the real existence of the impersonal standard. (See "Octaves," lines 7–14 on page 103 of *Collected Poems* of Robinson.) The poem illustrates a defect very obvious throughout the group of which it is a part, and often evident elsewhere in Robinson. The movement is stiff and insensitive—Robinson's ear is in general so deficient that he usually needs the support of rime and of a compact form—and the lines read as if they ought to be rimed and were left unrimed through an oversight. The lines stop so emphatically at the ends that the expression *on earth,* at the beginning of the sixth line, has the effect of an awkward afterthought, and its redundancy is made obvious. The eleventh octave is one of the best written, but offers no solution to the problem posed; it deals merely with the unsatisfied search for the solution. (See "Octaves," lines 23–26 on page 103 and lines 1–4 on page 104 of *Collected Poems* of Robinson.) The language applied in these poems to the evidence for a belief in God, language, for example, like "spirit-gleams of Wisdom" in the eighth, is likely to be both vague and more or less romantic in its connotations; such a phrase as the one just quoted, in fact, would perhaps appear to indicate a belief in the discovery of God through pure intuition and lend some support to those who find a strong trace of Emerson in Robinson; but there is not sufficient evidence in the poems to prove that the intuition is Emersonian intuition or that the God is Emerson's God, and there is explicit contrary evidence elsewhere. The worst one can say of the poems is that in general they are carelessly thought and carelessly written. Emerson used language reminiscent of Edwards without being a Christian;[9] Robinson could easily have used language reminiscent of Emerson without having been an Emersonian. Robinson, especially in his earlier years, might well have resembled a good many learned scholars of my acquaintance who claim to admire Emerson and who quote him by phrases, but who fail to understand or for sentimental reasons refuse to admit the total effect of his work. This kind of thing is fairly common and seems merely to indicate a normal and healthy capacity on the part of superior minds. "The Sage" appears to be a poem in praise of Emerson, but it does not define his doctrine. One could adduce a little more evidence of this kind from the shorter poems, but I believe that all of it would be similarly inconclusive.

V

Aside from explicit expressions of theory, however, there are occasional indications of a romantic attitude in Robinson, an attitude belonging especially to the 1890's, the period of his youth. "Flammonde" will do as an example. The poem praises an individual whom one might characterize as the sensitive parasite or as the literary or academic sponge. (See "Flammonde," lines 9–16 on page 3 and lines 12–19 on page 4 of *Collected Poems* of Robinson.) Now the near-genius of this kind, who represents an especially unfortunate type of failure, and who is frequently, as in the case of Flammonde, a somewhat unpleasant specimen, obsessed Robinson throughout his life for reasons which were largely personal. Frequently the poverty in which he lived threw him into the company of such people, and he may at times have visualized himself as one

[9] See "Jonathan Edwards to Emerson," by Perry Miller, *The New England Quarterly,* XIII, 4. See also the essays called "The Puritan Heresy" and "Emerson," *The Hound and Horn,* Vol. V, and reprinted in *The Pragmatic Test,* by H. B. Parkes. The Colt Press, San Francisco, 1941.

of them, though he could scarcely have visualized himself as Flammonde. But this obsession is not in itself an explanation of the language which Robinson uses, language which is reminiscent of the worst sentimentalism of the nineties, or even of lachrymose popular balladry. (See "Flammonde," lines 20–23 and 28–30 on page 4 and lines 13–14 on page 6 of *Collected Poems* of Robinson.) The classicism, the precision, of Robinson's great work is not in this poem; there is nothing here of it but an empty mannerism. The substance as a whole and phrase by phrase is repulsively sentimental. Yet the poem has been repeatedly offered as one of Robinson's great achievements; it perhaps comes as close to the classical as the average critic of our time is able to follow. In "Richard Cory," another favorite, we have a superficially neat portrait of the elegant man of mystery; the poem builds up deliberately to a very cheap surprise ending; but all surprise endings are cheap in poetry, if not, indeed, elsewhere, for poetry is written to be read not once but many times. Such poems, however, although there are more like them, are relatively rare.

VI

Robinson wrote a small but definite group of poems dealing with his political and social ideas, and although some of them are of greater length than the other poems discussed in this chapter, I shall take them up here for the sake of convenience. Most of these poems are poor and none are of his best; in general, they indicate the abilities and disabilities to which I have already pointed: the best adhere most closely to the case of the individual man, the worst adventure farthest into general theory. I have in mind "The Master," "The Revealer," "Cassandra," "Demos," "On the Way," "Dionysus in Doubt," and "Demos and Dionysus."

"The Master," a poem on Lincoln, and "The Revealer," a poem on Theodore Roosevelt, are primarily poems in praise of their respective subjects; but they indicate, perhaps not very clearly, Robinson's distrust of the common man and his belief in the superior leader as the only hope for democracy. They are the best poems in this group, "The Master" especially standing well up among the best of Robinson's secondary poems. "Cassandra" is a poem warning the nation against the naively enthusiastic commercialism of the early part of this century. (See "Cassandra," lines

9–12 on page 12 of *Collected Poems* of Robinson.) The admirable sharpness of such satirical statements as this is not equaled by his statements in praise of the virtues which he defends. (See "Cassandra," lines 20–28 on page 12 of *Collected Poems* of Robinson.) He does not tell us what old verities he has in mind nor how old they are—whether, for example, they are the verities of Emerson or those of Aquinas. Nor does he define the nature of the price in the last stanza, and a good many divergent definitions would be possible. He is quite as vague here as in his references to a positive theology; yet the force of a didactic poem depends precisely upon the clarity and validity of the ideas expressed.

"Demos," a double sonnet, warns us that "the few shall save the many, or the many are to fall"; but Robinson is again too vague. Does he mean, for example, that democracy cannot survive unless it is regularly governed by great men? If so, there is small hope for it, for great men rise to power in a democracy only occasionally and as a result of their being incidentally great politicians or as a result of some other chance. Robinson may mean that the common mass should be improved little by little by the teachings of great men as those teachings after many years reach them and become a part of tradition. I should place my own modest hopes in this latter formula, and in the belief that for the immediate present the common man is guided in some measure by such traditional wisdom, imperfectly as he may apprehend it and profit by it, and by a fairly acute sense of where the economic and social shoe pinches; this is not the formula for an Utopia, but I think it works reasonably well. But Robinson, unfortunately, does not say what he means, and he seems at times to be recommending a Carlylean leader-worship, or a doctrine of an elite class, either of which in practice would result in a Hitler or in an oligarchy.

"On the Way" is a dialogue spoken by Hamilton and Burr at a time when they were still superficially friendly with each other. Burr expresses the personal jealousy of a politician for a man greater than himself—that is, Washington—and Hamilton expresses an admiration for Washington similar to that expressed elsewhere by Robinson for Lincoln and Theodore Roosevelt. (See "On the Way," lines 24–30 on page 480 and lines 1–10 on page 481 of *Collected Poems* of Robinson.) With the admiration for Washington one cannot quarrel, nor can one quarrel with the unkind but essentially true statements about the common man; but again one is at a loss to discern the relationship of Washington to the common man, the way in which he may be said to guide the common man or be of value to him. In the nature of this relationship lies all the difference between barbarism and civilization, however halting. For Washington will be merely a menace to the nation if the common man depends upon him blindly. Unless the influence of Washington can outlast Washington, can teach the common man a few truths and give him a few perceptions, so that he can hope to survive the intervals between Washingtons, then the common man is lost.

"Dionysus in Doubt" deals immediately with the Prohibition Amendment of the 1920's, but more generally with the impropriety of legislation upon questions which are matters of personal morality rather than public. (See "Dionysus in Doubt," line 34 on page 860 and lines 1–6 on page 861 of *Collected Poems* of Robinson.) With this as a starting point, he deals sketchily with common personal attitudes which he finds a menace to society. (See "Dionysus in Doubt," lines 10–26 on page 865 of *Collected Poems* of Robinson.) These attitudes, and others which he attacks, are, as he says, a danger; but they are no more common and no more dangerous in democracies than elsewhere. Robinson appears to have confused the vices of humanity with the vices of his country. The writing, moreover, is lax and indolent, whereas satiric and didactic poetry should be compact and sharp; the confusing of the trite figure of the watch-dog with the equally trite figure of the dog in a manger is an especially bad example of this laxness. Dionysus goes on to meditate on the dangers of the standardization of the human mind implicit in the kind of legislation to which he is objecting. (See "Dionysus in Doubt," lines 20–26 on page 866 of *Collected Poems* of Robinson.) But once more Robinson seems to read into his own age and country a danger common to all times and countries: Socrates, Galileo, Abelard and Columbus suffered from this vice in human nature no less surely than anyone has done more recently. The tendency for the mediocre norm to impose itself and for the superior individual to combat and escape this norm or to be sacrificed to it have always existed and I imagine always will; and as for the Prohibition Amendment, we eventually got rid of it. I have no objection to the castigation of vices, and the vices which Robinson castigates are real; but unless they are rightly located, the poem suffers and there is the possibility that society may suffer.

The reader may assume, for example, that there was less standardization and more individual freedom under Louis XIV of France or Phillip II of Spain; but although the reigns of those monarchs may have been marked by important values which we lack, yet freedom was not one of them, and it strikes me as doubtful that the values in question would be recovered by the re-establishment of comparable political systems. Before we blame our spiritual defects on a political system which it has cost blood and centuries to establish, merely because the defects and the system coincide in time, we would do well to make a careful study of historical causes. And this issue is not irrelevant to the question of poetry; a poem which embodies so careless an outburst is not an adult performance —that is, it is not a good poem. "Demos and Dionysus" develops much the same argument, and with no greater distinction.

VII

In conclusion, I shall repeat that nearly all of Robinson's best poems appear to deal with particular persons and situations; in these poems his examination is careful and intelligent, his method is analytic, and his style is mainly very distinguished. If we are to risk pushing historical influences for all they are worth, we may say that in such poems Robinson exhibits the New England taste for practical morality, a passionate curiosity about individual dramas, and that in examining them he is guided by the moral and spiritual values of the general Christian tradition as they have come down to him in the form of folk wisdom or common sense, although in the application of these values he shows a penetration and subtlety which are the measure of his genius. In his more generalized, or philosophic, poems, he is almost always careless in his thinking and equally careless in his style, and it is in these poems that one may see—often in the method and sometimes in the form of the thought—the influence of Emersonian romanticism. "Hillcrest" is the most notable exception to this last statement.

Robinson is thus a poet whose thought is incomplete and in a measure contradictory; he would have been a greater poet had this not been so, but we should remember that he is no worse in this respect than Wordsworth, Hardy, Arnold or Bridges, if indeed he be as bad. Furthermore, within certain definitely delimited areas during the greater part of his career, his approach to his material is sound; we have seen this approach defined in "Hillcrest" and practiced in a number of other poems. The approach is what we may call critical and rationalistic; and the poetry is reasoning poetry. It is true that reasoning poetry has often been written to attack the reason—Pope's *Essay on Man* and most of Emerson may serve as examples—but these poems by Robinson are not written to attack the reason, they are written to illustrate it. It is an extremely careful poetry. I do not mean this in any superficial sense; I mean that Robinson not only scrutinizes his thought but also is watchful of his feeling. His New England heritage here is not a defect, even though he chooses occasionally to ridicule it; the feeling which *ought* to be motivated by his comprehension of the matter is what he seeks to express—he is not simply on a tour in search of emotion. And since his matter is often important and his comprehension sometimes profound, this exact adjustment of feeling to motive results on certain occasions in poetry of extremely great value.

The greatest poems, not all of which achieve perfection, are probably the following: from *The Children of the Night* (1890–97), "Luke Havergal" and "The Clerks"; from *Captain Craig, Etc.* (1902), none; from *The Town Down the River* (1910), "For a Dead Lady"; from *The Man Against the Sky* (1916), "Hillcrest," "Eros Turannos," "Veteran Sirens" and "The Poor Relation"; from *The Three Taverns* (1920), "The Wandering Jew"; from *Avon's Harvest, Etc.* (1921), "Lost Anchors" and "Many Are Called"; from *Dionysus in Doubt* (1925), "The Sheaves." After this there is only one volume, *Nicodemus* (1932), containing any short poems, and that contains only a few and none of importance. These eleven poems can be equaled, I think, in the work of only four or five English and American poets of the past century and a half.

To list all of the secondary poems of importance would be tedious and might lead to a number of unduly fine decisions, but I offer an incomplete list of my favorites as an introductory guide to the reader who may not be familiar with Robinson; this list alone, I suspect, would suffice to give Robinson a permanent reputation, had he done nothing better: from *Children of the Night,* "Horace to Leuconoë" and "George Crabbe"; from *Captain Craig, Etc.,* "The Growth of Lorraine"; from *The Town Down the River,* "The Master," "The White Lights," "Doctor of Billiards," "Miniver Cheevy" and "Two Gardens in Linndale"; from *The*

Man Against the Sky, "Another Dark Lady" and "The Voice of the Age"; from *The Three Taverns,* "The Valley of the Shadow," "The Mill," "Dark Hills" and "Souvenir"; from *Avon's Harvest, Etc.,* "Mr. Flood's Party," "Vain Gratuities" and "The Long Race"; from *Dionysus in Doubt,* "The Haunted House," "Karma," "New England," "Reunion," "A Christmas Sonnet."

I have not listed any of the Browningesque monologues and dialogues, such as "The Clinging Vine" and "John Gorham," poems which have no doubt contributed heavily to Robinson's popularity; for reasons which I have given elsewhere, these do not impress me as being serious poetry, and I have tried to select poems more concentrated and less obviously derivative. It should be remembered that these selections are from the shorter works only; not even the poems of moderate length, such as "The Three Taverns," have been considered—I shall deal with these in one of my last chapters.

E. A. Robinson: The Lost Tradition

by Louis O. Coxe

To the contemporary reader it seems strange that Allen Tate, in 1933, should have referred to E. A. Robinson as the "most famous of living poets" and again as the writer of "some of the finest lyrics of modern times." As far as most of us are concerned, nowadays Robinson ekes out a survival in "anthological pickle," as he called it, and few readers try to go beyond, for if any poet has been damned by the anthologists it is Robinson. Why the decline in his reputation? Did critics puff him far beyond his deserts? Can a critic today judge him on the basis of the old chestnuts, "Miniver Cheevy," "Flammonde," "Richard Cory"? Should criticism reiterate that he ruined himself writing those interminable narratives and dismiss him as a "transition figure" between somebody and somebody else, both presumably more "important"? Yvor Winters, in his recent book, has gone far to disestablish the transitional, and place the essential, Robinson, yet neither he nor Mr. Tate has told why he considers the poems he praises praiseworthy. Mr. Winters has in his brief study given an excellent analysis of Robinson's failings and failures, but there is still the problem of the kind of excellence readers who come to Robinson these days should expect. Vicissitudes of temper and fashion apart, I think much of the neglect of Robinson's work has derived from the deceptively old-fashioned appearance it presents and from the very stern cosmology out of which the poetry arises. The texture of the poetry is of a sort we are not used to; the subject-matter can be misunderstood. Above all, Robinson's technique lends itself to abuse (and he abused it frequently) so that very often the

"E. A. Robinson: The Lost Tradition" by Louis O. Coxe. From *Sewanee Review,* LXII, number 2 (Spring, 1954), 247–66.

reader may not detect that under an appparently calm surface many forms are in motion.

Robinson is a poet with a prose in view. Read "Eros Turannos" or "For a Dead Lady" or "The Gift of God" and you will feel that the scope of a long naturalistic novel has emerged from a few stanzas. Yet Mr. Tate, in his brief essay, says that Robinson's lyrics are "dramatic" and that T. S. Eliot observes this to be a characteristic of the best modern verse. I really do not know what the word "dramatic" means in this regard; Robinson's poetry is not dramatic in any sense of the word commonly accepted, unless it be that Robinson, like James, likes to unfold a scene. To look for anything like drama in the poems is idle, in that the excitement they convey is of a muted sort, akin to that which James himself generates. This poet wears no masks; he is simply at a distance from his poem, unfolding the "plot," letting us see and letting us make what applications we will. This directness, this prose element, in Robinson's verse is easy enough to find; less so to define or characterize. One can say this, however: just as Pope was at his best in a poetry that had morality and man in society as its subject matter and its criterion, so Robinson is happiest as a poet when he starts with a specific human situation or relationship, with a "story." By the same token, he fails most notably when he engages in philosophic speculation, when he writes poems, such as the "Octaves," or many of the sonnets, that have no real subject-matter, no focus of events or crisis seen objectively. The parallel between his method and that of Pope is patently incomplete, yet each poet, basing his whole scheme on certain immutable moral convictions and concerning himself primarily with man as a social creature, strove for a poetry that would be external, transparent, unified. Neither made elaborate experiments with form but each was content to exploit with dexterity a few common meters, because for both Pope and Robinson the real business was what was finally said and communicated. Both used their individual idioms, each far removed from anything we find today: spare where we are lush, general where we are specific, detailed where we are reticent or silent. The twentieth century has learned to dislike abstractions as the result of being badly cheated by them, yet the fear should perhaps be of the susceptibility to fraud, however pious.

Whatever Robinson's weaknesses, his frauds are few and those few easy to expose. The best poems work toward a condition of total communication by means of suggestion and statement, with no regard for the poet as speaker; that is, the attitudes out of which the poems emerge we take as our own, and there is no need to ascertain those of the speaker since Robinson is everywhere the same. His irony is not "in" the poem but external, one constituent of a cosmology that sees the human condition as comic in the largest sense—sees life as a desperate business but essentially, immutably unalterable. This is not childish disillusionment; it works out in the poetry as a cosmology that seems to us, scions of the liberal-romantic stock, bitter, profitless, perhaps old-fashioned. And because Robinson so early in his career found and grasped his ultimate beliefs, the modern reader does not find what he must naturally look for: progress, novelty, enlightenment. This poetry does not intend certain things, and discussion of the kind of verse Robinson wrote may clear the ground and allow the reader to go to the poetry with some idea of what not to expect or look for.

Many critics have spent too much time saying that Robinson was obsessed with failure, thereby accounting for his lapse into the profitless slough of the long narratives. Yet none has shown how vital a force the failure is as theme, how it contains within itself a possibility of vision and maturity, as well as of pathos. For to Robinson life and humanity were failures inasmuch as they consistently, unalterably fall short of, not the ideal, but their own proper natures. Robinson was never so romantically disillusioned that he could be for long disturbed over the discrepancy between actual and ideal, illusion and reality; for him the real irony, the comedy, lay in man's wilful misconception of life and his role in it. The very wilfulness may have a magnificence of its own, as in "The Gift of God," and the people in his poems who come through to an awareness of the true proportion do not simply rest there in smug knowledge, but rather for the first time see that it is from such vision of things as they are that a man starts:

> He may by contemplation learn
> A little more than what he knew,
> And even see great oaks return
> To acorns out of which they grew.

What may be irony from one point of view may be comedy or pathos, perhaps a kind of muted tragedy, from another. At all events, the point of view is essentially the same, with only a pace back, forward or to one side that gives the particular vision its specific color and shape.

The attitudes which have dominated the writing of our century have been rather different from Robinson's. We seem for the most part willing to contemplate life as a tragic affair, to command the ironic tone in our writing in order to express successfully the tragic division we see gaping between what we are and what we would be. Yet one wonders at times if we actually do *believe* this or whether it is another kind of myth-making, a device for getting poetry written and read, like Yeats's visions. If we really do believe, then we must accept the consequences of our faith, for in a world that is ultimately tragic, happiness is irrelevant, despair the resort of the thin-skinned, and total acceptance the only *modus vivendi*. The acceptance itself must entail a kind of transubstantiation: the Aristotelian essence of life turns to something else while the "accidents" of evil and death remain. This is the realm of miracle; the poetry of Robinson has nothing to do with it, for his work merely tries to come to a naked vision of the human condition without lusting after schemes of revision, without trying to discover something that is not, can not in nature be, there. In "Veteran Sirens" all the terrible irony of mankind's wilful refusal to face facts emerges in the pitying portrait of superannuated whores:

> The burning hope, the worn expectancy,
> The martyred humor and the maimed allure,
> Cry out for time to end his levity,
> And age to soften his investiture.

And we are all life's whores. What strikes Robinson as ironic is not the old discrepancy between illusion and reality, not the wastage of time, but the supreme dissipation of the expense of spirit in a waste of shame, folly and deceit. The stern, still-Calvinist view of carnal sin here has become a trope for life, for the way we all bargain with life for a living and are finally cheated.

The best of Robinson's poems have to do with such plots, such expense of the soul's life, and usually have as their center the single, crucial failure of a man or woman to commit that destruction of the beloved self, to make that complete disavowal of a precious image which alone and finally leaves the individual free. The price of such freedom comes high, "costing not less than everything," and is paid for by a crucial failure in which the image referred to is destroyed, in many such cases along with the life itself; in *Amaranth,* for instance, Atlas and Miss Watchman, both self-deluding artists, are destroyed along with their work, although Fargo, who sees the truth, manages to alter his whole nature and his way of life. The variations on the theme are many; the tone can be somber and tragic, or it can be pastoral and elegiac as in "Isaac and Archibald," or angry and bitter as in "For a Dead Lady." Yet all tones, all attitudes, are part of the one dominating view as the language, however bald or rich by turns it may be, serves the one narrative and ratiocinative end.

If Robinson's attitudes are not common ones, similarly his idiom finds little immediate sympathy in modern readers. Unfortunately we have been accustomed to read Robinson as though he were Edgar Lee Masters from Maine, a crabbed New Englander who should have read Walt Whitman, and unconsciously we judge him by a standard we would reject were it applied to Eliot or Ransom. Here is an old language, reborn, sometimes abstract and involved, unusually sparing of metaphor, though the imagery when it occurs is crucial, perhaps the more so because of its very compression and sparseness. Above all, Robinson organizes his poems to a disarming extent, often building a structure that is so symmetrically proportioned that only the closest reading discovers the articulation. Such a reading I shall attempt here in the hope that the effort will supply an insight into the poems themselves as well as a justification of the foregoing remarks.

"Eros Turannos" emerges to the mind as a narrative, compressed and suggestive yet without the trickery that occasionally irritates us, as in the case of "The Whip" or "How Annandale Went Out." Most noticeably, the language is general, the tone expository, the purpose of the poem communication rather than expression. Adumbrated in the first stanza, certain images, whose latent power and meanings are reserved until the final lines, have the function of motifs, repeated constantly and expanded as the poem opens out into suggestion. There are three such images or symbols: waves, tree, stairs leading down. Throughout, these symbols control and provide a center for the meanings possible to the poem, and from the mention of "downward years" and "foamless weirs" in the first stanza to the triple vision of the last four lines these elements recur, the same but altered. As is the case with so many Robinson poems, the reader must supply, from the general materials provided, his own construction, yet the poet has seen to it that there can be only one possible final product. The poem contains two complementary parts: the abstract, generalized statement and the symbolic counterpart of that statement, each constituting a kind of gloss upon the other; each moves through the poem parallel to the other, until at the end they become fused in the concrete images. In addition to the three symbols mentioned, we find also that of blindness and dimness, summed up in the single word "veil" yet continually present in the words mask, blurred, dimmed, fades, illusion. All this culminates in the sweeping final image: "Or like a stairway to the sea/Where down the blind are driven." Yet such inner order, such tight articulation as these examples may indicate derives no more from the concrete than from the generalized; contrary to Marianne Moore's professed belief, not all imaginary gardens need have actual toads in them, nor, conversely, do we have to bother with the toad at all if our garden is imagined truly enough. What we must have is room—for toads, or non-toads, but room anyhow, and Robinson seems to say that there will be more room if we don't clutter the garden with too many particular sorts of fauna and flora. For in "Eros Turannos" we are not told the where or the wherefore; only, and it is everything, the how and the just so. In the hinted-at complexity of the woman's emotion, in the suggested vagueness of the man's worthlessness, lies the whole history of human trust and self-deception: none shall see this incident for what it really is, and the woman who hides her trouble has as much of the truth as "we" who guess and guess, yet, the poem implies, coming no nearer to the truth than men usually do.

"Eros Turannos" is the Robinsonian archetype, for in it we can find the basic elements, the structural pattern, that he was to use frequently and with large success. The most cursory reading affords a glimpse into the potential power as well as the dangers of such a form; Robinson's use of it provides examples of both. In the poem in question he reaches an ultimate kind of equipoise of statement and suggestion, generalization and concretion. The first three words of the poem set the tone, provide the key to a "plot" which the rest will set before us. "She fears him": simple statement; what follows will explore the statement, and we shall try to observe the method and evaluate its effect.

She fears him, and will always ask
  What fated her to choose him;
She meets in his engaging mask
  All reasons to refuse him;
But what she meets and what she fears
Are less than are the downward years
Drawn slowly to the foamless weirs,
  Of age, were she to lose him.

The epigrammatic tone of the verse strikes one immediately; we are aware that here is a kind of expository writing, capable in its generality of evoking a good deal more than the words state. Important though unobtrusive imagery not only reinforces and enriches the exposition but by calculated ambiguity as well sets a tone of suspense and fatality. The man wears a mask: he conceals something that at once repels and attracts her; notice the play on "engaging" and the implications that involves. The motif is an important one for the poem, as is that contained in the metaphor of "weirs," since these two suggestions of deception, distrust, entrapment, blindness, and decline will be continually alluded to throughout the poem, to find an ultimate range of meaning in the final lines. The second stanza will in such expressions as "blurred" and "to sound" keep us in mind of the motifs mentioned, without actually requiring new imagistic material nor forcing us to reimagine the earlier metaphors. The intent here is not to be vague but to retain in the reader's consciousness what has gone before as that consciousness acquires new impressions. Hence, in stanza three, Robinson can now introduce a suggestive sketch of the man's nature while he reminds of the woman's and continues to explore it:

A sense of ocean and old trees
  Envelopes and allures him;
Tradition, touching all he sees,
  Beguiles and reassures him;

That engaging mask of his becomes apparent to us here in this man who finds a solace and security in the love of his wife and in her solid place in the community, and yet the sinister note first sounded in the image of "weirs" is lightly alluded to in the phrase "a sense of ocean." Moreover, that he too is "beguiled" presents a possibility of irony beyond what has yet been exploited. The stanza extends the narrative beyond what I have indicated:

> And all her doubts of what he says
> Are dimmed with what she knows of days—
> Till even prejudice delays
>   And fades and she secures him.

The possibilities are many. We grasp readily enough the pathos of her situation: a woman with a worthless husband, proud and sensitive to what the town is whispering yet ready to submit to any indignity, to close her eyes and ears, rather than live alone. Surely a common enough theme in American writing and one that allows the poet to suggest rather than dramatize. Again, in "dimmed" we catch an echo of what has gone before, and in the last two lines the abstract noun "prejudice" with its deliberately general verbs "delays" and "fades" presents no image but rather provokes the imagination to a vision of domestic unhappiness familiar to us all, either in fiction or empirically. And of course the finality of "secures," ironic neither in itself nor in its position in the stanza, takes on irony when we see what such security must be: the woman finds peace only by blinding herself and by seeing the man as she wishes to see him.

Stanza four once again recapitulates and explores. Statement alternates with image, the inner suffering with the world's vision of it:

> And home, where passion lived and died,
> Becomes a place where she can hide,
> While all the town and harbor-side
>   Vibrate with her seclusion.

If this stanza forms the climax of the plot, so to speak, the next comes to a kind of stasis, the complication of events and motives and themes we see so often in Henry James. The outside world of critical townspeople, hinted at before, now comes to the foreground, and we get a complication of attitudes and views—the world's, the woman's, the man's, our own—and the poet's is ours too. Yet even in a passage as seemingly prosaic and bare as this Robinson keeps us mindful of what has gone before. In stanza four such words as "falling," "wave," "illusion," "hide" and "harbor" have served to keep us in mind of the various themes as well as to advance the plot, and in the fifth stanza Robinson presents us with a series of possible views of the matter, tells us twice that this is a "story," reiterates that deception and hiding are the main themes, as in the metaphorical expression "veil" as well as in the simple statement, "As if the story of a house/Were told or ever could be." And at last, in the final lines, thematic, narrative and symbolic materials merge in the three images that accumulate power as they move from the simple to the complex, from the active to the passive, from the less to the more terrible:

> Though like waves breaking it may be,
> Or like a changed familiar tree,
> Or like a stairway to the sea
>   Where down the blind are driven.

For the attentive reader the narrative can not fail; Robinson has given us the suggestive outline we need and told us how, in general, to think about this story. He has kept us constantly aware of place, time, actors and action even though such awareness is only lightly provoked and not insisted on. In the last stanza the curious downward flow of the poem, the flow of the speculation, reaches an ultimate debouchment—"where down the blind are driven." Apart from the metrical power, the movement of the poem is significant; Robinson has packed it with words that suggest descent, depth and removal from sight, so that the terrible acceptance of the notion that we must "take what the god has given" becomes more terrible, more final as it issues out in the logic of statement and imagery and in the logic of the plot.

If much of the poem's power depends upon the interaction of statement and suggestion, still another source of energy is the metric. Robinson here uses a favorite device of his, feminine rhymes, in alternating tetrameter and trimeter lines, and gives to soft-sounding, polysyllabic words important metrical functions; as a result, when he does invert a foot or wrench the rhythm or use a monosyllable, the effect is striking out of all proportion to its apparent surface value. Surely the plucking, sounding quality of the word "vibrate" in the last line of the fourth stanza is proof of this, though equally effective is the position of "down" and "blind" in the final line of the poem.

Contemporary verse has experimented with meters, rhyme and

rhythm to such an extent that one has to attune the ear to Robinson's verse; at first it sounds jingly and mechanical, perhaps inept, but after we make a trial of them, the skill, the calculation, have their way and the occasional deviations from the set pattern take on the greater power because they are deviations:

Pity, I learned, was not the least
Of time's offending benefits
That had now for so long impugned
The conservation of his wits:
Rather it was that I should yield,
Alone, the fealty that presents
The tribute of a tempered ear
To an untempered eloquence.

This stanza from "The Wandering Jew" shows the style. This is mastery of prosody—old-fashioned command of the medium. The reversing of feet, use of alternately polysyllabic and monosyllabic words, of syncopation ("To an untempered eloquence") are devices subtly and sparingly used. The last stanza of the same poem gives another instance, and here the running-on of the sense through three-and-a-half lines adds to the effect:

Whether he still defies or not
The failure of an angry task
That relegates him out of time
To chaos, I can only ask.
But as I knew him, so he was;
And somewhere among men today
Those old, unyielding eyes may flash,
And flinch—and look the other way.

Deviation implies a basic pattern, and although in many cases, particularly in the blank verse narratives, syllable-counting mars the prosody, nonetheless the best poems subtly attune themselves to the "tempered ear," syncopate on occasion, and jingle to good effect.

This analysis is technical and only partial; it seems to presuppose that we must lapse into Mr. Brooks's "heresy of paraphrase." Granted. Yet this but begs a question, inasmuch as all of Robinson's poetry assumes that one will want to find the paraphrasable element the poet has carefully provided. These are poems *about* something, and what the something is we must discover. That is why we should consider Robinson as a poet with a prose in view, according to the description of "prose" earlier suggested. "Eros Turannos" is *about* the marriage of untrue minds, but specifically it is not about just untrueness and minds; it is about untrue man A and suffering, self-deluding woman B, as well as about those worldly wisemen who conjecture and have all the dope. Notably unsuccessful in speculative verse, Robinson excels in just this naturalistic case-history, this story of a Maine Emma Bovary. If the theme is still failure, Robinson rings a peculiar change upon it, since at last the poem forces us to accept the implication that there *is* and must be a "kindly veil between/Her visions and those we have seen"; that all of us must "take what the god has given," for failure is, in Robinson's world, the condition of man and human life. We do the best we can. In "Old Trails," the best one can is not often good, and what is indeed success in the world's eyes has a very shoddy look to those who recognize the success as merely "a safer way/Than growing old alone among the ghosts." It is the success of Chad in *The Ambassadors,* who will go home to the prosperous mills and Mamie and Mom, not that of Strether, who could have had the money and the ease but took the way of "growing old among the ghosts." But a briefer, more compact poem than "Old Trails," one that deals with another aspect of the theme, is the sonnet "The Clerks," which for all its seeming spareness is a very rich, very deft performance.

The octave opens colloquially, gives us a general location and an unspecified number of clerks; the speaker is the poet, as poet and as man. Robinson draws an evocative, generalized sketch of the clerks' past, of their prime as well as of the slow attrition of time and labor, and affirms that despite the wear they have sustained these men are still good and human. It is in the sestet that the poem moves out into suggestion, that it implies a conceit by which we can see how all men are clerks, time-servers, who are subject to fears and visions, who are high and low, and who as they tier up also cut down and trim away. To call the poem a conceit is no mere exercise of wit, for Robinson has clearly punned on many unobtrusive words in the sonnet. What is the clerks' "ancient air"? Does it mean simply that the men are old and tired? or that their manner is one of recalling grand old times of companionship that never really existed? or that one must take "air" literally to mean their musty smell of the store? These possibilities are rendered the more complex by the phrase "shop-worn brotherhood" immediately following, for then the visual element is reinforced, the atmosphere of shoddiness and shabbiness, of Rotary-club good-fellowship, and the simple language has invested itself with imagistic material that is both olfactory and visual. And of course, one may well suspect sarcasm in the assertion that "the men were just as good,/And just as human as they ever were." How good were they? Yet lest anyone feel this is too cynical, Robinson carefully equates the clerks with "poets and kings."

As is the case with "Eros Turannos," this poem proceeds from the general to the specific and back to the general again, a generality now enlarged to include comment on and a kind of definition of the human condition. Throughout there have been ironic overtones, ironic according to the irony we have seen as peculiarly Robinsonian in that it forms one quadrant of the total view. It has to do here with the discrepancy between the vision men have of their lives and the actuality they have lived. The poet here implies that such discrepancy, such imperfection of vision is immutably "human" and perhaps therefore and ironically, "good." That the clerks (and we are all clerks) see themselves as at once changed and the same, "fair" yet only called so, serves as the kind of lie men exist by, a lie that becomes an "ache" on the one hand and the very nutriment that supports life on the other. You, all you who secretly cherish some irrational hope or comfort, you merely "feed yourselves with your descent," your ancestry, your career, your abject position miscalled a progress. For all of us there can be only the wastage, the building up to the point of dissatisfaction, the clipping away to the point of despair.

Despite the almost insupportable duress of Robinson's attitude, we can hardly accuse him of cynicism or of hopelessness. In every instance his view of people is warm and understanding, not as the patronizing seer but as the fellow-sufferer. Such feeling informs the poems we have discussed and fills "The Gift of God" with humanity no cynic could imagine, no despair encompass. For in this poem the theme of failure turns once more, this time in an unexpected way so that we see Robinson affirming self-deception of this specific kind as more human, more the gauge of true love than all the snide fact-finding the rest of the world would recommend. The poem is about a mother's stubborn, blind love for a worthless (or perhaps merely ordinary) son, and this in the teeth of all the evidence her neighbors would be delighted to retail. Again, the poem is a compact narrative; again the irony exists outside the poem, not in its expression. As in so many of the best poems, Robinson says in effect: here is the reality, here is the illusion. *You* compare them and say which is which and if possible which is the correct moral choice.

The metaphorical material we can roughly classify as made up of imagery relating to royalty, apotheosis, sacrifice, and love. From the first few lines we are aware of a quality which, by allusion to the Annunciation and the anointing of kings, establishes the mother's cherished illusion and thereby makes acceptance of the emergent irony inescapably the reader's duty; he must compare the fact and the fiction for and by himself; Robinson will not say anything in such a way as to make the responsibility for choice his own rather than the reader's. He will simply render the situation and leave us to judge it, for all of Robinson's poems presuppose an outside world of critics and judges, of ourselves, people who see and observe more or less clearly. His irony is external; it lies in the always hinted-at conflict between the public life and the private, between the thing seen from the inside and from the outside, with the poet, the speaker presenting a third vision, not one that reconciles or cancels the other two, but one which simply adds a dimension and shows us that "everything is true in a different sense."

If the dominant motifs in "The Gift of God" are as indicated above, the progression of the poem follows undeviatingly the pattern suggested. In the first stanza Annunciation; the second, Nativity; the third, vision; the fourth, a stasis in which the mother seems to accept her son's unusual merit and her own vision of him as real; the fifth, a further extension of vision beyond anything actual; the sixth, the culmination of this calculated vision in the apotheosis. More than a schematized structure, the poem depends not only on the articulation of motifs and a plot, but equally on symbolic material that interacts with the stated or implied events in the "plot." Thus, from the outset the poet has juxtaposed the illusory vision and the "firmness" of the mother's faith in it; the language has a flavor of vague association with kingship, Biblical story, and legend, notably conveyed by such words as "shining," "degree," "anointed," "sacrilege," "transmutes," and "crowns." Yet in the careful arrangement of his poem Robinson has not oversimplified the mother's attitude. She maintains her "innocence unwrung" (and the irony of the allusion is not insisted on) despite the common knowledge of people who know, of course, better, and Robinson more than implies the innocence of her love in the elevated yet unmetaphorical diction he uses. Not until the final stanza does he open the poem out, suddenly show the apotheosis in the image of "roses thrown on marble stairs," subtly compressing into the last three lines the total pathos of the poem, for the son ascending in the mother's dream is "clouded" by a "fall": the greatness his mother envisions is belied by what we see. And who is in the right? For in the final turn of the "plot," is it not the mother who gives the roses of love and the marble of enduring faith? Is the dream not as solid and as real as human love can make it? If we doubt this notion, we need only observe the value Robinson places on the verb "transmutes" in stanza five: "*Transmutes* him with her faith and praise." She has, by an absolute miracle of alchemy, transmuted base material into precious; by an act of faith, however misplaced, found the philosopher's stone, which is love wholly purged of self. What we have come to realize is that in these poems we have been considering we are concerned with narrative—narrative of a peculiar kind in which the story is not just about the events, people and relationships but about the very poetic devices which are the vehicle of the narration and its insights. In "The Gift of God" symbol and theme have a narrative function; they must do in brief and without obtrusiveness what long passages of dialogue, exposition and description would effect in a novel. As a result, the reader is compelled to take the entire poem in at once; he either "understands" it or he does not. Naturally there are subtleties which emerge only after many readings; yet because these poems are narratives, Robinson must concentrate upon communication, upon giving us a surface that is at once dense yet readily available to the understanding.

As one apart, immune, alone,
Or featured for the shining ones,
And like to none that she has known
Of other women's other sons,—
The firm fruition of her need,

He shines anointed; and he blurs
Her vision, till it seems indeed
A sacrilege to call him hers.

This is on one hand simple telling of plot: the mother sees her son as unique and feels unworthy to be his mother. Simple enough. But the story is more than this, more than a cold telling of the facts about the mother's vision of her son. We see on the other hand that it is her need of the son, and of the vision of him, which complicates the story, while the suggestion of kingship, ritual, and sacrifice in the diction, the implication of self-immolation and deception, further extends the possibilities of meaning. All this we grasp more readily than we may realize, for Robinson prepares for his effects very early and while he extends meaning is careful to recapitulate, to restate and reemphasize the while he varies and complicates:

She sees him rather at the goal,
Still shining; and her dream foretells
The proper shining of a soul
Where nothing ordinary dwells.

In these lines Robinson affirms the mother's illusion: it is a "dream" that "foretells," and recapitulates the theme of kingship, of near-divinity in the repetition of "shining." The stanza that follows gives the poem its turn, states specifically that the son is merely ordinary, that the mother deludes herself, that her motive in so doing is "innocent," and in stanza five the poem, as we have seen, turns once more, pivots on the verb "transmute," turns away from the simple ironical comparison we have been experiencing and reveals a transmuted relationship: son to mother, vision to fact, and an ultimate apotheosis of the mother under the guise of a mistaken view of the son. The poem is about all these things and is equally about the means of their accomplishment within the poem. This is a poetry of surfaces, dense and deceptive surfaces to be sure but none the less a poetry that insists upon the communication of a whole meaning, totally and at once:

She crowns him with her gratefulness,
And says again that life is good;
And should the gift of God be less
In him than in her motherhood,
His fame, though vague, will not be small,

As upward through her dream he fares,
Half clouded with a crimson fall
Of roses thrown on marble stairs.

The recapitulation, the tying together, of the symbolic and thematic materials serves in this, the last stanza, a narrative as well as an expressive purpose. The tone is epigrammatic rather than prosaic and must shift delicately, come to the edge of banality, then turn off and finally achieve a muted sublimity that runs every risk of sentimentality and rhetoric yet never falters. The verse requires of us what it requires of itself: a toughness that can encompass the trite and mawkish without on the one hand turning sentimental itself or on the other resorting to an easy irony. The technique is the opposite of dramatic in that Robinson leaves as much to the reader as he possibly can; he uses no persona; the conflict is given not so much as conflict-in-action before our eyes as it unfolds itself at once, passes through complications, and returns to the starting point, the same yet altered and, to some degree, understood. To this extent Robinson is ratiocinative rather than dramatic; what we and the characters themselves think about the "plot" is as important as the plot, becomes indeed the full meaning of the plot.

Observably this ratiocinative and narrative strain tends towards a kind of self-parody, towards a formula. Robinson resorted to trickery too often in default of a really felt subject-matter, as in "The Whip." Yet we must not feel that between the excellence of such poems as "For a Dead Lady" and the dullness of *King Jasper* there lies only a horde of mediocre poems; on the contrary, there is no American poet who has approached Robinson in the number of finished poems of high merit. Mr. Winters' list seems to me an excellent one, though it may seem overly strict to some. In any case, it clearly indicates that Robinson is *the* major American poet of our era, with only T. S. Eliot as a peer. Of possible rivals, there is none whose claim rests on the number of *finished* poems nor on wholly achieved effects nor on the range and viability of subject. Of course, this is a controversial statement in many quarters and odious comparisons are far from the purpose; nevertheless, until such time as serious readers of serious poetry make an attempt to read and evaluate Robinson's poetry, they must take somebody else's word for it. The poetry is there—a fat volume with all the arid narratives at the end for convenience, the better poems scattered throughout. It may be that the time has come for readers of poetry to place Robinson where he belongs, to read him at any rate. This discussion has attempted to get at some of the more striking virtues of the poetry and to dispel some misconceptions, and while I suppose there are readers who do not like Robinson's *kind* of poetry, I have tried to show what we must not look for in it. It is to me important to get beyond fashion if we can and take stock of our best writers, not being deterred by what we have been trained to think about them nor discouraged by faults that loom large to us because they are not our own. If we can understand if not believe in his external irony, his cosmology, then we shall be equipped to recognize his worth in the same way that we recognize that of Swift, for example, or Mauriac. Time and fashion will have their effects, true enough, but unless we can rise above the predilections of the moment in our reading, there is little possibility of our understanding what we read.

Edwin Arlington Robinson: The Many Truths

by James Dickey

A reevaluation of the work of a poet as established as Edwin Arlington Robinson should involve us in some of the fundamentals we tend to forget when we read any poetry that happens to come to hand—the poetry that is thrust upon us by critics and in courses in literature as well as the poetry that we seek out or return to. As should be true of our encounter with any poetry, reevaluation requires that we rid ourselves of preconceptions and achieve, if we can, a way of reading an established poet as though we had never heard of him and were opening his book for the first time. It requires that we approach him with all our senses open, our intelligence in acute readines, our critical sense in check but alert for the slightest nuance of falsity, our truth-sensitive needle—the device that measures what the poet says against what we know from having lived it—at its most delicate, and our sense of the poet's "place," as determined by commentary, textbook, and literary fashion, drugged, asleep, or temporarily dead.

Like most ideal conditions, this one cannot be fully attained. But it is certainly true that an approximation of such a state is both an advantage and a condition productive of unsuspected discoveries in reading poets we thought we knew, particularly poets whom we thought we knew as well as Robinson. In Robinson's special case it is even more difficult than usual, for the course of poetry has to a certain extent turned away from him, making his greatest virtues appear mediocre ones and directing public scrutiny from his intro-

"Edwin Arlington Robinson: The Many Truths" by James Dickey. From *Selected Poems,* ed. Morton Dauwen Zabel (New York: The Macmillan Company, 1965), pp. xi–xxviii.

spective, intellectual, and ironic verse toward poetry in which more things seem to be taking place in a smaller area—poetry in which the poetic line is compressed and packed to the point of explosion and the bedazzlement of the reader is considered synonymous with his reward.

Robinson achieved unusual popularity in his lifetime. When he died in 1935, at the age of sixty-five, he had won the Pulitzer Prize three times and had gained a distinction rare for a poet—his book-length poem *Tristram* had become a best seller. But in the public mind, Robinson has during recent years been regarded as only his vices of prolixity, irresolution, and occasional dullness would have him. Yet if we could manage to read Robinson as if we did not know him—or at least as if we did not know him quite so well as we had believed—or if we could come to him as if he were worth rereading, not out of duty and obedience to literary history but as a possible experience, we would certainly gain a good deal more than we would lose.

I

Suppose, eager only for the experience of poems, we were to look through this book before reading it, noting only the shapes of the poems on the page. We would see a good many short, tight-looking poems in different structural forms, all of them severely symmetrical, and page after page containing long vertical rectangles of blank verse. Though this selection leaves out the Arthurian poems on which Robinson's popular reputation was made as well as the other later narratives of his declining years, there are still a number of middling-long poems that no editor interested in Robinson's best work could possibly eliminate. The chances are that we would be inclined to skip these and first read one of the shorter ones. What would we find if it were this one?

We go no more to Calverly's,
For there the lights are few and low;
And who are there to see by them,
Or what they see, we do not know.
Poor strangers of another tongue
May now creep in from anywhere,
And we, forgotten, be no more
Than twilight on a ruin there.

We two, the remnant. All the rest
Are cold and quiet. You nor I,
Nor fiddle now, nor flagon-lid,
May ring them back from where they lie.
No fame delays oblivion
For them, but something yet survives:
A record written fair, could we
But read the book of scattered lives.

There'll be a page for Leffingwell,
And one for Lingard, the Moon-calf;
And who knows what for Clavering,
Who died because he couldn't laugh?
Who knows or cares? No sign is here,
No face, no voice, no memory;
No Lingard with his eerie joy,
No Clavering, no Calverly.

We cannot have them here with us
To say where their light lives are gone,
Or if they be of other stuff
Than are the moons of Ilion.
So, be their place of one estate
With ashes, echoes, and old wars—
Or ever we be of the night,
Or we be lost among the stars.

It is a poem that opens, conventionally enough, with a reference to a place—one suspects from the beginning that it is one of those drinking places where men gather against the dark and call it fellowship—where there were once parties or at least conviviality of some sort; of that company, only two are left, and one of these is speaking. We feel the conventionality of the theme because we are aware that the contrast between places formerly full of animation and merriment with the same places *now* is one of the most haggard of romantic clichés and the subject of innumerable mediocre verses (though infrequently, as in some of Hardy, it can be memorable and can serve to remind us that such contrasts, such places, do in fact exist and *are* melancholy and cautionary). Yet there is a difference, a departure, slight but definitive, from the conventional. This difference begins to become apparent as we read the last two stanzas, which are mainly a roll call of the missing. The Robinsonian departure is in the way in which these dead are characterized. What, for example, are we to make of the reference to "Clavering/Who died because he couldn't laugh?" Or of "Lingard with his eerie joy"? What of these people, here barely mentioned, but mentioned in connection with tantalizing qualities that are hard to forget, that have in them some of the inexplicably sad individuality that might be—that might as well be—fate? I suspect that one who began as even the most casual reader might wish to know more of these people, and he might then realize that in Robinson's other poems, and only there, he would have a chance of doing so.

A first perusal of "Calverly's" might also lead the perceptive reader to suspect that the poet is more interested in the human personality than he is in, say, nature; that he is interested in people not only for their enigmatic and haunting qualities but also for their mysterious exemplification of some larger entity, some agency that, though it determines both their lives and their deaths, may or may not have any concern for them or knowledge of them. Of these men, the poet cannot say "where their light lives are gone," and because he cannot say—and because there is nothing or no way to tell him—he cannot know, either, what his own fate is, or its meaning; he can know only that he himself was once at Calverly's, that the others who were there are gone, and that he shall follow them in due time. He cannot say what this means or whether, in fact, it means anything. Though he can guess as to what it might mean, all he finally *knows* is what has happened.

This condition of mind is a constant throughout all but a very few of Robinson's poems. It links him in certain curious ways with the existentialists, but we are aware of such affinities only tangentially, for Robinson's writings, whatever else they may be, are dramas that make use of conjecture rather than overt statements of ideas held and defended. It is the fact that truth is "so strange in its nakedness" that appalled and intrigued him—the fact that it takes different forms for different people and different situations. Robinson believed in the unknowable constants that govern the human being from within; in addition, he had the sort of mind that sees history as a unity in which these human constants appear in dramatic form. This explains why he had no difficulty at all in projecting Welsh kingdoms and biblical encounters out of houses and situations he had known in New England, much as his own

Shakespeare was able to fill "Ilion, Rome, or any town you like/Of olden time with timeless Englishmen."

The unity of the poet's mind is a quality that is certain to make its presence felt very early in the reader's acquaintance with Robinson. One can tell a great deal about him from the reading of a single poem. All the poems partake of a single view and a single personality, and one has no trouble in associating the poems in strict forms with the more irregular ones as the products of the same vision of existence. The sensibility evidenced by the poems is both devious and tenacious, and it lives most intensely when unresolved about questions dealing with the human personality. Robinson is perhaps the greatest master of the speculative or conjectural approach to the writing of poetry. Uncertainty was the air he breathed, and speculation was not so much a device with him—though at its best it is a surpassingly effective technique—as it was a habit of mind, an integral part of the self. As with most powerful poets, the writing proceeded from the way in which Robinson naturally thought, the way he naturally *was,* and so was inextricably rooted in his reticent, slightly morbid, profoundly contemplative, solitary, compassionate, and stoical personality and was not the product of a conscious search for a literary "way," an unusual manner of speaking which was invented or discovered and in which the will had a major part.

Robinson's tentative point of view was solidly wedded to a style that has exactly the same characteristics as his mind. It makes an artistic virtue, and often a very great one, of arriving at only provisional answers and solutions, of leaving it up to the reader's personality—also fated—to choose from among them the most likely. Thus a salient quality of Robinson's work is the extraordinary roundness and fullness he obtains from such circumlocutions of his subjects, as though he were indeed turning (in William James's phrase) "the cube of reality." One is left with the belief that in any given situation there are many truths—as many, so to speak, as there are persons involved, as there are witnesses, as there are ways of thinking about it. And encompassing all these is the shadowy probability that none of them is or can be final. What we see in Robinson's work is the unending and obsessional effort to make sense of experience when perhaps there is none to be made. The poet, the reader, all of us are members of humanity in the sense Robinson intended when he characterized the earth as "a kind of vast spiritual kindergarten where millions of people are trying to spell God with the wrong blocks."

It is through people that Robinson found the hints and gleams of the universal condition that he could not help trying to solve. Like other human beings, he was cursed with intelligence and sensibility in a universe made for material objects. "The world is a hell of a place," he once said, "but the universe is a fine thing," and again, "We die of what we eat and drink,/But more we die of what we think." Robinson has been perhaps the only American poet—certainly the only one of major status—interested *exclusively* in human beings as subject matter for poetry—in the psychological, motivational aspects of living, in the inner life as it is projected upon the outer. His work is one vast attempt to tell the stories that no man can really tell, for no man can know their real meaning, their real intention, or even whether such exists, though it persistently appears to do so. In all Robinson's people the Cosmos seems to be brooding in one way or another, so that a man and woman sitting in a garden, as in "Mortmain," are, in *what* they are, exemplars of eternal laws that we may guess at but not know. The laws are present in psychological constitutions as surely as they are in physical materials, in the orbital patterns of stars and planets and atoms, only deeper hid, more tragic and mysterious, "as there might somewhere be veiled/Eternal reasons why the tricks of time/Were played like this."

Robinson wrote an enormous amount of poetry (how one's mind quails at the sheer *weight,* the physical bulk, of his fifteen-hundred-page *Collected Poems!*), but at the center of it and all through it is the Personality, the Mind, conditioned by its accidental placement in time and space—these give the individuations that make drama possible—but also partaking of the hidden universals, the not-to-be knowns that torment all men. In these poems "The strange and unremembered light/That is in dreams" plays over "The nameless and eternal tragedies/That render hope and hopelessness akin." Like a man speaking under torture—or self-torture—Robinson tells of these things, circling them, painfully shifting from one possible interpretation to another, and the reader circles with him, making, for want of any received, definitive opinion, hesitant, troubling, tentative judgments. The result is an unresolved view, but a view of remarkable richness and suggestibility, opening out in many directions and unsealing many avenues of possibility: a multidimensional view that the reader is left pondering as the poem has pondered, newly aware of his own enigmas, of what he and his own life—its incidents and fatalities—may mean, could mean, and thus he is likely to feel himself linked into the insoluble universal equation, in which nature itself is only a frame of mind, a projection of inwardness, tormenting irresolution, and occasional inexplicable calms.

> . . . she could look
> Right forward through the years, nor any more
> Shrink with a cringing prescience to behold
> The glitter of dead summer on the grass,
> Or the brown-glimmered crimson of still trees
> Across the intervale where flashed along,
> Black-silvered, the cold river.

II

As has been said, Robinson's method—which on some fronts has been labeled antipoetic—would not amount to as much as it does were not the modes of thought presented in such powerful and disturbing dramatic forms. For an "antipoet," Robinson was an astonishing craftsman. One has only to read a few of his better poems in the classic French repetitive forms, such as "The House on the Hill," to recognize the part that traditional verse patterns play in his work. This much is demonstrable. It is among those who believe the poetic essence to lie somewhere outside or beyond such considerations, somewhere in the image-making, visual, and visionary realm, that Robinson's position has been challenged. And it is true that his verse is oddly bare, that there are few images in it—though, of these, some are very fine indeed—and that most of it is highly cerebral and often written in a scholarly or pseudoscholarly manner that is frequently more than a little pedantic. Many of his poems contain an element of self-parody, and these carry more than their share of bad, flat, stuffy writing.

> There were slaves who dragged the shackles of a precedent unbroken,
> Demonstrating the fulfillment of unalterable schemes,
> Which had been, before the cradle, Time's inexorable tenants
> Of what were now the dusty ruins of their fathers' dreams.

Infrequently there is also a kind of belaboring-beyond-belaboring of the obvious:

The four square somber things that you see first
Around you are four walls that go as high
As to the ceiling.

And now and then one comes on philosophical pronouncements of a remarkable unconvincingness, demonstrating a total failure of idiom, of art:

Too much of that
May lead you by and by through gloomy lanes
To a sad wilderness, where one may grope
Alone, and always, or until he feels
Ferocious and invisible animals
That wait for men and eat them in the dark.

At his worst, Robinson seems to go on writing long after whatever he has had to say about the subject has been exhausted; there is a suspicious look of automatism about his verse instrument. The reader, being made of less stern stuff, will almost always fail before Robinson's blank verse does.

Robinson certainly wrote too much. Like Wordsworth—even more than Wordsworth, if that is possible—he is in need of selective editing. In the present book,[1] this is what the late Morton Dauwen Zabel has done, and I believe with singular success. The Robinson of this book is much more nearly the essential, the permanently valuable Robinson than the Robinson of the *Collected Poems,* though there are unavoidable exclusions—particularly of the good book-length poems, such as *Lancelot* and *Merlin*—which one might legitimately regret and to which it is hoped that the reader will eventually have recourse. Yet even in the present volume one is likely to be put off by the length of many of the pieces. Then, too, if the casual reader skims only a little of a particular poem and finds that nothing much is happening or that event, action, and resolution are taking place only in various persons' minds, he is also likely to shy away. But once *in* the poem, committed to it, with his mind winding among the alternative complexities of Robinson's characters' minds—that is, winding with Robinson's mind—the reader changes slowly, for Robinson hath his will. One is held by the curious dry magic that seems so eminently unmagical, that bears no resemblance to the elfin or purely verbal or native-

[1] [Mr. Dickey's essay was written to introduce Mr. Zabel's edition of Robinson's *Selected Poems* (New York: Macmillan, 1965).]

woodnote magic for which English verse is justly celebrated. It is a magic for which there is very little precedent in all literature. Though external affinities may be asserted and even partially demonstrated with Praed and Browning, though there are occasional distant echoes of Wordsworth, Keats, Hardy, and Rossetti, Robinson is really like none of them in his root qualities; his spell is cast with none of the traditional paraphernalia, but largely through his own reading of character and situation and fate, his adaptation of traditional poetic devices to serve these needs—an adaptation so unexpected, so revolutionary, as to seem not so much adaptation as transformation.

Another odd thing about Robinson is that his best work and his worst are yet remarkably alike. The qualities that make the good poems good are the same qualities that make the bad poems bad; it is only a question of how Robinson's method works out in, "takes to," the situation he is depicting, and often the difference between good, bad, and mediocre is thin indeed. This difficulty is also compounded by the fact that Robinson is equally skilled as a technician in both memorable poems and trivial ones. In the less interesting poems, particularly the longer ones, Robinson's air of portentousness can be tiresome. Reading these, one is tempted to say that Robinson is the most prolific *reticent* poet in history. Though he gives the impression that he is reluctant to write down what he is writing, he often goes on and on, in a kind of intelligent mumbling, a poetical wringing of the hands, until the reader becomes restive and a little irritated. In these passages, Robinson's verse instrument has a certain kinship with the salt maker in the fairy tale, grinding away of its own accord at the bottom of the sea. Then there is the gray, austere landscape of the poems, the lack of background definition. One is accustomed to finding the characters in a poem—particularly a narrative poem—in a *place,* a location with objects and a weather of its own, a world which the reader can enter and in which he can, as it were, live with the characters. But there is very little of the environmental in Robinson's work. What few gestures and concessions he makes to the outside world are token ones; all externality is quickly devoured by the tormented introversion of his personages. In Robinson, the mind eats everything and converts it to part of a conflict with self; one could say with some justification that all Robinson's poems are about people who are unable to endure themselves or to resolve their thoughts into some meaningful, cleansing action. So much introversion is not only harrowing; it can also be boring, particularly when carried on to the enormous lengths in which it appears in "Matthias at the Door" and "Avon's Harvest."

And yet with these strictures, the case against Robinson's poetry has pretty much been stated, and we have on our hands what remains after they have been acknowledged.

III

No poet ever understood loneliness or separateness better than Robinson or knew the self-consuming furnace that the brain can become in isolation, the suicidal hellishness of it, doomed as it is to feed on itself in answerless frustration, fated to this condition by the accident of human birth, which carries with it the hunger for certainty and the intolerable load of personal recollections. He understood loneliness in all its many forms and depths and was thus less interested in its conventional poetic aspects than he was in the loneliness of the man in the crowd, or alone with his thoughts of the dead, or feeling at some unforeseen time the metaphysical loneliness, the *angst,* of being "lost among the stars," or becoming aware of the solitude that resides in comfort and in the affection of friend and family—that desperation at the heart of what is called happiness. It is only the poet and those involved who realize the inevitability and the despair of these situations, "Although, to the serene outsider,/There still would seem to be a way."

The acceptance of the fact that there is no way, that there is nothing to do about the sadness of most human beings when they are alone or speaking to others as if to themselves, that there is nothing to offer them but recognition, sympathy, compassion, deepens Robinson's best poems until we sense in them something other than art. A thing inside us is likely to shift from where it was, and our world view to change, though perhaps only slightly, toward a darker, deeper perspective. Robinson has been called a laureate of failure and has even been accused (if that is the word) of making a cult and a virtue of failure, but that assessment is not quite accurate. His subject was "the slow tragedy of haunted men," those whose "eyes are lit with a wrong light," those who believe that some earthly occurrence in the past (and now forever impossible) could have made all the difference, that some person dead or otherwise beyond reach, some life unlived and now unlivable, could have been the answer to everything. But these longings were seen by Robinson to be the delusions necessary to sustain life, for human beings, though they can live without hope, cannot live believing that no hope ever could have existed. For this reason, many of the poems deal with the unlived life, the man kept by his own nature or by circumstance from "what might have been his," but there is always the ironic Robinsonian overtone that what might have been would not have been much better than what is—and, indeed, might well have been worse; the failure would only have had its development and setting altered somewhat, but not its pain or its inevitability.

Though Robinson's dramatic sense was powerful and often profound, his narrative sense was not. His narrative devices are few, and they are used again and again. The poet is always, for example, running into somebody in the street whom he knew under other circumstances and who is now a bum, a "slowly-freezing Santa Claus," a street-corner revivalist, or something equally comical-pathetic and cut off. The story of the person's passing from his former state to this one then becomes the poem, sometimes told by the derelict, the "ruin who meant well," and sometimes puzzled out by the poet himself, either with his deep, painful probing or, as in some of the later long poems, such as "The Man Who Died Twice," with an intolerable amount of poetical hemming and hawing, backing and filling.

And yet Robinson's peculiar elliptical vision, even when it is boring, is worth the reader's time. The tone of his voice is so distinctive, his technique so varied and resourceful, and his compassion so intense that something valuable comes through even the most wasteful of his productions. Not nearly enough has been made of Robinson's skill, the chief thing about which is that it is able to create, through an astonishing number of forms and subjects, the tone of a single voice, achieving variety within a tonal unity. And it is largely in this tone, the product of outlook (or, if I may be forgiven, inlook), technique, and personality, that Robinson's particular excellence lies; thus the tone is worth examining.

Robinson's mind was not sensuously rich, if by that is meant a Keatsian or Hopkinsian outgoingness into nature as a bodily experience and the trust and delight in nature that this attitude implies. His poetic interests are psychological and philosophical; he examines the splits between what is and what might have been, what must be and what cannot be. That Robinson sees these differences to matter very little, finally, does not mean that they do not matter to the people who suffer from them; it is, in fact, in this realm of delusionary and obsessive suffering that Robinson's poems take place. Though his mind was not rich in a sensuous way, it was both powerful and hesitant, as though suspended between strong magnets. This gives his work an unparalleled sensitivity in balance; and from this balance, this desperately poised uncertainty, emanates a compassion both very personal and cosmic—a compassion that one might well see as a substitute for the compassion that God failed to supply. It is ironic at times, it is bitter and self-mocking, but it is always compassion unalloyed by sentimentality; it has been earned, as it is the burden of the poems themselves to show. This attitude, this tone, runs from gentle, rueful humor—though based, even so, on stark constants of human fate such as the aging process and death—to the most terrible hopelessness. It may appear in the tortuous working out of a long passage, or it may gleam forth for an instant in surroundings not seen until its appearance to be frightening, as in the poem below.

"Isaac and Archibald" is a New England pastoral in which a twelve-year-old boy takes a long walk with an old man, Isaac, to visit another old man at his farm. Nothing much happens, except that both Isaac and Archibald manage to reveal to the boy the signs of mental decline and approaching death in the other. The two men drink cider; the boy sits and reflects, prefiguring as he does the mature man and poet he will become. The boy's awareness of death is built up by small, affectionate touches, some of them so swift and light that they are almost sure to be passed over by the hurried reader.

> Hardly had we turned in from the main road
> When Archibald, with one hand on his back
> And the other clutching his huge-headed cane,
> Came limping down to meet us.—"Well! well! well!"
> Said he; and then he looked at my red face,
> All streaked with dust and sweat, and shook my hand,
> And said it must have been a right smart walk
> That we had had that day from Tilbury Town.—
> "Magnificent," said Isaac; and he told
> About the beautiful west wind there was

Which cooled and clarified the atmosphere.
"You must have made it with your legs, I guess,"
Said Archibald; and Isaac humored him
With one of those infrequent smiles of his
Which he kept in reserve, apparently,
For Archibald alone. "But why," said he,
"Should Providence have cider in the world
If not for such an afternoon as this?"
And Archibald, with a soft light in his eyes,
Replied that if he chose to go down cellar,
There he would find eight barrels—one of which
Was newly tapped, he said, and to his taste
An honor to the fruit. Isaac approved
Most heartily at that, and guided us
Forthwith, as if his venerable feet
Were measuring the turf in his own door-yard,
Straight to the open rollway. Down we went,
Out of the fiery sunshine to the gloom,
Grateful and half sepulchral, where we found
The barrels, like eight potent sentinels,
Close ranged along the wall. From one of them
A bright pine spile stuck out alluringly,
And on the black flat stone, just under it,
Glimmered a late-spilled proof that Archibald
Had spoken from unfeigned experience.
There was a fluted antique water-glass
Close by, and in it, prisoned, or at rest,
There was a cricket, of the soft brown sort
That feeds on darkness. Isaac turned him out,
And touched him with his thumb to make him jump . . .

Until the introduction of the cricket and the few words that typify it, there is nothing startling in the passage, though it is quite good Robinson, with the judicious adverb "alluringly" attached to the protrusion of the pine spile and the lovely affectionate irony of Archibald's "unfeigned experience" with the cider. But the cricket, of the *sort* that feeds on darkness, changes the poem and brings it into the central Robinsonian orbit. Here, the insect is a more terrifying and mysterious creature—a bitter symbol for the context—than a maggot or dead louse would be, for it is normally a benign spirit of household and hearth. This simple way of referring to it, as though the supposition that it "feeds on darkness' were the most obvious and natural thing in the world to say about it, produces a haunting effect when encountered along with the gentle old farmers' proximity to death and the boy's budding awareness of it.

It may be inferred from the above passages that Robinson is not a writer of unremitting brilliance or a master of the more obvious technical virtuosities. He is, rather, as has been said, a poet of quick, tangential thrusts, of sallies and withdrawals, of fleeting hints and glimpsed implications. In his longer poems, particularly, the impacts build up slowly, and it is only to those who have not the sensitivity to catch the sudden, baffling, half-revealing gleams—those who are "annoyed by no such evil whim/As death, or time, or truth"—that Robinson's poems are heavy and dull. Though he has a way, particularly in the later poems, of burying his glints of meaning pretty deeply in the material that makes them possible, Robinson at his best manages to use the massiveness of discourse and the swift, elusive gleam of illumination—the momentary flashing into the open of a stark, tragic hint, a fleeting generalization—as complementaries. And when the balance between these elements is right, the effect is unforgettable.

At times it appears that Robinson not only did not seek to avoid dullness but courted it and actually used it as a device, setting up his major points by means of it and making them doubly effective by contrast, without in the least violating the unity of tone or the huge, heavy drift of the poem toward its conclusion. He is a slow and patient poet; taking his time to say a thing as he wishes to say it is one of his fundamental qualities. This has worked against him, particularly since his work has survived into an age of anything but slow and patient readers. The pedestrian movement of much of his work has made him unpopular in an era when the piling on of startling effects, the cramming of the poetic line with all the spoils it can carry, is regarded not so much as a criterion of good or superior verse of a certain kind, but as poetry itself, other kinds being relegated to inferior categories yet to be defined. But Robinson's considered, unhurried lines, as uncomplicated in syntax as they are difficult in thought, in reality are, by virtue of their enormous sincerity, conviction, and quiet originality, a constant rebuke to those who conceive of poetry as verbal legerdemain or as the "superior amusement" that the late T. S. Eliot would have had it be.

The Robinson line is simple in the way that straightforward English prose is simple; the declarative sentence is made to do most of the work. His questions, though comparatively rare, are weighted with the agony of concern, involvement, and uncertainty. It is the thought, rather than the expression of the thought, that makes some of Robinson difficult, for he was almost always at pains to write simply, and his skills were everywhere subservient to this ideal. My personal favorite of Robinson's effects is his extremely subtle use of the line as a means of changing the meaning of the sentence that forms the line, the whole poem changing direction slightly but unmistakably with each such shift.

> What is it in me that you like so much,
> And love so little?

And yet for all his skill, Robinson's technical equipment is never obvious or obtrusive, as Hopkins', say, is. This is, of course, a tribute to his resourcefulness, for in his best pieces the manner of the poem is absorbed into its matter, and we focus not on the mode of saying but on the situations and characters into whose presence we have come.

IV

Robinson's favorite words, because they embody his favorite way of getting at any subject, are "may" and "might." The whole of the once-celebrated "The Man Against the Sky," for example, is built upon their use. When the poet sees a man climbing Mount Monadnock, it is, for the purposes of his poem, important that he *not* know who the man is or what he is doing there, so that the poem can string together a long series of conjectural possibilities as to who he might be, what might happen to him, and what he might conceivably represent.

> Even he, who stood where I had found him,
> On high with fire all round him,
> Who moved along the molten west,
> And over the round hill's crest
> That seemed half ready with him to go down,
> Flame-bitten and flame-cleft,
> As if there were to be no last thing left
> Of a nameless unimaginable town—
> Even he who climbed and vanished may have taken
> Down to the perils of a depth not known . . .

When he reaches the words "may have," the reader is in true Robinson country; he lives among alternatives, possibilities, doubts, and delusionary gleams of hope. This particular poem, which not only uses this approach but virtually hounds it to death, is not successful mainly because Robinson insists on being overtly philosophical and, at the end, on committing himself to a final view. Another shortcoming is that he is not sufficiently close to the man, for his poems are much better when he knows *something* of the circumstances of a human life, tells what he knows and *then* speculates, for the unresolved quality of his ratiocinations, coupled with the usually terrible *facts,* enables him to make powerful and haunting use of conjecture and of his typical "may have" or "might not have" presentations of alternative possibilities.

It is also true of this poem that it has very little of the leavening of Robinson's irony, and this lack is detrimental to it. This irony has been widely commented upon, but not, I think, quite as accurately as it might have been. Though it infrequently has the appearance of callousness or even cruelty, a closer examination, a more receptive *feeling* of its effect, will usually show that it is neither. It is, rather, a product of a detachment based on helplessness, on the saving grace of humor that is called into play because nothing practical can be done and because the spectator of tragedy must find some way in which to save himself emotionally from the effects of what he has witnessed.

> No, no—forget your Cricket and your Ant,
> For I shall never set my name to theirs
> That now bespeak the very sons and heirs
> Incarnate of Queen Gossip and King Cant.
> The case of Leffingwell is mixed, I grant,
> And futile seems the burden that he bears;
> But are we sounding his forlorn affairs
> Who brand him parasite and sycophant?
>
> I tell you, Leffingwell was more than these;
> And if he prove a rather sorry knight,
> What quiverings in the distance of what light
> May not have lured him with high promises,
> And then gone down?—He may have been deceived;
> He may have lied—he did; and he believed.

The irony here is not based on showing in what ridiculous and humiliating ways the self-delusion of Leffingwell made of him a parasite and sycophant; it works through and past these things to the much larger proposition that such delusion is necessary to life; that, in fact, it is the condition that enables us to function at all. The manufacture and protection of the self-image is really the one constant, the one obsessive concern, of our existence. This idea was, of course, not new with Robinson, though it may be worth mentioning that many psychiatrists, among them Alfred Adler and Harry Stack Sullivan, place a primary emphasis on such interpretations of the human mentality. What should be noted is that the lies of Leffingwell and of Uncle Ananias are in their way truths, for they have in them that portion of the truth that comes not from fact but from the ideal.

> All summer long we loved him for the same
> Perennial inspiration of his lies . . .

There is something more here, something more positive, than there is in the gloomy and one-dimensional use of similar themes in, say, Eugene O'Neill's *The Iceman Cometh,* for in Robinson's poems the necessity to lie (and, with luck, sublimely) is connected to the desire to remake the world by remaking that portion of it that is oneself. Robinson shows the relation between such lies and the realities they must struggle to stay alive among, and he shows them with the shrewdness and humor of a man who has told such lies to himself but sadly knows them for what they are. The reader is likely to smile at the absurdity—but also to be left with a new kind of admiration for certain human traits that he had theretofore believed pathetic or contemptible.

V

These, then, are Robinson's kinds of originality, of poetic value—all of them subtle and half-hidden, muffled and disturbing, answering little but asking those questions that are unpardonable, unforgettable, and necessary.

It is curious and wonderful that this scholarly, intelligent, childlike, tormented New England stoic, "always hungry for the nameless," always putting in the reader's mouth "some word that hurts your tongue," useless for anything but his art, protected by hardier friends all his life, but enormously courageous and utterly dedicated (he once told Chard Powers Smith at the very end of his life, "I could never have done *anything* but write poetry"), should have brought off what in its quiet, searching, laborious way is one of the most remarkable accomplishments of modern poetry. Far from indulging, as his detractors have maintained, in a kind of poetical know-nothingism, he actually brought to poetry a new kind of approach, making of a refusal to pronounce definitively on his subjects a virtue and of speculation upon possibilities an instrument that allows an unparalleled fullness to his presentations, as well as endowing them with some of the mysteriousness, futility, and proneness to multiple interpretation that incidents and lives possess in the actual world.

Robinson's best poetry is exactly that kind of communication that "tells the more the more it is not told." In creating a body of major poetry with devices usually thought to be unfruitful for the creative act—irresolution, abstraction, conjecture, a dry, nearly imageless mode of address that tends always toward the general without ever supplying the resolving judgment that we expect of generalization—Robinson has done what good poets have always done: by means of his "cumulative silences" as well as by his actual lines, he has forced us to reexamine and finally to redefine what poetry is—or our notion of it—and so has enabled poetry itself to include more, to *be* more, than it was before he wrote.

One Kind of Traditional Poet

by Edwin S. Fussell

"The more extensive your acquaintance is with the works of those who have excelled," wrote Sir Joshua Reynolds in his *Discourses,* "the more extensive will be your powers of invention, and what may appear still more like a paradox, the more original will be your composition." Shakespeare and the Bible may demonstrate how Robinson's creative talent was sharpened by acquaintance with great writing; Emerson and Ibsen and Wordsworth may stand for all those poets whose influence partly accounts for his originality and whose spirit permits a description of his uniqueness. Indeed, Robinson's whole poetic career may profitably be read as a concrete elaboration of Reynolds' propositions, for it is clear that Robinson's own views were substantially similar and that these views explain much of his quality as a poet. The title-page quotation of Robinson's first book is conclusive on this point: "Whom should I imitate in order to be original?"

There is even better and earlier evidence in a sonnet that Robinson began at Harvard and published in 1896. Comparison of the early plan with the finished poem is instructive chiefly in showing Robinson's rapidly maturing feelings for literary tradition. In 1892 he wrote:

> I have made a little verse today, however—part of a sonnet beginning:
>
> "I make no measure of the words they say
> Who come with snaky tongues to me and tell
> Of all the woe awaiting me in Hell
> When from this goodly world I go my way, etc."

"One Kind of Traditional Poet" by Edwin S. Fussell. From *Edwin Arlington Robinson: The Literary Background of a Traditional Poet* (Berkeley: University of California Press, 1954), pp. 171–86. Reprinted by permission of the publisher.

> Eventually I shall go on to say how the appearance of a good wholesome white-haired man who never told a lie or drank Maine whiskey impresses me, and how I draw a lesson from the unspoken sermon of his own self and begin to realize the real magnificence of better things —the which I have an idea will make the closing line.[1]

This is vague enough, but it is easy to see that the poem as finally written is quite different. Although some of the framework was retained and only one word of the final line changed, the whole point of the poem was shifted significantly. The initial concept was broad and infirm, Robinson obviously intending a simple platitudinous *exemplum* of the kind he inherited from Longfellow. But as his feeling for his art grew, the sonnet came to be defined in a way that is important for our understanding of his work. The "Wholesome white-haired man" (whatever originally lay behind this phrase) becomes a great artist. His example now inspires, instead of moral rejuvenation, submission to the discipline of history (unfortunately "better things" was carried over to the new version). The young writer must cultivate his individual talent in the light of the "long-tutored consciousness"[2] of the past. The oxymoron, "living sunset," attempts to define Robinson's sense of how the past and the future coalesce in the heat of present composition. And the octave, which seems to have been originally conceived as a rather general defiance of the Puritan doctrine of work, becomes in the changed context Robinson's serious protest against the habit of utilitarian societies to defile the artist's integrity. Since this important poem was not collected by Robinson, I give it here:

I make no measure of the words they say
Whose tongues would so mellifluously tell
With prescient zeal what I shall find in hell
When all my roving whims have had their day,—
I take no pleasure of the time they stay
Who wring my wasted minutes from the well

[1] [*Untriangulated Stars: Letters of Edwin Arlington Robinson to Harry de Forest Smith, 1890–1905,* ed. Denham Sutcliffe (Cambridge: Harvard University Press, 1947)], pp. 59–60. April 17, 1892.

[2] This remarkably wise phrase is also curiously prophetic of subsequent aesthetic theory. Compare, for example, Richard Blackmur's definition: "those modes of representing felt reality persuasively and credibly and justly, which make up, far more than meters and rhymes and the general stock of versification, the creative habit of imagination, and which are the indefeasible substance of tradition" (*The Expense of Greatness,* New York, 1940, p. 47).

Of cool forgetfulness wherein they dwell
Contented there to slumber on alway;—

But when some rare old master, with an eye
Lit with a living sunset, takes me home
To his long-tutored consciousness, there springs
Into my soul a warm serenity
Of hope that I may know, in years to come,
The true magnificence of better things.[3]

This was written in 1896, the year in which Robinson was also rebelling against the present course of English poetry. And it is only in the resolution of this apparent paradox that Robinson's poetry and its relation to literary history may be understood. It is no simple matter of "convention" and "revolt," and Robinson is not to be labeled too quickly as either "conservative" or "radical." His attitude is too complex to be so summarily disposed of, and this complexity cannot be appreciated without taking into account the particulars on which it was based.

The situation can be somewhat simplified by considering some of the implications of Robinson's relation to the whole course of poetry from 1890 to 1935. The difficulty in grasping this relationship inheres less in Robinson's career than in the literary background of the period, "a period whose instability Robinson emphasized by his steady purpose and isolation." [4] It is the evident fact that poetry as a whole changed more during his lifetime than his own poetry did that partly explains why Robinson seemed a rebel at the first and a reactionary at the end. "It is the present fate of poetry to be always beginning over again," [5] writes Allen Tate. Unless the modern poet has Yeats' extraordinary capacity for always beginning over again, his relation to the poetry written around him is bound to be a shifting one. A few months before he died, Robinson complained: "I must be very far behind the times. Once I was so modern that people wouldn't have me." [6]

Robinson's exact historical position cannot be too much empha-

[3] Charles B. Hogan, *A Bibliography of Edwin Arlington Robinson* (New Haven, 1936), p. 173.

[4] Morton D. Zabel, "Robinson: the Ironic Discipline," *Nation,* CXLV (August 28, 1937), 222.

[5] Allen Tate, *On the Limits of Poetry* (New York, 1948), p. 370.

[6] [Unpublished letter] to Mrs. Laura E. Richards. December 2, 1934. [Houghton Library, Harvard University, Cambridge, Mass.]

sized: he was one generation older than such groups as the "lost generation" or the "new critics," and nearly a generation older than most of the poets who participated in the "poetic renaissance." Because he is the only major American poet of his own generation and because his early work seems to anticipate the "new poetry," he often suffers a unique injustice: first he is grouped with much younger poets and then, in comparison with them, he is damned as "too traditional." It is easier to keep our bearings if we remember what the World War I years seemed to mean to the generation of Hemingway and E. E. Cummings, and then remember that at this time Robinson was in his late forties, with his two best decades of work behind him. Dreiser is the American writer whose dates most nearly match Robinson's. He was born two years before and died ten years after Robinson. A list of poets born five years before or after 1869 would include Robinson, Yeats, Kipling, Æ., Dowson, Synge, De la Mare, Hovey, Moody, Masters, Stephen Crane, Amy Lowell. Housman's first book of poems was published in the same year as Robinson's, Hardy's two years later.

Positively, there is an initial revolt to take into account. Richard Crowder's summary description of the poetic scene in America when Robinson began to write helps us to understand some of the immediate causes of this early intransigence, and it also suggests why Robinson's innovations occasioned so little wonder:

> Among the established poets in America when the first books of Edwin Arlington Robinson appeared were Riley and Field; the Negro Paul Lawrence Dunbar; the lady poets Edith Matilda Thomas, Louise Chandler Moulton, Elizabeth Stoddard, Louise Imogen Guiney, and Lizette Woodworth Reese; the perfectionists Aldrich, Gilder, Bunner, and Sherman; Ambrose Bierce, Emily Dickinson, Richard Hovey, Stephen Crane, Father Tabb, Henry Van Dyke, Madison Cawein, Lloyd Mifflin, and George Santayana. With few exceptions the emphasis in verse-writing at this time was on form; there was an excessive reliance on symbols long since sterile; experience and genuine emotion went for naught. In general, readers of poetry wanted only highly polished verses, no matter how remote and cold. Robinson's poetry, cast in the usual forms, appeared conventional enough to draw only modest notice from most readers.[7]

Admittedly, some of Robinson's early poetry was conventional

[7] Richard Crowder, "Emergence of E. A. Robinson," *South Atlantic Quarterly*, XLV (January, 1946), 89. Emily Dickinson's poems were published during the 1890's, but she had died in 1886.

in every possible way. But in those poems in which he had truly discovered his talent, what was the nature of his divergence? Most important, perhaps, was his refusal to admit that nature, and not man, was the proper study of mankind. His skepticism on this point marked the end of one of the strongest conventions of romantic poetry. If man was to be the subject, the dormant dramatic instincts would return to English poetry. Robinson brought them back in 1896. Wit, generally suppressed in English poetry for more than a century, returned in Robinson's poetry, together with irony and a sterner intellectual discipline. His contribution to the purification of poetic language was equally substantial: ridding his verse of the stilted romantic diction that had been accreting since the early nineteenth century, he turned instead to a conversational and argumentative manner, reintroduced the language of genuine erudition, and provided poetry with a medium that had power and resiliency and was capable of intellectual distinctions. All these qualities were to prove of central importance in the later development of twentieth-century poetry, although most critics continue to be unconscious of Robinson's contribution to this development.

Most of his life Robinson seems to have been more conservative. He steadily objected to free verse and imagism; although he liked some of the poetry that came out of these movements, he was convinced that they were based on totally erroneous assumptions. He always emphasized what was "universal" and "unchanging" in any art. "There is always a new movement in poetry," he said. "There is always a new movement in everything . . . But if you mean to ask me if this new movement implies necessarily any radical change in the structure or in the general nature of what the world has agreed thus far to call poetry, I shall have to tell you that I do not think so." [8] In "The False Gods" and again in *Amaranth* Robinson satirized the art that had developed as his own career was reaching its peak and that he feared might overturn his most deeply held convictions on the nature and function of poetry. In *Amaranth* it may be the old master lecturing his upstart successors:

"I lean to less rebellious innovations;
And like them, I've an antiquated eye

[8] Lloyd R. Morris, ed., *The Young Idea: An Anthology of Opinion Concerning the Spirit and Aims of Contemporary American Literature* (New York, 1917), pp. 193–194.

For change too savage, or for cataclysms
That would shake out of me an old suspicion
That art has roots. . . ."

But in "The False Gods" it is the poet at the height of his own powers expressing his mature sense of tradition, continuity, and order:

"And you may as well observe, while apprehensively at ease
With an Art that's inorganic and is anything you please,
That anon your newest ruin may lie crumbling unregarded,
Like an old shrine forgotten in a forest of new trees.

"Howsoever like no other be the mode that you employ,
There's an order in the ages for the ages to enjoy;
Though the temples you are shaping and the passions you are singing
Are a long way from Athens and a longer way from Troy."

With further vacillations in taste behind us, the rebels that so disturbed Robinson now seem neither so rebellious nor so worthy his scorn. It has become equally evident that it is primarily with Eliot that Robinson ought to be compared. There are many obvious points of similarity, but it is perhaps in comparing the ways in which they may be considered "traditional" poets that their relation comes out most sharply. Both, of course, began as rebels and grew more conservative. But they should immediately be distinguished from another kind of rebel—Sandburg or Masters or Amy Lowell, for example—by emphasizing the fact that each had something substantial to fall back on. Instead of "rebel" it might be better to say "reactionary." The difference between the areas to which Eliot and Robinson retreated determined, at least in part, the different qualities of their verse. Eliot went back to the metaphysical poets, to the Elizabethan dramatists (but was shy of Shakespeare), to Dante, and to the French symbolists. A comparison of this pattern of interest with Robinson's shows immediately how complementary they are. They overlap at a few places, of course, but even here the differences are striking—for example, their attitudes toward *Hamlet* or Donne or Dante might be contrasted. Eliot's reaction carried him almost completely beyond the nineteenth century in England and America, but he was skeptical about much of Shakespeare and hostile to Milton. Robinson's "curve," on the other hand, is anchored at one end in Shakespeare and Milton and at the other in the nineteenth-century literature of America and Western

Europe. Robinson's tradition, to put the matter crudely, is that of romantic naturalism, whereas Eliot's is primarily that of a symbolic classicism. The traditions to which Robinson and Eliot turned, both convinced that poetry could not continue without going back to regain ground that had been lost, were substantially opposed and excluding. Such a schematization, it goes without saying, is of instrumental value only; obviously this kind of description does no sort of justice to the complexity and catholicity of either poet. But these would seem to be the chief traditions of modern poetry. Yeats and Hart Crane could be placed with Eliot. Frost would obviously be with Robinson, and so would Hardy and Auden and Pound. According to this view, Wallace Stevens might represent the center.

Except for one important specific difference. Robinson's attitude toward tradition somewhat anticipates Eliot's. As he told one interviewer, "I think there is a main road in all the arts. These young fellows, I think, are off the road. But that doesn't mean that everything which rolls over it must be like what went before." [9] Eliot and Robinson, of course, differ radically about the definition of the "main road." Here is Robinson again on the way a tradition operates: "My theory of art is very simple, and is not new. The great bulk of art consists merely in the giving out of what has been absorbed from others. The best, however, is a miracle of sheer genius, producing what the world has never before had." [10] Tradition and inspiration—these are the polar concepts in Robinson's view of art.

[9] Karl Schriftgeisser, "An American Poet Speaks His Mind," *Boston Evening Transcript,* November 4, 1933, Book Section, p. 1. This was a characteristic position. In a 1913 interview Robinson said: "I don't know anything about the poetry of the future except that it must have, in order to be poetry, the same eternal and unchangeable quality of magic that it has always had. Of course, it must always be colored by the age and the individual, but the thing itself will always remain unmistakable and indefinable" (William Stanley Braithwaite, "America's Foremost Poet," *Boston Evening Transcript,* May 28, 1913, p. 21). And in 1929: "I am essentially a classicist in poetic composition, and I believe that the accepted media for the masters of the past will continue to be used in the future. There is, of course, room for infinite variety, manipulation and invention within the limits of traditional forms and meters, but any violent deviation from the classic mean may be a confession of inability to do the real thing, poetically speaking" (Lucius Beebe, "Robinson Sees Romantic Strain in Future Verse," *New York Herald Tribune,* December 22, 1929, Pt. I, p. 19.

[10] Walter Tittle, "Edwin Arlington Robinson," the *Century Magazine,* CX (June, 1925), 192 (an interview).

Perhaps Robinson's feeling for literary tradition was sharpest concerning formal values. His own program was to revive and continue traditions that appeared moribund, and his emphasis was generally, as he put it, "to command new life into that shrunken clay." One sentence from Eliot's essay on Massinger joins the issue: "Changes never come by a simple reinfusion into the form which the life has just left." [11] Elsewhere he has given a fuller explanation of what he meant:

> Some forms are more appropriate to some languages than to others, and all are more appropriate to some periods than to others. At one stage the stanza is a right and natural formalization of speech into a pattern. But the stanza—and the more elborate it is, the more rules to be observed in its proper execution, the more surely this happens—tends to become fixed to the idiom of the moment of its perfection. It quickly loses contact with the changing colloquial speech, being possessed by the mental outlook of a past generation; it becomes discredited when employed solely by those writers who, having no impulse to form within them, have recourse to pouring their liquid sentiment into a ready-made mould in which they vainly hope that it will set. In a perfect sonnet, what you admire is not so much the author's skill in adapting himself to the pattern as the skill and power with which he makes the pattern comply with what he has to say. Without this fitness, which is contingent upon period as well as individual genius, the rest is at best virtuosity.[12]

Robinson's admirers would counter that here precisely is one of his great successes: that he was able to mold the forms he found into a fresh way of saying, that he was able to make the very pattern of the sonnet part of his ironic statement, that he constantly played off colloquial speech against the social connotations

[11] T. S. Eliot, *Selected Essays, 1917–1932* (New York, 1932), p. 190. At least one of Eliot's critics claims, however, that the early Eliot was really doing exactly what Robinson consciously intended: "Up to *The Waste Land* Mr. Eliot is on the whole doing what Bridges says the Romantics did: trying to put new content into old forms, and to revive the forms by returning to older handlings of them." Helen Gardner. *The Art of T. S. Eliot* (London, 1949), p. 22.

[12] T. S. Eliot, "The Music of Poetry," *Partisan Review,* IX (November–December, 1942), 463–4. This quotation represents, I think, Eliot's general *emphasis;* but his view is more complicated when taken in context. He goes on to say, for example, "Elaborate forms return: but there have to be periods during which they are laid aside." I do not think Robinson would have agreed that such extreme iconoclasm is ever necessary; and Eliot certainly has felt that Robinson's period was one in which elaborate forms should have been laid aside.

of traditional stanza forms. All this was one of his ways of fusing the past and present, of thereby escaping the limitations of his own age and thus achieving the impersonality and universality that he and Eliot both found in the ideal order of art.

But Robinson was bewildered by Eliot's poetry. In 1930 he wrote: "I found the Eliot book waiting for me here and have read it with some wonder as to what poetry is coming or going to. I like some of his things, but this is too much for my elementary brain." [13] And three years later he wrote: "I don't know much about Eliot except that he appears to have the younger generation at his heels. I like some of his things, but he seems to me to be going the wrong way." [14] The repeated phrase "I like his things, but" epitomizes Robinson's attitude.[15] Eliot's subsequent move in the direction of more conventional structures would doubtless have pleased Robinson. He would probably have liked the *Four Quartets,* and have been even enthusiastic about the plays.

Whatever the respective merits of these two views of tradition, it is clear that Robinson's initial revolt was of another kind than Eliot's. "Ballade of Broken Flutes," in Robinson's first book of poems, reveals more precisely what his intention was. It is not an

[13] A letter to James R. Wells. June 6, 1930. Quoted in *Edwin Arlington Robinson, A Collection of his Works from the Library of Bacon Collamore* (Hartford, 1936), p. 48.

[14] [Unpublished letter] to Mrs. Laura E. Richards. April 9, 1933. [Houghton Library, Harvard University, Cambridge, Mass.] "For those who accept tradition as a discipline and the private intelligence, sober or ironical, as a matter of importance, Robinson still offers his annual example. 'Talifer' and 'Amaranth' are the latest versions of the interminable rumination in scruple that has filled twenty volumes or more, now attenuated to sardonic dryness and the unfaltering accent of a grim satisfaction. This passive agnosticism is opposed by Eliot's recent zeal for religious and ethical leadership in three books, 'The Use of Poetry,' 'After Strange Gods,' and 'The Rock.' . . . Robinson and Eliot cannot be reconciled." Morton D. Zabel, "American Poetry: 1934," *New Republic,* LXXXI (December 12, 1934), 134–35.

[15] Perhaps the issue ought to be raised whether Robinson is not, in terms of American poetry, the last figure in a tradition going back to the Renaissance, and Eliot the first major figure in a new. See Joseph Frank, "Spatial Form in Modern Literature," *Sewanee Review,* LIII (1945), 221–40, 433–56, 643–53. If Mr. Frank's conjectures are correct, then it is possible to conclude that Robinson's adaptation to the "new century" was not radical enough, and that his failure to reckon with "spatial form" accounts for his bewilderment over so much modern poetry, painting, and music. But Robinson's own tentative strivings in this direction would then have to be dealt with: [see chapter 5 of Edwin S. Fussell, *Edwin Arlington Robinson: The Literary Background of a Traditional Poet* (Berkeley: University of California Press, 1954)], and also the structures of most of [Robinson's] long narrative poems.

"easy" poem, however, chiefly because it is so difficult to separate Robinson's own attitudes from the posturing associated with the form. Many of its assumptions, and its view of the decline of English poetry, were commonplaces of the 'nineties. But two quotations from Robinson's favorite Gleeson White anthology, *Ballades and Rondeaus,* should help put a frame around this poem so that one can discern what Robinson was doing in the foreground. Here are the opening lines of Oscar Fay Adams' "Where Are the Pipes of Pan?" which Robinson would have found on the first page of White's collection:

In these prosaic days
  Of politics and trade,
Where seldom fancy lays
  Her touch on man or maid,
  The sounds are fled that strayed
Along sweet streams that ran;
  Of song the world's afraid;
Where are the Pipes of Pan? [16]

Robinson shared the belief that materialism, especially in its utilitarian clothes, was largely responsible for the decadence of English poetry, but he equally despised the inconsequential twittering that Adams seems to believe constitutes poetry. Austin Dobson's "With Pipe and Flute" is even closer to Robinson's poems:

With pipe and flute the rustic Pan
Of old made music sweet for man;
  And wonder hushed the warbling bird,
  And closer drew the calm-eyed herd,—
The rolling river slowlier ran.

Ah! would,—ah! would, a little span,
Some air of Arcady could fan
  This age of ours, too seldom stirred
    With pipe and flute!

But now for gold we plot and plan;
And from Beersheba unto Dan,
  Apollo's self might pass unheard,
  Or find the night-jar's note preferred . . .

[16] Gleeson White, ed. *Ballades and Rondeaus* (London, 1887), p. 3.

Not so it fared, when time began
With pipe and flute! [17]

A few years earlier Yeats, emerging from a literary background similar to Robinson's (Yeats was four years older), had written a somewhat similar poem, "The Song of the Happy Shepherd":

The woods of Arcady are dead,
And over is their antique joy;
Of old the world on dreaming fed;
Grey Truth is now her painted toy;
Yet still she turns her restless head:
But O, sick children of the world,
Of all the many changing things
In dreary dancing past us whirled,
To the cracked tune that Chronos sings,
Words alone are certain good.

It should be easier now to cut through the tissue of conventional pleasantries that encases Robinson's poem and to see what it means when taken in historical context. The first stanza is routine complaint about the decay of poetry, though the concentrated images of death, sterility, and silence give it more power than might be expected. The second stanza renders the contrast between past and present both more explicit and more graphic, Robinson's contemporaries now appearing as "a ghostly band of skeletons." The third stanza is more personal, and clarifies Robinson's relation to this state of affairs:

No more by summer breezes fanned,
The place was desolate and gray;
But still my dream was to command
New life into that shrunken clay.
I tried it. And you scan to-day,
With uncommiserating glee,
The songs of one who strove to play
The broken flutes of Arcady.

Robinson's statement of purpose now seems clear enough: briefly, it was to revive a tradition in poetry that was considered dead by nearly everyone. And it was primarily the great tradition of the nineteenth century that he had in mind. At this time he had very little notion what directions modern poetry might take; and he

[17] *Ibid.*, p. 160.

probably underestimated the seriousness of the situation, as Eliot twenty years later may have overestimated it. With his second book Robinson was experimenting more daringly, feeling that he had not yet broken sharply enough with the immediate past. The ballade itself ends in disillusion. If this is not merely conventional, it may reflect dissatisfaction with the work he had done so far, or it may perhaps represent an awakening suspicion that it was now too late for a simple revival of the older tradition—this is not at all clear in the poem. A half century later we may surely read the poem with irony, for the songs referred to include such characteristic landmarks of modern American poetry as "The House on the Hill," "Richard Cory," "Reuben Bright," "The Clerks," "Credo," and "Luke Havergal."

One of the broken flutes Robinson had in mind was the sonnet. His sonnet on the sonnet, "The master and the slave go hand in hand" (the allusion is to Wordsworth's "Intimations" Ode), typically joins a nineteenth-century literary tradition with the poet's personal idealism. Wordsworth and Rossetti, among others, had written such poems, and Robinson follows their lead in declaring his eager submission to form. And it is also clear that Robinson considers the form decadent:

> The master and the slave go hand in hand,
> Though touch be lost. . . .

The sonnet is one item in Robinson's program "to command new life into that shrunken clay."

There is probably no better form to keep in mind when considering Eliot's principle that a decadent form cannot be resuscitated. For the sonnet, of all the intricate metrical arrangements of English poetry, has most clearly followed a steady pattern of desuetude and rejuvenescence. It has been revived successively by Shakespeare, Milton, Wordsworth, and Robinson; each renewal, moreover, although it involved some new principle of extension, has established its validity by reference to the past history of the form. Shakespeare starts with the contrast of everyday experience with the Petrarchan conventions. The Miltonic sublimity depends for its effect upon our awareness of the effects so achieved by Shakespeare (and Donne); all three must be kept in mind in order to measure the lyric departures of Wordsworth. Robinson's use of the sonnet for his concise narrative and dramatic portraiture represents what is probably his most skillful adaptation of an apparently decadent form to a dynamic and realistic contemporary purpose. Paradoxically, it was the sonnet—perhaps, of all the structures Robinson used, the hoariest with conventional frost—that led him to discover his unique talent.

A better-known sonnet, "Oh for a poet," was also in this first volume. Its argument again illuminates the complex blend of rebellion, conservatism, and reaction that determined the quality of Robinson's product. Like the "Ballade of Broken Flutes," it assumes the necessity to reinvigorate a dying tradition. But it also depends upon Emerson's sturdy assumption that any age is as good as any other. Thus Robinson is determined that great poetry shall not die in his time, though he is bewildered by the apparent decline of the past several decades. More important, the poem provides further evidence what kind of tradition Robinson fell back on: even the revisions Robinson made in the poem reveal his feeling that he was going back to regain a particular lost ground and to make that ground tenable for the twentieth-century poet.

As in "George Crabbe," "flicker" is Robinson's word for the 'nineties' version of "the light that never was." Contemporary poetry is marked by sterility, monotony, and the falsely feminine gentility of the superficial passion it reflects. Robinson's call for a new poet is in terms that Whitman might have approved:

> Oh for a poet—for a beacon bright
> To rift this changeless glimmer of dead gray.

The poem appeared in the *Critic,* November 24, 1894, and was Robinson's first commercial publication. When he printed it in *The Torrent and the Night Before,* he was more aware of his relation to the stream of English poetry. Thus "Shall not one bard arise" was replaced by "Shall there not one arise," a Wordsworthian revision that strengthens Robinson's objection to poetic banality. And in line eleven "as of yore" gave way to "as before." Not only did the change remove another stilted phrase, it also shifted emphasis from a vague tribute to ancient times to a more precise reference to the immediately preceding period, *that is, the early and middle years of the century.*

"Momus," a poem of the 1910 *Town Down the River* collection, illustrates Robinson's continuing and sensitive concern with literary history. Here Robinson's attitude is more complex, registering for the first time his consciousness of being a poet in a late stage of civilization. "Momus" is also another of Robinson's attacks on the Philistine, and thus looks back to such an early poem as "I make no measure of the words they say." Through Momus, the god of mockery so often used in Lucian's dialogues, Robinson puts the objections of the utilitarian, and then answers them in his own person. The first objection is that poetry is no longer needed by a scientific age that has "progressed" beyond such illusion. But the poet who never believed in time has little difficulty with this argument, and counters simply that King Kronos is still young and that all gods (including Apollo) are wild enough to resist such superficial formulation anyway. Next, it is supposed that poetry is not wearing well any more. Robinson, of course, had for a long time felt that parts of Browning, Byron, and Wordsworth merited such criticism. It is part of his skill as ironist that he allows the opposition so good a talking point, and it is also significant that he chose poets toward whom his own feelings were personal and mixed. We know, too, that Robinson worried privately over an apparent acceleration in literary history that he feared might eventually invalidate his whole concept of order and meaning in the poetry of the past. But here his conviction of "an order in the ages for the ages to enjoy" is established with an oblique allusion:

"Shut the door,
Momus, for I feel a draught;
Shut it quick, for some one laughed."

"Some one" is never identified further, though it is certain that he is "the Lord Apollo, who has never died." The final stanza insinuates that poetic material has been exhausted, that poets by this time can only go over and over the same ground, that what the nineteenth century called "wonder" is dead and the poetic attitude no longer feasible. This argument is quickly turned back on the Philistine: as a last resort, poetry can always fight for its own existence. But Robinson's optimistic faith enabled him to postpone this miserable possibility to the infinite future:

When the stars are shining blue
There will yet be left a few
Themes availing—
And these failing,
Momus, there'll be you.

Because his own poetry was based so firmly on his personal and sensitive appropriation of what was unchanging and available in the poetry of the past, Robinson was finally able to contemplate the future with some equanimity. Subsequent revolutions in taste have somewhat impaired the reputation he finally won toward the end of his career, but these revolutions have also shown that some of Robinson's poetry did attain the stature at which he aimed and that it will not be quickly forgotten. There can be little doubt that his best work is now part of the ideal order by which he always wished to be measured.

Robinson's Inner Fire

by Josephine Miles

The title of Edwin Arlington Robinson's early book, *The Children of the Night,* suggests its place in romantic tradition and its participation in the late nineteenth-century poetics of starlight, dream, and death. The first poem begins:

> Where are you going tonight, tonight,—
> Where are you going, John Evereldown?
> There's never the sign of a star in sight,
> Nor a lamp that's nearer than Tilbury Town.
> Why do you stare as a dead man might?
> Where are you pointing away from the light?
> And where are you going tonight, tonight,—
> Where are you going, John Evereldown?

Many characteristics of Robinson's poetry are found in these lines—the strong formal use of repetition, the conversational tone, the ballad-like mysteries and assumptions, the language of dreariness. Robinson's contemporaries in British poetry were Swinburne, Hardy, Housman, Wilde, and Yeats; after the death of Emily Dickinson, his American contemporaries were Sill, Lanier, Guiney, Moody, Sterling, and Frost. Robinson is of their number in his frequent use of atmospheres from the earlier world of Coleridge.

Another important part of Robinson's poetry is so traditional as to comprise the major vocabulary of English poetry: basic terms like *good, day, god, man, time, world, come, give, go, know, make,* and *see.* With the exception of one term, *sun.* Robinson made use of the full panoply of traditional poetic language.

Another set of qualities in his early poetry is more uniquely Robinsonian; not that he alone made use of it, but he shared it with a few poetic allies and set his name upon it for the future. His especially are the adjectives *desolate, human, lonely, lost,* and *sad;* the nouns *faith, flame, gleam, glory, shame, truth, thought, touch, hell, music, song, woman, wisdom,* and *wall;* the verbs *call* and *feel.* His connectives are characteristically few, except for the relative pronoun *that.* The atmosphere, the yearning, the generalizing of human values in inner hope and shame are evident in:

> Go to the western gate, Luke Havergal,
> There where the vines cling crimson on the wall,
> But go, and if you listen she will call.
> No, there is not a dawn in eastern skies
> To rift the fiery night that's in your eyes;
> God slays Himself with every leaf that flies,
> And hell is more than half of paradise.
> Nor think to riddle the dead words they say,
> Nor any more to feel them as they fall. . . .

The lines of every poem are loaded and reloaded with terms of value. From "Three Quatrains," for example, the music, with abstraction, "as long as Fame's imperious music rings." From "Dear Friends" too:

> So, friends (dear friends), remember, if you will,
> The shame I win for singing is all mine,
> The gold I miss for dreaming is all yours.

Emotional judgments are common in such poems as "The Story of the Ashes and the Flame":

> The story was as old as human shame

Or "Zola":

> Because he puts the compromising chart
> Of hell before your eyes, you are afraid;
> Never until we conquer the uncouth
> Connivings of our shamed indifference
> (We call it Christian faith) are we to scan
> The racked and shrieking hideousness of Truth. . . .

Or "The Pity of the Leaves":

> . . . Loud with ancestral shame there came the bleak
> Sad wind. . . .

One notes in "Supremacy," the weighted measure of "There is a drear and lonely tract of hell . . . ," and the full interpretive array of "Octaves,"

We thrill too strangely at the master's touch;
We shrink too sadly from the larger self . . .
We dare not feel it yet—the splendid shame
Of uncreated failure; we forget,
The while we groan, that God's accomplishment
Is always and unfailingly at hand. . . .

With conscious eyes not yet sincere enough
To pierce the glimmered cloud that fluctuates
Between me and the glorifying light
That screens itself with knowledge, I discern
The searching rays of wisdom that reach through
The mist of shame's infirm credulity,
And infinitely wonder if hard words
Like mine have any message for the dead.

And in "L'Envoi," again, the combination of sense, in *music,* with idea, in *transcendent:*

Now in a thought, now in a shadowed word,
Now in a voice that thrills eternity,
Ever there comes an onward phrase to me
Of some transcendent music I have heard;
No piteous thing by soft hands dulcimered,
No trumpet crash of blood-sick victory,
But a glad strain of some vast harmony
That no brief mortal touch has ever stirred.
There is no music in the world like this,
No character wherewith to set it down,
No kind of instrument to make it sing.
No kind of instrument? Ah, yes, there is;
And after time and place are overthrown,
God's touch will keep its one chord quivering.

These are the poems of the nineties, Robinson's first work. Thirty years later, in *Avon's Harvest* and in *Tristram,* the culmination of the Arthur sequence, the same characteristic phrasings prevail.

Fear, like a living fire that only death
Might one day cool, had now in Avon's eyes
Been witness. . . .

He smiled, but I would rather he had not. . . .

I was awake for hours,
Toiling in vain to let myself believe
That Avon's apparition was a dream. . . .

Robinson emphasized the mystery and interiority, sometimes the horror or majesty, of human feelings scarcely formulable—the "old human swamps" of Avon, the phantom sound of Roland's horn for Mr. Flood. The vividly implicative narrative turns inward, as is characteristic of the English nineteenth century in the poetry of Coleridge, Browning, and Yeats. "Modernities" is a fine and explicitly thoughtful example in concentration. The same pattern can be traced in *Tristram,* but the development is more leisurely: "Isolt of the white hands . . . white birds . . . remembered . . . her father . . . smiling in the way she feared . . . Throbbing as if she were a child . . . For making always of a distant wish/A dim belief . . . How many scarred cold things that once had laughed . . . a cold soul-retching wave . . . And body and soul were quick to think of it . . . Smiling as one who suffers to escape/Through silence and familiar misery, . . . Lost in a gulf of time where time was lost . . . and at the end,—He smiled like one with nothing else to do; . . . It was like that/For women sometimes, . . . Alone, with her white face and her gray eyes,/She watched them there till even her thoughts were white, . . . And the white sunlight flashing on the sea."

The terms which are new to the later poems are usually required by the content, like the *father, king, queen, forget, remember,* and *wait* of Isolt's life in the *Tristram* story. Some differences however, reveal significant shifts of attitude. *Sick* takes the place of *dead;* sensory *cold* and *white* replace more commenting *desolate, lonely,* and *sad.* Similarly, objective nouns like *bird, fire, moon,* and *shadow* take the place of more commenting *gleam, glory, faith,* and *shame.* The musical references are fewer. The ironic use of *laugh* and *smile* is heightened. In other words, objectivities do more of the work in the later verse; it is the same work, cooled.

We saw that fire at work within his eyes
And had no glimpse of what was burning there. . . .
. . . and there was now
No laughing in that house. . . .

> . . . without the sickening weight of added years.
> . . . a made smile of acquiescence, . . .
> . . . he who sickens . . . over the fire of sacrifice . . .
> He smiled, but I would rather he had not.

These lines and many more in their vein are in "Avon"; and, in "Rembrandt," "shadows and obscurities,"

> Touching the cold offense of my decline,
> . . . like sick fruit . . . our stricken souls . . .
> Your soul may laugh . . . or grinning evil
> In a golden shadow . . .
> Forget your darkness in the dark, and hear
> No longer the cold wash of Holland scorn.
> The moon that glimmered cold on Brittany . . .
> How many scarred cold things that once had laughed
> And loved, and wept, and sung, and had been men, . . .
> . . . a cold soul-retching wave
> . . . And body and soul were sick to think of it.
> . . . White birds . . . Before his eyes were blinded
> by white irons . . .
> . . . The still white fire of her necessity.
>
> And when slow rain
> Fell cold upon him as upon hot fuel,
> It might as well have been a rain of oil
> On faggots round some creature at a stake
> For all the quenching there was in it then
> Of a sick sweeping beast consuming him
> With anguish of intolerable loss.

With these backward looks of his, metaphysical *fire,* romantic *white* and *rain,* Robinson also looked forward. If not an innovator, he was at least an early participator in new developments. Although he was, with Frost, one of the last to stress thought and thinking, he shared his *feeling, telling, singing, song,* and *music* with his contemporary William Vaughn Moody, with Chivers and Sterling, and later with Wallace Stevens. His verb *touch* he shared with Sill and Swinburne; his *human,* with Sterling and Stevens; his *face* and *nothing* with Poe and Stevens. He shared with the young poets of the mid-twentieth century his implicative *cold, small, bird, flame, dream, shadow,* and his especial *sick.*

Writers on Robinson have agreed with Redman's conclusion that the first books revealed the method and matter of Robinson's maturity and that New England childhood, Harvard education, New York and MacDowell work and writing, all kept him to "the seasons and the sunset as before." He was neither explorer nor revolutionary. He saw each man trying to cope with his own demon, as in "Rembrandt"; and each as a child "trying to spell *God* with wrong blocks." [1] He often saw a conflict between experience and expectation; thus his characteristic early vocabulary gives us the heart of his poetry with its blend of sense—in *touch, sing, shine, flame, gleam*—and interpretation—in *desolate, lonely, human, shame, wisdom, truth*—while *Avon* and *Tristram* add *cold, sick, white, shadow, smile,* and *remember* to *nothing* and *time.* This was a world already established by Coleridge and Poe, and enforced by Robinson's contemporaries, yet he was right to insist that he looked forward. Much of his terminology has been used intensively by the poets of the mid-twentieth century. Sill's *small, still, touch,* and *watch;* Sterling's *vision* and *gleam;* Moody's *low, sick,* and *road;* Stevens' *large, human,* and *music;* Williams' *flame, call,* and *seek;* W. T. Scott's *memory* and *remember;* and Hecht's *cold;* all move into Rothenberg's *lost, hell, grow, leave, white,* and *shadow;* the *cold* of Gary Snyder and others; David Ray's *woman;* Robert Kelly's *music* and *song;* and Michael McClure's *sick, dream, flame, memory, nothing, wall, remember,* and *touch.* Robinson foreshadowed the modern poet's connotative, implicative, nostalgic sense of beauty in the world today.

Esther Willard Bates reported that Robinson "told me that he was, perhaps, two hundred years in advance of his time, indicating in brief half-statements, with pauses in between, that his habit of understatement, his absorption in the unconscious and semi-conscious feelings and impulses of his characters were the qualities in which he was unlike his contemporaries. . . . He said he wondered if he wasn't too dry, too plain, if he wasn't overdoing the simple, the unpoetic phrase." [2]

Yet this was the poet who "knew his Bible" (p. 29) and who was quoted by his biographer Hagedorn as characteristically writing, "In the great shuffle of transmitted characteristics, traits, abilities, aptitudes the man who fixes on something definite in life that he

[1] Ben Ray Redman, *Edwin Arlington Robinson* (New York: McBride, 1926), pp. 28, 33.

[2] Esther Willard Bates, *Edwin Arlington Robinson and His Manuscripts* (Waterville, Maine: Colby College Library, 1944), p. 3.

must do, at the expense of everything else, if necessary, has presumably got something that, for him, should be recognized as the Inner Fire. For him, that is the Gleam, the Vision, and the Word! He'd better follow it." [3]

What have the Gleam, the Vision, and the Word to do with dry, plain, and unpoetic understatement? How does Robinson reconcile objects of nature with concepts of desire, Tennyson's atmospheres with Browning's interior psychologizing, rich sense with metaphysical thought, so that he seems at once archaic and modern, reminiscent and inventive? His major vocabulary suggests one answer: that his chief material is romantic natural beauty, but that his treatment of it is skeptical and unhappy, in a metaphysics of *shame, lonely,* and *sick.* Such a tone preserves him his modernity through a moonlit world. *Desolate, human, shame, truth,* and *wisdom* are the terms of interpretive comment which his critics call literary. Such terms distinguish him from metaphysicians like Frost on the one hand and, in their negativity, from the American poets of praise like Whitman on the other hand. He praises with nostalgia and he blames with apprehension; many young poets today share his combination of attitudes and even his vocabulary of dismayed values.

[3] Herman Hagedorn, *Edwin Arlington Robinson, A Biography* (New York: Macmillan, 1938), p. viii.

The "New" Poetry: Robinson and Frost

by Warner Berthoff

For poetry the important consequences of the renewed impulse toward "realism" in this rising generation were formal and stylistic. It is hard now, after the experimental novelties and triumphs of another half-century, to imagine the indifference of established critical taste around 1900 to the kind of poetic language Edwin Arlington Robinson and Robert Frost (thirty-one and twenty-six respectively at the turn of the century) had begun teaching themselves to write in. It is also hard to imagine how unsure they themselves could be as to when in fact they had achieved what they wanted—in Robinson's case the "sense of reality" (letter to Harry de Forest Smith, February 3, 1895) which he had found in no poet of his time so much as in the prose of Hawthorne and Thomas Hardy; in Frost's, those "effects of actuality and intimacy," communicating the special thrill of "sincerity," which he once called (letter to W. S. B. Braithwaite, March 22, 1915) "the greatest aim an artist can have."

A more direct and substantial confrontation of actual experience than can be found in the propriety-ridden verse of the preceding thirty years in American writing—the period of Edwin Rowland Sill, Joaquin Miller, Sidney Lanier, John Boyle O'Reilly, Father Tabb, James Whitcomb Riley, Edwin Markham, Lizette Woodworth Reese—is surely a main part of Robinson's and Frost's achievement. But the language for embodying it in poems was not created all at once. It is curious to leaf through Frost's first collection, *A Boy's Will* (published in 1913 but consisting mostly of poems written six, ten, even fifteen years earlier) and discover how

"The 'New' Poetry: Robinson and Frost" by Warner Berthoff. From *The Ferment of Realism* (New York: The Free Press, 1965), pp. 263–77. Copyright 1965 by The Macmillan Company. Reprinted by permission of The Macmillan Company.

little Frostian the run of it sounds. His early poems, Malcolm Cowley has remarked, "gave his own picture of the world, but in the language of the genteel poets." Surely verbal texture was not what encouraged Frost to go on reprinting poems beginning, "Thine envious fond flowers are dead, too," or "Lovers, forget your love,/ And list to the love of these,/ She a window flower,/ And he a winter breeze." The first example dates back to 1895, but the point, historically, is that even then Frost knew better. His twenty-year struggle to establish a satisfactory verse language is one of the significant episodes in modern literary history. "I was under twenty," he wrote in the letter already quoted,

> when I deliberately put it to myself one night after good conversation that there are moments when we actually touch in talk what the best writing can only come near. The curse of our book language is not so much that it keeps forever to the same set phrases (though Heaven knows those are bad enough) but that it sounds forever with the same reading tones. We must go out into the vernacular for tones that haven't been brought to book. We must write with the ear on the speaking voice.

—we must achieve, he said in the same letter, and was saying in all his correspondence and conversation of the time, not merely fine sounds or important sense but something more vital than either: the very "sound of sense," caught as if at the instant of its coming alive.

Robinson's command of tone (so defined: the "sound of sense") does not seem as supple and varied or as distinctly individual as Frost's came to be, but it is perhaps more consistently "major" in the body of his work, just as the body of his work represents a more abundant and a steadier creative energy. We observe that he secured his verse style sooner than any of his nearer contemporaries—Masters, Frost, Amy Lowell, Sandburg, Wallace Stevens; "modern" poetry in the United States begins with Robinson's volumes of 1896 and 1897, *The Torrent and The Night Before* and *The Children of the Night*. Yet he too had his troubles breaking through the flaccidity of contemporary verse conventions. Two versions of one of his early successes, the much-anthologized villanelle, "The House on the Hill," show him groping toward the characteristic style of his maturity, distinguished (though the advance is slight and uncertain in this instance) by a more concentrated specification of feeling and, coincidentally, a provocative obliquity of statement.

The first version, written out in a letter of February, 1894, antedates the second and published version by more than two years:

I	II

They are all gone away,
  The house is shut and still:
There is nothing more to say.
	They are all gone away,
	  The House is shut and still,
	There is nothing more to say.

Malign them as we may,
  We cannot do them ill:
They are all gone away.
	Through broken walls and gray
	  The winds blow bleak and shrill:
	They are all gone away.

Are we more fit than they
  To meet the Master's will?—
There is nothing more to say.
	Nor is there one to-day
	  To speak them good or ill:
	There is nothing more to say.

What matters it who stray
  Around the sunken sill?—
They are all gone away,
	Why is it then we stray
	  Around that sunken sill?
	They are all gone away.

And our poor fancy-play
  For them is wasted skill:
There is nothing more to say.
	And our poor fancy-play
	  For them is wasted skill:
	There is nothing more to say.

There is ruin and decay
  In the House on the Hill:
They are all gone away,
There is nothing more to say.
	There is ruin and decay
	  In the House on the Hill:
	They are all gone away,
	There is nothing more to say.

Two versions of his rendering in sonnet form of Horace, Book I, Ode XI, which can be dated to May, 1891, and December, 1895, show the same development toward verbal plainness, emotional concentration, dramatic obliquity.

A morally serious apprehension of life joined to a steady determination to make poetry once again an adult calling: these motives are fundamental to Robinson's and Frost's progress beyond the dead level of competent verse rhetoric of the '80s and '90s. Yet other ambitious young poets of the same generation worked from the same motives—in particular the group of university poets, mostly Harvard-educated, among whom William Vaughn Moody (1869–1910), Trumbull Stickney (1874–1904), and William Ellery Leonard (1876–1944) seem now the most gifted, and Santayana (who published *Sonnets and Other Verses* in 1894 and a verse tragedy, *Lucifer,* in 1899) appears as a kind of unofficial senior tutor. The special historical interest of this group has been pointed out by Malcolm

Cowley, in remarking how the "tradition" they participated in, with its classical learning, its use of myth-themes, its French exposure, and its assumption that verse drama is the supreme literary form, is the local tradition that nourished T. S. Eliot.[1] Through Eliot we can see that these allegiances were not necessarily stultifying. But reading the published work of these undoubtedly thoughtful and sincere poets we can also see the essential inertness of their verse language, in syntax, in phrase cadence, in diction and metaphor. Perhaps we can see, too, why certain ideas—an "objective correlative" for emotion; artistic creation as an "escape from personality"—gained a special prominence in Eliot's early thinking. It is in technique first of all, in the securing of a fresh voice and a greater concentration of form, that the poetic renaissance of the early 1900s declares itself. For Robinson and Frost not less than for Eliot and Pound, technique becomes the critical test of a poet's "sincerity." Certainly nothing is more fundamental to the actual creation of a "new" poetry than this: the transfer of ambition from the lining out of important subjects and weighty themes to the achievement of a disciplined, freshly viable craftsmanship.

In feeling and in imaginative grasp there is a narrowness and monotony about the poetry of Edwin Arlington Robinson (1869–1935) which, at first encounter, may make nearly inexplicable the ranking which more than one commentator has felt it impossible to withhold from him: the foremost talent in American poetry between Whitman and Eliot. Reading one after another of his severe narrative portraits, with their dry skepticism and sensuous bareness, we may wonder whether he was not himself a leading victim of that American blight which seems his central, perhaps obsessive, subject. Robinson is the poet of casualties; of broken lives and exhausted consciences; of separateness;[2] and of the calm that comes with resignation and defeat—perhaps only with death. He writes of an "ethical unrest" ("Flammonde") or "querulous selfish-

[1] *The Literary Situation,* 1955, p. 244. Robinson and Frost were also at Harvard briefly in the '90s, but with this difference: both matriculated when already into their twenties and when—so it appears from early letters—they had already learned to read and to think critically for themselves; and both came away before having to commit themselves to the pursuit of a degree.

[2] More separateness than isolation: his most compact monologues and analyses invariably assume a listener or observer, the irony of whose uncomprehending presence intensifies dramatically the suggested emotion.

ness" ("Captain Craig") undercutting every philosophic reassurance, every visionary refuge, men may think to guard their lives with. Robinson's sense of life has, of course, its regional sources. His links with the older New England consciousness—the "folk atmosphere of the upper levels of New England society," in Yvor Winter's phrase—and also the timing of his absorption into it, at the dry climax of its long dissolution, have not gone unremarked. The Puritan concept of life as a wearing state of spiritual probation; the Puritan-Transcendentalist passion for "the light" and for right relationship; the inexhaustible, humanly exhausting concern of both Puritan and Transcendentalist for defining the sovereign laws of life ("lords of life," in Emerson's phrase) through the minutely detailed testimony of certain representative men: these motives receive perhaps their last direct expression in Robinson's poems. But it is typical of the state of the New England tradition when he came to inherit it that the opening lines of an early sonnet called "Credo" should affirm only negations—"I cannot find my way: there is no star. . . ."—and that thirty years later his address to this tradition in another sonnet, "New England," should be derisively ironic.

Inheritance, temperament, imaginative consciousness blend almost indistinguishably in Robinson. His most casual words are suffused with the tones and accents of his best poems. At twenty-four he remarked in a letter to Harry de Forest Smith: "I am afraid that I shall always stand in the shadow as one of Omar's broken pots. I suspect that I am pretty much what I am, and that I am pretty much a damned fool in many ways; but I further suspect that I am not altogether an ass, whatever my neighbors may say." The damned and the fooled—these are the recurring subjects of Robinson's verse portraits; and a great part of his strength as a poet is his ability to specify as if from interior knowledge both the magnitude and the inscrutability of the forces that have prevailed over them. His poems convey a real awe, a sense of the actual mystery and translatedness, of those who have met and endured these forces to the full. A few poems celebrate the even more mysterious and select company of those who have themselves somehow prevailed in their lives, though such figures, typically, are all but nameless in the poems devoted to them—"The Master" (Lincoln), "Walt Whitman," "Ben Jonson Entertains a Man from Stratford"; the fine "Rembrandt to Rembrandt" is the exception in this respect, and there the speaker, unhonored, is left to name himself. These heroes survive not as imaginable persons but as "flying words," as "piercing cadences" too pure and triumphant to be heard directly, as vanished yet unforgettable impressions.

Words and cadences rather than generalizing argument; the emotion not to be contested rather than the thought seeking to complete itself—these (almost against his intellectual will, it seems) are the particular means of Robinson's accomplishment. In his first maturity he accepted the notion that the duty of the learned man was to consider what it was that he "believed"; to search out a system of philosophic or religious truth which he could give a proper name to, perhaps even live by. So we find Robinson at the time of his first book trying to define his religion—"a kind of optimistic desperation" was his own early description of it—and earnestly considering the merits and claims of "idealism" over against "materialism" as "the one logical and satisfactory interpretation of life." We note how Christian Science attracted him until he came up against its theological and sectarian pretensions, and how late in life he was still pointing out (to an interviewer in 1932) the "Transcendentalism" in certain poems. What bearing do such matters have upon his achievement as a poet? Robinson's "thought," we can say, was neither more nor less impressive than that of many sensitive and serious-minded contemporaries. Neo-Darwinist generalities and post-Protestant absolutes concerning human fate and the order of the cosmos rumbled through his head as monotonously as may be imagined, given his times and background—and that might indeed be the principal interest of his poems if he had not written them out so carefully; if he had not, that is, coincidentally committed himself to that other way of truth-seeking which is the vocation of the artist. Robinson matters as a poet, not as a philosopher. His thought counts as it is articulated in the words, measures, serial figures of his verse. He is not even a philosophical poet, really—certainly not so much of one as, say, Eliot or Stevens. His saving grace is that he will not say what he cannot take technical possession of; he is sincere and pursues truth within his capacity to complete the expressive figures he composes in.

That would seem to be the point of Frost's charming, scarcely improvable tribute in a preface to the posthumous *King Jasper* (1935): "For forty years it was phrase on phrase on phrase with Robinson"—and every one, Frost added, "the closest delineation of argumentative syntax and of prosody. Frost seems to have had his eye on one aspect of it in praising Robinson for "the way the shape of the stanza is played with [in the developing statement], the easy way the obstacle of verse is turned to advantage." The young poet and critic Jane Hess has discussed it in more specific detail:

> Although Robinson was at ease with a variety of forms (one criterion for a major poet), including blank verse and the sonnet, his ear was most naturally tuned to balanced cadences, the ballad measure, and the resolution of true rhymes. Into lyric stanza forms he forced studied analyses, composing an abstract, bony kind of verse the elements of which remain constantly in tension and reflect in their actual construction the tension of the characters they portray.

Within the chosen measures of his verse it is always the firmly wrought phrase- and sentence-figure—"phrase on phrase on phrase" —that carries attention forward. This is the means by which his apprehensions reach us. Figures of predication and address, metrical and stanzaic figures, figures of expression and description: they come into being together and cannot be dissevered. They act along the line of their own advance; they are how his poems speak. Like any settled way of speaking, of course, this of Robinson's creates its own dangers. The capacity to produce these basic figures of statement in consistent abundance, the "formulary ingenuity" in Robinson that Yvor Winters speaks of, is also what frequently creates, especially in long poems, the damping impression of a kind of automatic writing. Certain devices become mannerisms and begin to seem self-proliferating: in particular the use, like a speech tic, of abstract relative clauses for primary statement (thus, successfully enough, in "Flammonde": "How much it was of him we met/ We cannot ever know; nor yet/ Shall all he gave us quite atone/ For what was his, and his alone"),[4] and also a corresponding trick of negative identification (not this, not this, not even this, but possibly that, though perhaps not that either). Sometimes these devices are precisely suited to the unfolding of the argument; sometimes they

[4] It is characteristic of Robinson, whose verse idiom is grounded in the broad range of Romantic and Victorian poetry, to have spotted an occasional fine effect in a poet like Longfellow and adapted it to his own uses. See the fourth stanza of Longfellow's "The Fire of Driftwood": "We spake of many a vanished scene,/ Of what we once had thought and said,/ Of what had been, and might have been,/ And who was changed, and who was dead. . . ."

something that *is* something." Phrase rather than image: Robi language is notoriously abstract and unsensuous. His meta tend to be apparitional; they are verbal signals not so muc bodying the theme or the emotion in concrete detail as lighti its progress through the bare statement of the poem. Dark, gleams, voices, fire and flame, music, years, waves, dreams basic vocabulary is composed almost entirely of the familiar " metaphors of common rhetoric (and of Romantic wisdom verse decadence). But one sign of Robinson's rather powerful tac poet is that half the time such metaphors are used parodist to cover with doubt or irony or pathos the turns of though feeling that commonly lean on them. A case can be made, i for their special appropriateness in poems so many of whi built upon the imaginative setting of the congregated Am village and its befogged way of looking at things (whether Ga Maine, or the New York City of his 1910 volume, *The Town the River*); poems which consistently produce, as Conrad Aike suggested, the effect of something deviously known rather directly seen. But the basic strength of Robinson's poeti guage resides in something even more elemental than this metaphor. Robinson surely has the most flexible working ulary in modern American poetry—and has it (in contrast to like Pound and Stevens) entirely within the framework plain style. In large part it is sheer unaided verbal and den tive resourcefulness that enlivens his poems, restoring the full ulary of ordinary prose discourse to verse statement, and that him as a main defense against argumentative monotony (wi perfect success) in the long verse narratives of his later The elaborations, the refinements, the suspended complexi stated meaning would be quite strangling in Robinson's poems without this continual infusion of fresh linguistic c

Robinson's poetic authority involves something more of than this ordinary verbal resourcefulness, though that is a r part of it. What it centrally consists in is a matter at o

[8] About this later work—the Arthurian poems, *Merlin* (1917), *Lancelo* and *Tristram* (1927), and the psychological verse novels like *Roman Ba* (1923), *The Man Who Died Twice* (1924), *Cavender's House* (1929), and *at the Door* (1931)—the comment has been made more than once that, else may be said about them, it cannot be said that they are badly Almost any passage, tested at random, will show the same resourcef petence at phrase-balancing and verse-making.

are the means to what seems a willful obscurity, a pointless circumlocution. But in the main Robinson's predicative style, as we may call it, is a style equal to the most demanding occasions in his poetry. It is the instrument, for example, which makes "The Man Against the Sky" (1916), his meditative ode on the mysteries of mortal being and the shadow our consciousness of mortality throws over the reasoned conduct of life, one of the most fitly eloquent of modern poems; here as elsewhere it seems an admirable vehicle for expressing the restless yet finely balanced skepticism of Robinson's mind.

His best-remembered poems are mostly the shorter dramatic monologues and narrative portraits or biographies: "Luke Havergal," "Charles Carville's Eyes," "Cliff Klingenhagen," "Richard Cory," "Eros Turannos" (justly praised), "Mr. Flood's Party," "Flammonde," to name only the most frequently anthologized. But anthologies are a means of forgetting as well as remembering. They are also a means of simulating critical principles where lack of space is what really decides; so they regularly conspire to perpetuate Poe's curiously long-lived thesis that the coherent long poem is a practical impossibility. In any case nobody anthologizes Robinson's 2016-line poem of 1902, "Captain Craig," the climactic work of his first maturity. Yet it is possible to think that this "rather particular kind of twentieth century comedy," as he called it, is his greatest achievement. Most of the poem's effort goes into defining—which is to say, surrounding, blanketing, wholly occupying—an attitude or mind style of which the Captain himself is first spokesman and, in his reported life, chief exemplar. Space is lacking to suggest the variety and energy and sheer surface interest of the line-by-line fashioning of the poem. It must do to say that this effort of definition goes forward by contrasts, dialectically; Robinson's ironic humor has the firmness of syllogism, of argument pursued until it has embraced, or disarmed, its invoked opposite. Humor is the determining mode. Captain Craig, by his own account, is above all a "humorist"—"Shrewd, critical, facetious, insincere." What he propounds is propounded with "an ancient levity/ That is the forbear of all earnestness." A stoical, derisive, yet garrulous and congenial humor is his refuge from impossible alternatives: from "altruism," for example, for which the actual world is never quite ready; or from "sincerity"—the poem is a kind of anatomy of failed or overworked sincerity and thus bids for a place among the classics of skeptical or third-stage romanticism; or from a state which both altruism and sincerity will come down to in any case, that oppressive and irreversible exhaustion of spirit from which so much of modern literature (and modern catastrophe) takes its rise:

> . . . the spiritual inactivity
> Which more than often is identified
> With individual intensity,
> And is the parent of that selfishness
> Whereof no end of lesser *tions* and *isms*
> Are querulously born.

The abounding wordiness of "Captain Craig" (even these few lines display it) is both reinforced and moderated by the facetious, mock-pedestrian tone of the Captain's discourse. *Wordiness* becomes, in fact, the active metaphor for the mode or style of life, always inadequate, which the poem defines. In the metaphoric substructure of "Captain Craig" wordiness is set against the ideal mode of *music* (a conjunction is made at the end, ironically, in the presumptuous music of the brass band, blaring "indiscreetly," which marches the Captain to his grave). Appropriately, then, throughout the poem, counterpointing all its knotted figures of primary statement, the music of older poetic formulas sounds—cadences from Shakespeare, Milton, the Bible, Emerson, Byron, Wordsworth, Tennyson, Swinburne. Greece and Provence are mentioned: "Captain Craig" is one more early modern work—Pound's "Hugh Selwyn Mauberley" (1920) is another—that finds in allusions to the Greeks both a source of metaphor for its skeptical, ironic lamentation and also a kind of litany of consolation in its knowledge of their names. The Wordsworthian echoes are particularly significant with regard to the theme of "the Child"—the phoenix life within the overshadowed adult consciousness—which the Captain's comfortless, perilously insistent humor justifies itself by keeping in view.

Whether "Captain Craig" succeeds greatly or not and finds and entirely fulfills its own proper laws of form, it is historically of the greatest interest. Its moral and stylistic comedy stands, in American literature, midway between Melville's "Marquis of Grandvin" and Wallace Stevens's "The Comedian as the Letter C" (a poem surely influenced by it), and is stronger and steadier in running its course than either of those—as one may say with all due admiration for Stevens's copiously witty poem. A remarkable quantity of subsequent American writing seems an elaboration of the manner of address perfected in "Captain Craig." One may mention in particular all the ironic narratives—shifting between the facetiously verbose and the cynically proverbial—of what it is that lies beneath middle-class respectability, or of the doings of certain mortally disaffected though perhaps transfigured heroes who approach some rarer knowledge of the spirit's capacity for truth but go to ruin as a consequence: the fiction, that is, of writers like Cozzens, Penn Warren, Styron, Bellow, Wright Morris, Salinger and, as Louis Coxe has observed, of Robert Lowell in his verse narrative, *The Mills of the Kavanaughs*; of Henry Miller and of Faulkner when he gives rein to the compulsive talkers of his later stories; of, supremely perhaps, the Eugene O'Neill of *The Iceman Cometh* and *Long Day's Journey Into Night.* "Captain Craig" is a poem whose working co-ordinates embrace no small part of the expressive tradition it energetically advances.

The Alienated Self

by W. R. Robinson

> Since we live only in and by contradictions, since life is tragedy and tragedy is perpetual struggle, without victory or the hope of victory, life is contradiction.
>
> Miguel de Unamuno

Man, individual man, is the moral center of Robinson's poetry. He begins with a nineteenth-century interest in character and carries over its corresponding ideal of the whole or complete person. We know all too well that the twentieth century is the age of alienation, and alienated man can be found with ease and in abundance in Robinson's poetry. Though segregation and disintegration are there, to be sure, especially in the early and middle poems but also as the starting point for the later ones, they are not final but remediable conditions. Robinson's treatment of his characters, particularly the course of events he puts them through, is his most specific means for displaying the achievement and meaning of integration.

Probably the most frequent "character" to appear in Robinson's poetry is Tilbury Town, the fictional community that provides the setting for many of his poems and explicitly links him and his poetry with small-town New England, the repressive, utilitarian social climate customarily designated as the Puritan ethic. For Tilbury Town, more than simply a setting, is an antagonistic moral force in the drama of life as Robinson imagined it. In this capacity it is one pole in another aspect of the dualism he inherited from materialism—the dichotomy between self and society, one more obstacle in the way to being whole.

"The Alienated Self" by W. R. Robinson. From *Edwin Arlington Robinson: A Poetry of the Act* (Cleveland: The Press of Western Reserve University, 1967), pp. 75–95.

The first reference to Tilbury Town occurs in "John Evereldown," which appeared in *The Torrent and the Night Before* (1896), Robinson's first volume of poetry. Here, simply a place, it has not yet acquired a dramatic role. In other poems of the same volume, however, the small-town community, though unnamed, does begin to assume such a role, as for instance in "Richard Cory," where the collective "we" speaks as a character. By the time of "Captain Craig" (1902) Tilbury Town is fully dressed for its part and firmly established as a dramatic persona. Here, from the beginning of the poem, the town is Captain Craig's explicit antagonist. The captain defines their differences this way:

> Forget you not that he who in his work
> Would mount from these low roads of measured shame
> To tread the leagueless highways must fling first
> And fling forever more beyond his reach
> The shackles of a slave who doubts the sun.
> There is no servitude so fraudulent
> As of a sun-shut mind; for 'tis the mind
> That makes you craven or invincible,
> Diseased or puissant. The mind will pay
> Ten thousand fold and be the richer then
> To grant new service; but the world pays hard,
> And accurately sickens till in years
> The dole has eked its end and there is left
> What all of you are noting on all days
> In these Athenian streets, where squandered men
> Drag ruins of half-warriors to the grave—
> Or to Hippocrates. [166][1]

At issue, as the captain sees it, is the quality of life, with the two alternatives being the life-enhancing way of the sun-receptive mind and the life-squandering way of the world. The narrator of the poem, one of the few citizens of the town eventually to look after and listen to the captain, agrees with his views but even more explicitly criticizes the town when he remarks,

> a few—
> Say five or six of us—had found somehow
> The spark in him, and we had fanned it there,
> Choked under, like a jest in Holy Writ,
> By Tilbury prudence. [113]

[1] [Page references are to *Collected Poems of Edwin Arlington Robinson* (New York: Macmillan, 1937).]

Tilbury's prudence callously squanders life—literally, in this instance—but the captain does not blame the town, or some privileged faction of it, for his hard times; he is not interested in criticizing prevailing institutions in order to bring about social reform. Nor is the narrator, who writes,

> And he was right: there were no men to blame:
> There was just a false note in the Tilbury tune—
> A note that able-bodied men might sound
> Hosannas on while Captain Craig lay quiet.
> They might have made him sing by feeding him
> Till he should march again, but probably
> Such yielding would have jeopardized the rhythm;
> They found it more melodious to shout
> Right on, with unmolested adoration,
> To keep the tune as it had always been,
> To trust in God, and let the Captain starve. [114]

For both the captain and the narrator it is social or collective man, whose interests are in getting on well materially rather than in humanity or the quality of life, who is the object of their criticism.

By befriending the captain the narrator receives as reward for his generous sympathy a rediscovery of an old truth, which he states at the conclusion of his tale:

> The ways have scattered for us, and all things
> Have changed; and we have wisdom, I doubt not,
> More fit for the world's work than we had then;
> But neither parted roads nor cent per cent
> May starve quite out the child that lives in us—
> The Child that is the Man, the Mystery,
> The Phoenix of the World. [168]

Throughout the poem, much is made of the child's consciousness as the source of spiritual health, or as the saving power, and that consciousness is consistently linked with the imagery of light. Both the child and the light are excluded from Tilbury Town, and this repudiation of spirit is the town's most grievous sin. Its social materialism—its prudence, its righteousness and inhumanity, its "cent per cent" engrossment, its obsession with conventional worldly success—results in indifference to the captain as a suffering individual and to the eccentric, anticonformist ways of art, the soul, and the light for which he speaks. The town's prudence being a spiritual crassness and blindness that makes it an adamant enemy of the captain and what he values, the sun's light and the phoenix' fire are forever locked outside its walls.

Although Tilbury Town is not personified in "Captain Craig," as it is in "Richard Cory" and other poems where the collective "we" or a representative member is the speaker of the poem, "Captain Craig" provides the town with its biggest role. Never again does it rise to such explicit dramatic prominence. Yet whenever it appears thereafter, no matter how briefly, it bears the stamp of the spiritual crassness and blindness suggested in "Richard Cory" and fully and explicitly defined in "Captain Craig." For example, in "Isaac and Archibald," two old men of rough but ready friendship unconsciously instruct a boy, the narrator, in the ways of humanity, but that instruction takes place outside the town, as it must. And never again is Tilbury Town simply a place; it is always a character, the collective consciousness, antagonist of the peculiar, gifted, or far-seeing individual, who, a failure by conventional standards, dedicates himself to the interior life.

Although Tilbury Town, easily identified with Gardiner, Maine, is the most direct device Robinson could use for treating the individual's alienation from the community, it is not his only one. Shakespeare's obsession with Stratford and Rembrandt's troubles with Amsterdam, as well as St. Paul's with Rome, the Wandering Jew's with New York, and Merlin's and Lancelot's with Camelot are vehicles for the same theme. In fact, as this brief list suggests, Robinson's better known poems are usually on this subject. His personal troubles[2] permitted him to imagine concrete and profound

[2] In addition to being a literary theme, the conflict between individual and community treated in "Captain Craig" was a deeply disturbing personal problem for Robinson, because as Hermann Hagedorn remarks, "In his diffidence, as a man Robinson tacitly accepted the standards which, as a poet, he vehemently rejected, and judged himself by them. . . . He became obsessed by what, rightly or wrongly, he believed Gardiner thought of him" [Hermann Hagedorn, *Edwin Arlington Robinson* (New York: Macmillan, 1938), pp. 87–88]. Robinson indicated the degree to which Gardiner was much on his mind when he said of it: "it . . . makes me positively sick to see the results of modern materialism as they are revealed in a town like this . . . we need local idealism . . . I wonder if a time is ever coming when the human race will acquire anything like a logical notion of human life. . . ." [*Untriangulated Stars: Letters of Edwin Arlington Robinson to Harry de Forest Smith, 1890–1905,* ed. Denham Sutcliffe (Cambridge: Harvard University Press, 1943), p. 260.] This is only one of many displays of this obsession in his letters. He repeatedly refers to his home town and townsmen critically, and he anxiously returns over and over again to the subjects of money, his vocation, and success. Sorely plagued by the pressure Gardiner exerted upon him, he exclaimed, while a young man,

images of men caught in a sharp antagonism between the radically opposed values of poetry and materialism, whether the men were citizens of Tilbury Town, artists, religious men, or knights. He knew intimately the hostility of a money-based society to poetry. Its investment in superficial outer signs of power such as property and wealth precluded tolerance for the human spirit, and so drove a deep wedge between man's interior life and his outer social world. As a poet, as a spokesman for the life of the spirit in a materialistic society, he knew the social dualism challenged him to fight for his life.

Tilbury Town is the most direct geographical embodiment of Robinson's antagonism toward a materialistic community antipathetic to spirit, and "Captain Craig" is his largest dramatic rendering of that antipathy. But his most subtle and profound treatments of it are found in his deservedly well-known medium-length poems on the artist, in, for example, "Ben Jonson Entertains a Man from Stratford" and "Rembrandt to Rembrandt." Ben Jonson says of Shakespeare, in defining the source of his black depression, that "there's the Stratford in him; he denies it, / And there's the Shakespeare in him" (21). "Manor-bitten to the bone" (23) and at the same time "Lord Apollo's homesick emissary" (21), Shakespeare is torn between the contrary pulls of these two sides of his being. In trying to account for the hold of "that House in Stratford" (32) on Shakespeare, Jonson thinks Shakespeare is racked by

> . . . the fiery art that has no mercy
> But what's in that prodigious grand new House.
> I gather something happening in his boyhood
> Fulfilled him with a boy's determination
> To make all Stratford 'ware of him. [27]

The insights that art has made available to him have revealed to Shakespeare that all is worthless, even his ambition for the house, yet the demon driving him to be a citizen of rank in Stratford will not allow him freedom from this obsession.

"Business be damned" [*Untriangulated Stars,* p. 4]. Yet later, as a successful poet, he made a point of itemizing his income from poetry, evidently pleased to measure his success by conventional standards [*Selected Letters of Edwin Arlington Robinson,* ed. Ridgely Torrence (New York: Macmillan, 1948), p. 157.] The itemization could have been meant ironically, but that is of no consequence; Gardiner never left him in peace.

In Shakespeare the conflict is internalized, as it was personally for Robinson, so that he is the victim of the mutual animosity of both sides. Rembrandt, though he is caught in the same countercurrents, has a better time of it in that he makes the choice of art at the sacrifice of his fame and fortune in Holland and becomes free of the rending antagonisms within himself. "Sometimes a personage in Amsterdam / But now not much" (587), his "Me" addresses his "I,"[3] represented by his self-portrait on the canvas:

That was a fall, my friend, we had together—
Or rather it was my house, mine alone,
That fell, leaving you safe. Be glad of that.
There's life in you that shall outlive my clay
That's for a time alive and will in time
Be nothing—but not yet. You that are there
Where I have painted you are safe enough . . .
[586]

As always with Robinson, this life, like the fire in Shakespeare's art, is the life of the spirit:

We know together of a golden flood
That with its overflow shall drown away
The dikes that held it; and we know thereby
That in its rising light there lives a fire
No devils that are lodging here in Holland

[3] These terms, which I will rely upon somewhat heavily hereafter, are George Herbert Mead's, in *Mind, Self and Society*. Their meaning can be extracted from the following passages: There are "the selfish versus the unselfish sides or aspects of the self . . . the relation between the rational and primarily social side of the self and its impulsive or emotional or primarily anti-social and individual side" (p. 230). "The possibilities in our nature, those sorts of energy which William James took so much pleasure in indicating, are possibilities of the self that lie beyond our own immediate presentation. We do not know just what they are. . . . The possibilities of the 'I' belong to that which is actually going on, taking place, and it is in some sense the most fascinating part of our experience. It is there that novelty arises and it is there that our most important values are located. It is the realization in some sense of this self that we are continually seeking" (p. 204). "The 'I,' then, in this relation of the 'I' and the 'Me,' is something that is, so to speak, responding to a social situation which is within the experience of the individual. It is the answer which the individual makes to the attitude which others take toward him when he assumes an attitude toward them. Now, the attitudes he is taking toward them are present in his own experience, but his response to them will contain a novel element. The 'I' gives the sense of freedom, of initiative. The situation is there for us to act in a self-conscious fashion. We are aware of ourselves, and of what the situation is, but exactly how we will act never gets into experience until after the action takes place" (pp. 177–78).

Shall put out wholly, or much agitate,
Except in official preparation
They put out first the sun. [587]

Holland's scorn had frightened Rembrandt into submission and thus into self-denial, but latterly he had come to recognize the cost of his submission, which was

The taste of death in life—which is the food
Of art that has betrayed itself alive
And is the food of hell. [585]

And so he realizes that his life lies in his being and destiny as an artist:

Whether I would
Or not, I must; and here we are as one
With our necessity . . . [587]

You are the servant, Rembrandt, not the master,—
But you are not assigned with other slaves
That in their freedom are the most in fear.
One of the few that are so fortunate
As to be told their task and to be given
A skill to do it with, a tool too keen
For timid safety . . . [590]

The price of being true to himself is ostracism and banishment; he has to go forth alone into the darkness, with his only solace being that "if you are right / Others will have to see" (590).

These two poems reveal that even the most concrete representation of the conflict between self and society, which begins with an antagonism between an artist's worldly ambition and his devotion to his art, transcends the psychological and moral issue of art versus materialism and becomes an antipathy inherent in the dualistic nature of life. Two aspects of life, two realities, are pitted in eternal hostility, and when caught between them, a man's vital being is torn apart. When he chooses between them, he must pay the price of either self-betrayal or exclusion from the human community. There are two truths and each abhors the other, so that man is trapped in a dilemma in which every gain automatically entails a loss; every joy, suffering, no matter what choice he makes.

Other poems more explicitly universalize the alienation of self and society. In them the hostility is objectified even more than it is in "Rembrandt to Rembrandt": the antagonists become separate entities that stand over against one another. Both Rembrandt and Shakespeare are instances of inner conflict, which one man resolves and the other does not. But this is not so in the "Wandering Jew" (456–59), where a mythic figure angrily battles the society in which he finds himself—New York in this case. The narrator of the poem, an adult, reveals the nature of the Wandering Jew when he says, "I had known / His image when I was a child"; with "Captain Craig" as evidence, it is clear that this link with childhood connects the Wandering Jew with the Light. Robinson emphasizes the Wandering Jew's "loneliness" and the tragic dualism by asserting that "the figure and the scene / Were never to be reconciled." When he goes on to say that the Wandering Jew's eyes at times seem to look on a "Presence . . . One who never dies. / For such a moment he revealed / What life has in it to be lost," there can indeed be no doubt that the Wandering Jew represents the spirit in a spiritually desiccated world. Thus his very existence is "an angry task / That relegates him out of time / To chaos," and he knows with bitterness the "many a lonely time in vain / The Second Coming came and went." He is quite aware that he is doomed to failure in his task, and though his "old, unyielding eyes may flash" when he by chance comes face to face with another person, they will "flinch—and look the other way"; he knows that he can never enter society, that he is forever excluded from the human community, and that the waters of the spirit can never revive the arid "scene."

In "The Wandering Jew," where the protagonist is a mythical figure, myth replaces art as the enemy of society, the two being at heart the same, of course, except that myth is more inclusive. No longer do art and materialism simply offer a choice of contrasting values, if that is all they ever did; now they are clearly but one form of a much larger conflict. And that conflict extends even beyond myth and society: a still more inclusive form of it, found in such poems as "Three Taverns" and "Nicodemus," is the hostility between the religious experience and the social forms of religion—dogma and the church. In a critical remark on Gardiner, Robinson asked when the human race would acquire anything like a logical notion of human life, then added, "or, in other words, of Christianity." [4] These two poems could be regarded as his view of Chris-

[4] [*Untriangulated Stars: The Letters of Edwin Arlington Robinson to Harry de Forest Smith, 1890–1905,* ed. Denham Sutcliffe (Cambridge: Harvard University Press, 1943), p. 260.]

tianity in Gardiner, and it is significant that Christ, though his presence haunts the poems, never actually appears. They can also be regarded as portrayals of the alienation of spirit, the ultimate human reality, from society.

In "Three Taverns" St. Paul says that he had "had men slain / For saying Something was beyond the Law, / And in ourselves" (462) when he had been an orthodox Jew. But after his religious experience on the road to Damascus, he looks back upon his past and concludes he was "A prisoner of the Law, and of the Lord / A voice made free" (462). St. Paul tells his audience that now, after his conversion, "The man you see not— / The man within the man —is most alive" (463). And in finding his spiritual being he has "lost all else / For wisdom, and the wealth of it" (470) and is a "criminal . . . for seeing beyond the law / That which the Law saw not" (471). Though aware that he is a criminal and will be executed if apprehended, he nevertheless intends to enter Rome for the inevitable tragic encounter with entrenched authority. His religious experience has given him the terrible knowledge that the spirit, "the man within the man," is the radical enemy of social forms, religious and otherwise.

The antagonism between the mystical inner reality and society is stated in its most general form by Robinson at the end of *Lancelot*—though the antagonism must be understood to include personal relations (that of lovers, in this case) as well as that of an individual to a group. Here Robinson writes of Lancelot,

> . . . he rode on, under the stars,
> Out of the world, into he knew not what,
> Until a vision chilled him and he saw,
> Now as in Camelot, long ago in the garden,
> The face of Galahad who had seen and died,
> And was alive now in a mist of gold.
> He rode on into the dark, under the stars,
> And there were no more faces. There was nothing.
> But always in the darkness he rode on,
> Alone; and in the darkness came the Light. [449]

The Light and the world are not simultaneously available to man; he must choose between them; and what is finally at stake in that choice is life and death. As Nicodemus expresses it in an impassioned argument against Caiaphas, who defends the Law,

> You are a priest of death, not knowing it.

There is no life in those old laws of ours,
Caiaphas; they are forms and rules and fears,
So venerable and impressive and majestic
That we forget how little there is in them
For us to love. We are afraid of them.
They are the laws of death; and, Caiaphas,
They are the dead who are afraid of dying.
[1164]

Shakespeare's black depression, the Wandering Jew's anger, Rembrandt's and St. Paul's risking all for the Light, Nicodemus' impassioned attack—all reveal how the man with special knowledge of the spirit's truth reacts to society, to life in death. Inherent in man is a hostility between inner being and external forms and relations, between what Emerson called "the instantaneous instreaming causing power" [5] and the objects that can hinder or misdirect its flowing.

Despite his obvious sympathies with the spirit, Robinson never assumes an immediate or long-run triumph by the self over society in which social forms are "saved." As with every subject, his concern for truth led him to adopt an objective attitude toward the relation between self and society; he simply records from various points of view and with varying results things as they are, the simultaneous presence and irreconcilability of self with society. Rembrandt chooses art and is free; Shakespeare cannot choose and suffers; St. Paul discovers the inner man and is doomed; Nicodemus recognizes the truth but is impotent; the Wandering Jew is the truth, but he too is impotent. Richard Cory is viewed from the point of view of the town; the town is viewed from the point of view of Eben Flood. The first dies tragically; the second lives comically. Lancelot rides out of the world, but in the long poems after *Lancelot* the protagonist—for example, Fargo of *Amaranth,* who abandons art to become a plumber—in effect returns to the world. But in every poem, regardless of what happens, the initial truth, the given condition of human existence, is the alienation of self from society, a schism between art and social values, the spirit and social forms, the soul and doctrine, the Light and the world. And finally that schism is an irremediable dichotomy in man's being between his personal and his social self. The pressure of creative power against achieved form is never more than momentarily relaxed.

[5] *The Collected Works,* I, 73.

The materialism Robinson set out to reject not only killed nature but also threatened to socialize man. To preserve the uniquely human from metaphysical materialism, Robinson had to dissociate man from nature; to preserve it from "social materialism," he had to dissociate the self from society. Thus in getting rid of materialism Robinson sought to free the spirit from antispiritual society as well as from nature by giving the spirit an autonomous existence beyond both. William Barrett remarks, "It has become a law of modern society that man is assimilated more and more completely to his social function,"[6] and this succinctly describes the social development that Robinson, in addition to the epistemological and aesthetics problems previously cited, had to find a solution to in order to achieve his desired unity. Robinson struggled for integration and eventually attained it, but in his early and middle poetry not the integration but the disintegration of the individual from the group, the external world, and himself is emphasized.

Nowhere are the effects of alienation more apparent than in one of Robinson's favorite characters, the empowered person who can help others but not himself. Bearer of the secret knowledge of the spirit, he can see what others are blind to and work mysterious effects on their lives, but as a bearer of that knowledge he, like Rembrandt, is outlawed from intimate human relations and the human community. His knowledge bars him from worldly position and power, for having broken through to the higher truth, he can never take any social role seriously, and so can never do anything for himself as a social creature.

The empowered person's predicament, Robinson saw, is only one instance of the plight of the "I" in every man. If the "I" and the "Me" are antithetical aspects of life and self, how can they communicate with and tolerate one another? How can man survive as man? For if the "I" is "unsocializable," then communication and harmony between the "I" and "Me" are impossible. And if they are impossible, so is poetry, for it would be impossible to affirm consciously the "I" in aesthetic as well as discursive terms, art being a consciously created public object. In fact, the spirit, if it can be said ever to have existed, could not be known and would perish from neglect. Robinson sensed that separateness, hostility, alienation cannot be the whole truth, therefore; something beyond and encompassing division unites apparent antitheses.

[6] *Irrational Man*, p. 4.

The empowered person who can help others but not himself exemplifies all the problems resulting from the alienated self, including those arising from the relation of man to society, to man, and to himself. And his predicament, finally, raises all the nasty problems of communication, which strike right to the heart of the poet's responsibilities when he is as socially conscious as Robinson was. Robinson mulls these problems over again and again, considering them from varying perspectives and under various conditions. One of his best known poems on the subject is "Eros Turannos," which treats of human isolation in its most extreme form. Here, a woman, betrayed by the man she was depending upon to protect her against the "downward years" and estranged from the town where she lives, is divested of her illusions of love and is thrown back upon the terrible truth of her being. Commenting on her experience, the narrator, the collective "We," remarks:

> We tell you, tapping on our brows,
> The story as it should be,—
> As if the story of a house
> Were told, or ever could be;
> We'll have no kindly veil between
> Her visions and those we have seen,—
> As if we guessed what hers have been,
> Or what they are or would be.
>
> Meanwhile we do no harm; for they
> That with a god have striven,
> Not hearing much of what we say;
> Take what the god has given . . .
>
> [33]

The story of a house—symbol for an individual's life—cannot be told; the depth where an individual strives with the gods cannot be plumbed by another, whether the "We" be the collective consciousness or a storyteller. The poem asserts that the existential level of experience, which is the spirit's region, is inaccessible not only to the intellect ("our brows") but also to art. Under any and all circumstances it is true that, as Matthias says, "No man has known another / Since men were born" (1133). The man-within-the-man St. Paul spoke of is doomed to eternal isolation. Man is indeed alone.

If "Eros Turannos" tells the whole truth, man, society, and poetry could not exist as we know them, because there would be no way for the spirit to enter the world, society, or consciousness; and if it cannot enter these, then all of life is reduced to inert matter, and materialism is triumphant. But society, man, and the self do survive, however precariously. For Robinson the spirit does enter into the world and communication between men and within man does take place. Captain Craig, for instance, argues at great length that this communication is the mission of the poet and poetry. The empowered person who can help others but not himself is another instance of such communication. In "Captain Craig," a poem that is typical of a form Robinson uses also in "Isaac and Archibald," "Flammonde," and "The Man Who Died Twice," a narrator who apprehends with his conscious intellectual faculties tells the story of his encounter with an eccentric character who lives by a deeper spiritual awareness. The eccentric communicates his awareness to the narrator so that in the end the narrator's life is deepened. Although Captain Craig dies without altering the quality of life in Tilbury Town and is in part killed by the town's indifference, he does have influence; he produces a spiritual enhancement, an enlargement of consciousness, in the lives of five or six of its citizens. This transaction, as slight and vague as it may be, results in a dim self-discovery, enough to awaken and sustain the spirit.

Although the spirit can enter society, it can do so only at specific points and temporarily. Society as a whole, antithetical by nature to spirit, is not itself redeemable. The spirit enters only through specific persons, only in a dialogue between men, and is communicable only between individuals. And then it cannot enter directly or be straightforwardly communicated; it can enter only indirectly through an infinitesimal gap provided by compassion, the glint of eyes, or the tone of voice. The narrator of "Captain Craig" asserts that he and his friends could have been "wrecked on [the Captain's] own abstractions" (167) had they taken the captain's words for the Word; the narrator of "The Man Who Died Twice," though he professes to believe, cannot be sure that Fernando Nash's claims about the meaning of his mystical experience are true; and the Wandering Jew, Ponce de Leon, Rembrandt, and numerous others communicate spiritually through their eyes, not through language. Not negotiable through words or institutions, the transaction between man and man occurs obliquely. But it does occur, and with God and nature dead, this silent dialogue is the sole means by which the special knowledge of the "seer" can enter the consciousness of a normal person and the "I" can become known to the conscious mind.

It seems somewhat paradoxical that Robinson emphasizes the dialogue between man and man, which is a social relation, and denigrates society so thoroughly. But there is no paradox: the dialogue simply takes place on two levels, those of the "I" and the "Me." On the level of the "Me" the dialogue amounts to an exchange of acquired attitudes associated with roles, while on the level of the "I" it amounts to awakening the underground, personal, religious self. Little of value and much that is harmful is transferred in the communication between "Me's," whereas the existence, integrity, and realization of the spirit is made possible through the communication between "I's." It is for this reason that Robinson so heavily emphasizes the value of compassion, explicitly in "Zola" and implicitly in the poems in which a narrator, a sympathetic observer and listener, discovers his own deeper reaches through a seer.

And it is also for this reason that he returns repeatedly to the subject of guilt, which as he conceives it is the betrayal, not of God by man, but of man by man. A great number of his poems—"Bokardo," "Avon's Harvest," "Sisera," "Cavender's House," "King Jasper," for example—are devoted in whole or in large part to rendering the destructive effects of guilt on the self. Guilt, of course, presupposes conscience, and for Robinson conscience is a moral sense innate in the "I," for which the primary moral value is the sanctity of the individual person. In "Sisera," Jael for her own aggrandizement has treacherously killed Sisera while he slept. "Tell Deborah," she exultantly proclaims, "that a woman, / A woman filled with God, killed Sisera / For love of Israel" (1178). And she defends her act with the argument, "What is one man, or one man's way of dying, / So long as Israel has no more of him" (1177). A man is of no significance; Israel and God, superhuman entities, justify sacrificing him should one choose to serve them and seek their rewards. Everyone else in the poem, however, though impotent before an orthodox devotion to God and country, clearly reacts with horror and disgust to what Jael has done. Through vanity, the enemy of compassion, she destroys the bond between man and man, and thereby loses her humanity, the very life of the spirit that she ironically affirms in placing the murdered Sisera at the feet of God and Israel. By betraying another she betrays herself.

A way to testify to the spirit's existence and a means by which to release it more liberally into society and the "Me," greater communication through rejecting the abstract and valuing the concrete: these were the desiderata issuing for Robinson from the self's alienation. Their attainment had to wait until the later poems, however. In a sonnet on Erasmus, the major historical figure in humanism, Robinson wrote,

> When he protested, not too solemnly,
> That for a world's achieving maintenance
> The crust of overdone divinity
> Lacked ailment, they called it recreance;
> And when he chose through his own glass to scan
> Sick Europe, and reduced, unyieldingly,
> The monk within the cassock to the man
> Within the monk, they called it heresy.
>
> And when he made so perilously bold
> As to be scattered forth in black and white,
> Good fathers looked askance at him and rolled
> Their inward eyes in anguish and affright;
> There were some of them did shake at what was told
> And they shook best who knew that he was right. [193]

He is, of course, speaking for himself, although his target was society and sick America rather than the church and sick Europe: he protested against the crust of overdone socialization, and he reduced man to "the man within the man." He was not a romantic; he did not assume that paradise would be regained by returning to a natural state; rather, he felt, like Hawthorne, that social existence is prerequisite to humanity and requires the compromise of individual aberrations. But society itself, he recognized, suffers from severe limitations. By its very nature it is incapable of honoring and encouraging the individual or the man within the man. Of course, society is only the behavior of individuals in relation to one another, so that what the term actually refers to is the tendency of human beings to deny their spiritual being and that of others by preferring the social to the spiritual bond between men. Robinson acknowledged that it is only natural, therefore, that society and spirit be permanently at odds; they are radical alternatives within the self that the individual must choose between and take the consequences, as Rembrandt or any other artist must choose between the fashionable public taste and his own vision. And it is obvious that should an individual pursue economic or social ends—wealth, status, power, etc.—he must perforce neglect his soul. Society or social values are thus antithetical to humanistic ones, and the true bond between men, instead of being a social relation of "Me's," is a relation of "I's" based on identity, compassion, and conscience. Humanism, as it is commonly understood, simultaneously affirms man's dignity and accepts his limitations. With Robinson, this ambiguity takes the form of honoring the marvelous and mysterious spiritual life in man and recognizing that man is human only when he is moral, when, that is, he repudiates egotism and lives in accordance with his responsibility to man. The forces that produce society and the "Me," the instruments of socialization, block communication and the life of the spirit; but regardless how hidden that life must be or how estranged from society, the private, personal, presocial elements in experience do exist and are expressed, and man is thereby saved from social totalitarianism.

Robinson's most felicitous treatment of alienation is "Flammonde" (1–6), which states, more precisely and profoundly than any of his other poems, the multidimensions and full consequences (the central myth, it might be called) in the self's journey toward truth, at the stage before that journey can be completed. Yvor Winters, an avid admirer of Robinson's poetry, discarded "Flammonde" from the Robinson canon because it was "repulsively sentimental," [7] and his criticism of the poem as unadulterated romanticism would seem to be supported by biographical fact. It did result from storybook inspiration: "While sitting in a movie theatre," Robinson said, "suddenly I saw Flammonde and I could hear the poem quite clearly. All the lines were there and I only had to write them down." [8] But this romantic origin, this gift from the unconscious, could mean that this "spontaneous" creation represents in its deepest or truest form Robinson's own sense of life.

The poem is ostensibly about Flammonde, or more precisely, "the man Flammonde." He is one of those gifted persons ("Rarely at once will nature give / The power to be Flammonde and live") who sees but cannot do for himself. He comes for a brief sojourn

[7] *Edwin Arlington Robinson,* p. 51. [See Yvor Winters, "The Shorter Poems" in this collection.]

[8] Nancy Evans, "Edwin Arlington Robinson," [*Bookman,* LXXV (November, 1932), 675–81.]

in Tilbury Town, where in appearance and demeanor he is everything that its citizens are not; no one knows where he came from or where he went, only that he is characterized by a "firm address and foreign air"; has the "news of nations in his talk / And something royal in his walk"; a "glint of iron in his eyes / But never doubt, nor yet surprise"; stands "Erect, with his alert repose / About him, and about his clothes." He appears "As one by kings accredited." While he is in Tilbury Town Flammonde befriends a disgraced woman, recognizes the intellectual ability of a boy and provides for his education, and joins old enemies in friendship, among other good works. Through his superior vision and power he sees more deeply into men and is able to work wonders among a few individual citizens of the town by introducing an unaccustomed compassion and humanity into their lives. That is the man in Flammonde. But he is indeed an unusual man, for if he is a man at all, he is the essential spiritual being and power of man. As his name "the flame of the earth" implies, he is, like the Wandering Jew, a mythological figure. His flame, along with the glint of iron in his eyes and everything else about him, establishes him as an envoy of the Light who comes out of nowhere ("God knows where") into a community of futile people to work his wonders, then disappears without a trace. It is impossible for the townsmen to tell whether he is playing a role (assuming a "Me" as the "Prince of Castaways") or is genuine; but despite their uncertainty, he brings the Light, the mystic power, for a brief moment, redeeming a portion of the impotent community by introducing into it the capacity for creative action for good.

Flammonde is not, however, the subject of the poem: more properly, the subject, to take advantage of the pun, is the narrator's consciousness; Flammonde is the object. The poem is about the narrator's attempt to understand what Flammonde was; it is a dramatization in which the mind meets and interacts with the soul, the "Me" meets and interacts with the "I." The broad structural outlines of the poem are sufficient testimony of this. The first three stanzas describe Flammonde, and thus fix an image of him before the narrator's and the reader's eyes; the next five recount his exploits and reveal his powers; the concluding four are devoted to reflection upon what Flammonde was. The poem is a meditation in which the eyes fix themselves on an image while the mind, working upon the image, tries to comprehend its significance. And this is an action of consciousness in which awareness proceeds from its simplest form, sensory perception, to its higher forms.

But to understand what is involved in the higher forms of awareness, it is necessary to look much closer at what happens in the poem. In the first place, the narrator is trying to answer his question about Flammonde some time after his appearance in Tilbury Town, so that the narrator is not conducting an empirical investigation but is working on material provided by his memory, the storehouse of the impressions Flammonde made upon him. Sensory perception was the means of the narrator's acquaintance with Flammonde, the source of the "contact" of his consciousness with him, but during perception no understanding took place, only the awareness of physical features, bearing, and behavior. Although the conscious transaction between the speaker and Flammonde during perception was limited to appearances, the narrator was *touched* in the depths of his being, and in time this unconscious depth response erupts into the conscious through unabetted recollection. As the narrator says,

> We cannot know how much we learn
> From those who never will return,
> Until a flash of unforeseen
> Remembrance falls on what has been.
> [6]

Apparently the mysterious and strangely powerful man has set astir something in the darker recesses of the narrator's being. Perhaps a power present but not detected in the sensory images awakens his "I" through resonance. In time these aspects of his self gather force and emerge from darkness; then they are available for the reflective mind to ponder. It is at this moment and for this purpose that the narrator writes the poem, seeking an answer to the haunting question of who Flammonde was.

His question is obviously misplaced; it is not Flammonde but that part of his own being brought disturbingly alive by Flammonde that the narrator wants to understand. But, typically for Robinson, the "I" is viewed objectively, and so the narrator's attention is directed away from introspection toward an objectified, mythological embodiment of his inner being. He must work from the outside to the inside, and to go in that direction is not to go very far. The inescapable consequence is the inability of the narrator to answer his question; Flammonde remains unknown, a mystery. But that isn't the complete story: intellectual comprehension fails, true, but a transaction has taken place, as the narrator's writing of the poem testifies, and as the narrator points out when he says in conclusion that "from time to time / In Tilbury Town, we look beyond / Horizons for the man Flammonde." Tilbury Town has not been redeemed once and for all, but it has been made aware that something exists beyond its horizons. Although Tilbury Town and Flammonde are not permanently compatible, communication has taken place between them and the "We" has become aware—dimly, to be sure—of the deeper, hidden life of the spirit.

Such are the form, the dynamics, and the consequences of the meeting of self and society in "Flammonde." It should be noted that the meeting takes place on three levels: between an individual and the community (Flammonde and Tilbury Town); between man and man (Flammonde and the narrator); and between the "I" and the "Me" of the narrator. It is also of significance that Flammonde is linked with the cleansing heritage of tradition, which is collective memory, and that tradition represents the endurance of spirit through history, while society, with no roots outside of time or permanence within it, is caught in the flux of endless, meaningless change. Because self transcends society and the corrosive effects of time, it is also beyond conventional morality, and therefore Flammonde cannot be ethically judged. His was a hero's or a saint's fate, his vocation being with the divine, not with man, except when, Christlike, he passed through a community as bearer of the Word and left behind him a dim wake of Light. When that Light awakens some men spiritually, they are driven to ponder what lies beyond death as they continue their climb up the darkening hill of life. But Flammonde must continue on his way, enduring his special fate of wandering the earth like a bonze, alone and alienated. Though he possessed mythic power and exercised it, he could not escape his fate. What he accomplished was done by juxtaposition and resonance, not by overt words or force of will. He can never directly offer his gift, and he can never turn it to his own advantage.

Robinson's primary "myth," then, traces the soul's journey to self-awareness, under the conditions life provides and to the degree possible up to and during the time he wrote almost all the poems discussed in this chapter. At this point the alienated self, as in

"Captain Craig," is still on the defensive. An aggressive society expels it, or an eager mind reaches out to grasp it. Shy and self-defensive, the self warily moves about the periphery and eludes its pursuer, waiting for conditions more favorable to it. The animosity here is sharp, but Robinson is not done with psychological probing: he has not yet taken his characters as far as they can and will have to go.

E. A. Robinson: The Cosmic Chill

by Hyatt H. Waggoner

> As the physical world-picture grew and technology advanced, those disciplines which rested squarely on "rational" instead of "empirical" principles were threatened with complete extinction. . . . The truth is that science has not fructified and activated all human thought.
>
> Suzanne K. Langer in *Philosophy in a New Key*

1. THE CRUCIAL QUESTION

When Hawthorne in "Alice Doane's Appeal" described Salem during an ice storm and suggested that the ice was not limited to the trees and streets in the frozen village, he had found a symbol more perfectly suited to his purposes than the black veil, the birthmark, or the wedding knell. But he never used it again, preferring instead usually the laboriously conceived products of an active fancy and seldom achieving complete and perfect expression of his sensibility.

So, too, E. A. Robinson—who felt the chill of a frozen world as deep in the marrow as ever Hawthorne did—was, toward the end of his life, ordinarily unable to find the symbols he needed. His poetry gives evidence of the paralysis of the will that affected Wakefield, though few of his poems express it. The result is, of course, an impoverishment of his work which, were it not for a relatively few poems, would make it impossible to consider him a major poet. The common, the almost unanimous opinion that Robinson's best work was done in the short poems, and especially in the poems of

"E. A. Robinson: The Cosmic Chill" by Hyatt H. Waggoner. From *The Heel of Elohim* (Norman, Oklahoma: The University of Oklahoma Press, 1950), pp. 18–40.

the early and middle periods, seems to me justified; but no good reason for this has ever been suggested. There must have been a number of reasons why the poems to which Robinson devoted the major portion of his poetic energy during the last twenty years or so of his life are generally less satisfactory than his early and his casual poems, but one of the reasons and not the least significant will be found, I think, to be similar to that which prevented Hawthorne from completing, indeed even from satisfactorily starting, his late romances. Robinson's sympathy for Hawthorne was deep, and the parallel between them striking. The thought of each led to an impasse which paralyzed the sensibilities.

The framework of Robinson's thought was put together in the late nineteenth century, and not chiefly by the major thinkers of the age. The poet's contact with logic and philosophy in college produced a distaste for both. At the end of the century he was defending Herbert Spencer as *the* philosopher; he read William James with great distaste, felt that Santayana was bloodless, found something to admire in Schopenhauer and Nietzsche, and was impressed by Mary Baker Eddy's *Science and Health,* which seemed to him a remarkable book though he could not accept it "in detail." Notable here are both the emphases (Spencer, Schopenhauer, Nietzsche, and Mary Baker Eddy!) and the omissions or negative reactions (Bradley, Royce, Santayana, James—very nearly a list of the best philosophic minds of the day).

Unquestioning obeisance to science Robinson absorbed not only from Spencer but from the spirit of the times, whether or not he read *Popular Science Monthly,* which devoted itself to spreading Spencer's gospel. Yet at the same time he also absorbed a corrupted Emersonianism, which had become in his time and place like "common sense," an unexamined part of the furniture of the mind. So that, despite his reading of Nietzsche and Schopenhauer, his ideas have less in common with those of the major philosophers than they have with those of John Burroughs, who combined Emerson, Whitman, and Herbert Spencer in an optimistic synthesis, or John Fiske, who aspired by a positivistic method applied with a certain vagueness through nature to God. Despite his acquaintance with the work of Santayana, his early thoughts on religion reflect the popular solution of the time in Protestant America: drop theology with positive benefit to religion, a solution he might have found learnedly put forth in the nineties by Andrew Dickson

White's massive *History of the Warfare of Science with Theology in Christendom.* His early poems express contemporary popular "advanced" thought, without the customary enthusiasm for the conclusions of the thought.[1]

It is more enlightening, then, to compare his early thinking with that of the popular philosophers and minor spokesmen of the age than with that of the best minds. True, he knew James's "will to believe," was fully aware of the neutral world described by science which formed one strand of Santayana's thought, and was an idealist by inclination as was Royce; but much more evident in his poetry is that state of mind described by John Burroughs at the end of the century in *The Light of Day.* "Feeling, emotion," wrote Burroughs, "falls helpless before the revelations of science. The universe is going its own way with no thought of us. . . . This discovery sends the cosmic chill, with which so many of us are familiar in these days."

Burroughs might have been writing of the effect of scientific doctrines on any of a great number of literary people before or after Robinson's time, on Tennyson or Arnold, on MacLeish or Aldous Huxley; again, the passage might be from Krutch's *The Modern Temper* (1929) instead of from *The Light of Day* (1900), so generally true is it. But there are several reasons why it makes a particularly good starting point for a discussion of Robinson. First, the "revelations of science" lead Burroughs to a conception of an alien universe, not to a new conception of man. Purpose and meaning are gone *from the world;* the universe is fully revealed by physics and chemistry. So in Robinson's poetry the effect of sci-

[1] This seems to me to be the only conclusion one can reach despite Miss Estelle Kaplan's attempt to trace the influence of several major philosophers in Robinson's work (*Philosophy in the Poetry of Edwin Arlington Robinson* [New York, 1940]). Evidence of the nature and extent of Robinson's reading may be found in Hermann Hagedorn, *Edwin Arlington Robinson* (New York, 1938), *Selected Letters of Edwin Arlington Robinson* (New York, 1940), and Denham Sutcliffe (ed.), *Untriangulated Stars* (Cambridge, Mass., 1947), which are the chief sources of the facts I have just summarized. There seems to be a tendency for studies of Robinson's thought either to demonstrate the obvious or to end in silliness, with an inverse proportion between the elaborateness of the study and the value of its conclusions. One of the most sensible of such studies is also one of the earliest and briefest: Chapter 5 of Lloyd Morris's *The Poetry of Edwin Arlington Robinson* (New York, 1923). Of considerable value are F. I. Carpenter's "Tristam the Transcendent," *New England Quarterly,* Vol. XI, No. 3 (September, 1938), 501–23, and Floyd Stovall's "The Optimism Behind Robinson's Tragedies," *American Literature,* Vol. X, No. 1 (March, 1938), 1–23.

ence is chiefly what we should expect it to be in a poet reared in the century dominated by advances in biology and physics. It remained for the younger poets to be affected by the sciences developed in our century, especially psychology and sociology, and to impale themselves upon the other horn of the naturalistic dilemma, the dehumanization of man.

Second, the revelations of science, Burroughs says, paralyze feeling and chill the mind. Burroughs's language here is apt, though perhaps somewhat too rhetorical. T. S. Eliot and others who have deplored the "dissociation of sensibility" of the nineteenth century have not always set the fact in its historic context. When one is faced with a totally hopeless situation, one may continue to think, but the thinking will be without purpose so far as the situation is concerned; if the situation is all-inclusive, one's thought will take on the character of daydreaming. One may also continue to feel, but the emotion will not issue in action nor will it activate thought. The road from thought to action leads through emotion, and from emotion to sane action through thought; and either course requires a sense of purpose if the transit is to be completed. To the extent that an age thinks it has discovered ultimate meaninglessness, to the extent that it has lost a sense of security, it will be characterized by dissociation of sensibility. Neurosis is an individual matter, no doubt, but ages and peoples may exhibit neurotic symptoms.[2]

Robinson's poetry is that of a man whose mind and heart are at odds. His didactic poems are ordinarily his poorest work, and the more ambitious his effort in this direction the weaker the result. When "The Man Against the Sky" again and again breaks down into rhymed prose, the failure is not a "technical" one but the result of a breakdown of thought and feeling, an impasse of the soul. If the philosophic passages in his long narrative poems are frequently thin and verbose, unconvincing and even tedious, it is because they are most often on the theme of ultimate meaning and on this theme Robinson could only think and feel by turns.

Yet he worried the theme throughout his whole poetic career. His best poems—"Hillcrest," "Eros Turannos," "Isaac and Archibald," "Dark Hills," "New England," "Miniver Cheevy," and many others—concern it only indirectly or not at all. But from *The Children of the Night* to *King Jasper* much of his best effort was devoted to this theme which he was least able to handle. Further to

[2] Erich Fromm, *Escape from Freedom* (New York, 1941).

define the theme and the feeling with which for Robinson it was surrounded, I shall again avail myself of quotation. Lord Russell's essay "A Free Man's Worship" has been called by Mr. Eliot a piece of sentimental rhetoric, and from any point of view resembling Mr. Eliot's it no doubt deserves the description; but it expresses precisely, yet in terms general enough to fit both the early and late poems, the course of thought and the state of feeling which dominated Robinson's poetry from beginning to end. The question with which the passage ends is the question which Robinson devoted himself to attempting to answer in all of his philosophic poems:

> That man is the product of causes that had no prevision of the end they were achieving; that his origin, his growth, his hopes and fears, his loves and beliefs are but the outcome of accidental collocations of atoms; that no fire, no heroism, no intensity of thought and feeling, can preserve an individual life beyond the grave; that all the labors of the ages, all the devotion, all the inspiration, all the noonday brightness of human genius, are destined to extinction in the vast death of the solar system, and that the whole temple of man's achievement must inevitably be buried beneath the debris of a universe in ruins—all these things, if not quite beyond dispute, are yet so nearly certain, that no philosophy which rejects them can hope to stand. Only within the scaffolding of these truths, only on the firm foundation of unyielding despair, can the soul's habitation henceforth be safely built.
>
> How, in such an alien and inhuman world, can so powerless a creature as Man preserve his aspirations untarnished? [3]

2. THE ANTAGONIST

That the unhappy revelations of science did indeed provide Robinson with the chief stimulus to his thinking and determine the main course of his philosophic poems need not be demonstrated to anyone thoroughly acquainted with the whole body of Robinson's work, though it may not be apparent from a reading of the usual anthology pieces. Again, though an adequate biography of the poet remains to be written and not all of his letters have been published, there is sufficient external evidence to show that Robinson read the usual books on science and scientific philosophy and discussed the subject frequently with his friends. What is more

[3] The essay, first published in 1903, may be found in Russell's *Mysticism and Logic* (London, 1923).

to the point is the frequency and nature of his allusions to science in his poems.

It is clear upon even casual inspection that the significance of science for Robinson in the nineties and the earliest years of this century lay in the fact that it was in conflict with "the creeds." Just which religious doctrines were disproved by science, Robinson never made clear in his poetry, nor is it likely that he thought much about it. It simply seemed to him as to others that science had cut the ground out from under any supernaturalist interpretation of life and the world. So the "obsolescent creeds" must go; only the "common creed of common sense," the doing of "his will," could stand in the face of the new knowledge. Yet there must, he thought, be immortality; if there were not another chance, it would be better if we had never been born. One must somehow maintain confidence in "Life's purposeful and all-triumphant sailing." There must be a God, and He must be Love, and just. "It is the faith within the fear That holds us to the life we curse." The chief impression one gets from Robinson's earliest work is that he is whistling in what he customarily wrote as "the Dark."

The faith he longed for and at times thought he had was a sort of Emersonian romantic naturalism. "So let us in ourselves revere The Self which is the universe." God thrilled the first atom with a mystic touch. Evolution could—must—be interpreted idealistically and man would move forward into the light as he put off old superstitions. F. I. Carpenter has shown us the transcendental elements in Robinson's work, and we are grateful for the demonstration; but it seems to me that we should expect Robinson to adopt the Emersonian line and should be surprised only if we were to discover that he did not, the state of liberal opinion in late nineteenth-century New England being what it was. It would be quite possible, though I think not entirely worth while, to trace the correspondences between Robinson's early poetry and the sort of thought that Emerson's influence had contributed to so strongly, the "religion of humanity" of Robert Ingersoll, for instance, the idealism of John Fiske, and the published sermons of countless liberal Protestant preachers of the day. The point is that Robinson's thinking on the subject in his early years is indistinguishable from popular "advanced" thinking of the time.

But Emerson's solution of saving God by identifying Him with the whole course and nature of things seemed less and less like a solution to Robinson, as to the literate public generally, as the years went by.[4] Open skepticism became more prominent in the poems than the desperate hope, which became steadily more desperate and more attenuated. Like Cavender, Robinson knew a need to believe rather than a belief:

> And so there must be God; or if not God,
> A purpose or a law. Or was the world,
> And the strange parasites infesting it,
> Serpent or man or limpet, or what not,
> Merely a seeming-endless incident
> Of doom?

More and more frequently Robinson made the characters in his long narrative poems share Cavender's sensation that he could "feel atoms moving and conspiring Against him, and death rustling in the shadows." References to the creeds diminished and the problem came to be phrased in philosophic terms. The question was now simply whether the universe was purposeful or not, whether science told all. What had once seemed like the answer, dropping theology and keeping religion, was now seen to be merely a verbal solution. What was at stake was the status of value in a world in which the "chemistry of fate" seemed quite adequate to account for everything. In the years just before World War I Robinson faced the issue fully; from then on to the end of his life he pondered the scientific "news of an ingenious mechanism" and concluded that there was no way of countering the dismaying news by argument, that there was only, as he said in *King Jasper,* the final conviction that

> . . . No God
> No law, no purpose, could have hatched for sport
> Out of warm water and slime, a war for life
> That was unnecessary, and far better
> Never had been—if man, as we behold him,
> Is all it means.

I shall comment shortly on the quality of the poetry in which Robinson's convictions are expressed, but what concerns us at

[4] Robinson's omission of "The Children of the Night" from all editions of his *Collected Poems* is symptomatic of this shift in his opinions, as it is also of a change in his standards of taste. "The Children of the Night" is not only very weak poetry; it is also more forthright in its expression of faith than Robinson later felt able to be.

present is the convictions themselves, insofar as it is possible to separate matter from manner—and in this kind of poetry it is possible, up to a point. The convictions can be summarized quite simply, for the ideas involved are neither complex nor profound. We must recapture the atmosphere of the mechanist-vitalist controversy to set the terms in their proper context, and that is all. Robinson is concerned with the devastating implications of materialistic naturalism, which finds purpose, value, even quality as distinguished from measurable quantity, subjective or unreal. In an era when John B. Watson, then thought to be the leading American psychologist, was proclaiming that psychologists must start their work by ruling out the possibility of there being any soul, mind, will, purpose, or memory, Robinson was concerned to keep these entities. Humanistic knowledge must be of some real significance, but it could not be if life were "really" only "a riot of cells and chemistry," an "accident of nameless energies."

> . . . There is more of me
> I hope, than a pathetic mechanism
> Grinding itself to nothing. Possibly not,
> But let me say there is.

In an era when the universe was thought to have been revealed as a vast machine in which matter and motion were the only realities, Robinson found "a free man's worship" not enough. For him, as for so many others, knowledge was "cruel" and the need for faith great; but the "unanswered questions" remained and Robinson's faith continued to be like that of most men he knew, "whose faith, when they are driven to think of it, is mostly doubts and fears." To deny the total validity of what seemed to him the unarguable "facts" of science, he had to deny positivism. There are, he felt, areas of reality with which "myopic science" with its "inch-ruling of the infinite" cannot deal. The conviction toward which he was moving suggests Whitehead's position on the nature and result of abstraction in science, though I know of no evidence that Robinson was familiar at first hand with Whitehead's work. But his inability to formulate any clear statements about these areas left over after science has finished its work would seem to confirm not his convictions but those of the logical positivists.

I have said that the ideas in Robinson's poetry are neither complex nor profound. I should add that Robinson himself was the first to insist that they were not. In view of all the studies of his philosophy, it is interesting to note what he said in a letter written in 1930: "There is no 'philosophy' in my poetry beyond an implication of an ordered universe and a sort of deterministic negation of the general futility that appears to be the basis of rational thought." And there is a touch of pathos in his remark in a letter to a candidate for an advanced degree:

> I am naturally gratified to learn that you are writing a thesis on my poetry, but I am rather sorry to learn that you are writing about my "philosophy"—which is mostly a statement of my inability to accept a mechanistic interpretation of the universe and of life. . . . I still wish that you were writing about my poetry—of which my so-called philosophy is only a small part, and probably the least important.

3. "THE MAN AGAINST THE SKY"

"The Man Against the Sky" is Robinson's most ambitious attempt to set forth his thought on ultimate problems. Although modesty and insight made him declare that his ideas were probably the least important part of his poetry, this poem, on which as much as on any other his reputation was founded, is solely concerned with ideas. In it man's destiny is examined in the light of several current outlooks; various popular philosophies and attitudes toward life are discussed and rejected. And since the spur to thought here, as elsewhere in Robinson's poetry, is the question Lord Russell asked, I shall examine the poem in some detail.

The form is very loose. Irregularly rhymed and with lines of varying length, it seems to fall logically into three main parts, but there is no formal relation between its ten verse paragraphs and the logic of its structure. The language is very general, with the abstract diction, suggestive of philosophic or polemic prose, varied here and there by generalized and frequently traditional figures. Thus the commonly accepted goals, "a kingdom and a power and a Race," are said to end in "ashes and eternal night"; *eternity, death, faith, ambition, light,* and *dark* and their modifiers make up the core of the poem. The texture is thin, the method discursive.[5]

[5] If it were a part of my purpose here to attempt a complete evaluation of Robinson's language, I should try to show that his turn from the conventional poetic language of the late nineteenth century to a more natural language having recognizable connections with his own spoken idiom is an important part of his achievement as a poet, whereas his tendency toward the abstract discursive language of prose is often a weakness in his work. But to discuss this question

It seems to me that only Robinson's honesty and thoughtfulness save the poem from being completely uninteresting, and even these are not sufficient to make it a really distinguished poem, partly for the obvious reason that distinguished poems are not made by honesty and thoughtfulness and partly because even considered as a prose statement the poem is finally unsuccessful. But because its failure is so fully illustrative of Robinson's typical weaknesses, and because those weaknesses are closely connected with the aspects of his thought and sensibility which are my subject, I want to summarize what the poem says.

The man outlined against the sunset as he walks over the hill toward the west is any man—mankind—seen in the ultimate perspective of death. The "world on fire" against which he is outlined is at once the sunset, the conflagration of the World War I, and the universe described by science, with its live stars and dead stars, the electrical nature of matter, and so on. (And this, incidentally, is one of the few figures in the poem that have several levels of mean-

---

would take me beyond the limits set by the purpose of this book. [See Josephine Miles' discussion of Robinson's language in "Robinson's Inner Fire" in this collection.] The question is a very difficult one, involving such problems, central in contemporary criticism, as the nature and value of didactic poetry, a problem on which Mr. Yvor Winters gives one answer while most of the other new critics give a radically different one. All that I should insist on is that Robinson's tendency to make his longer poems all argument and speculation is a very different thing from his "plain," "dry," "factual" language. That poetry is at its best when it is symbolic in its own way (not necessarily when it is "pure" or incapable of being paraphrased) has been argued not only by the new critics but by two philosophers, Susanne K. Langer and W. M. Urban. As Mr. Urban puts it in *Language and Reality* (London, 1939, p. 500), "The poet . . . does well . . . to keep to his own symbolic form. For precisely in that symbolic form an aspect of reality is given which cannot be adequately expressed otherwise. It is not true that whatever can be expressed symbolically can be better expressed literally. For there *is* no literal expression, but only another kind of symbol." It seems to me that the weaknesses—though not all of the strength—in Robinson's poetry could be revealed by an analysis in terms of Mr. Allen Tate's principle of *tension* in poetry. [In his essay "Tension in Poetry," in *Collected Essays* (Denver: Alan Swallow, 1959), pp. 82–83, Tate remarks that he is using the term "not as a general metaphor, but as a special one, derived from lopping the prefixes off the logical terms *ex*tension and *in*tension. What I am saying, of course, is that the meaning of poetry is its 'tension," the full organized body of all the extension and intension that we can find in it. The remotest figurative significance that we can derive does not invalidate the extensions of the literal statement. Or we may begin with the literal statement and by stages develop the complications of metaphor: at every stage we may pause to state the meaning so far comprehended, and at every stage the meaning will be coherent."]

ing.) Robinson wonders how the man approaches death. The introduction of the poem ends with the second verse paragraph.

The second part of the poem, logically divided, sets forth various attitudes toward life and death. This section keeps to the original figure of the man against the sky and relates the outlooks discussed to appropriate character types. Thus, first, the figure may be a man of unshaken faith, an anachronism in an age of doubt; or, second, a practical, unthoughtful man who has been so fortunate as never to have known the trials that would shake an instinctive faith, a natural materialist; or, third, a cynical pessimist getting a kind of pleasure out of denial of meaning, a philosophic materialist; or, fourth, a man with religious instincts who has lost his faith and is now moved to terror and despair by his vision of "the living death Assigned alike by chance To brutes and hierophants," a "world without meaning" in which "molecules" are the ultimate realities; or, last, an ambitious and worldly man who, absorbed in his pride and search for power, finds no reason to question his importance in the scheme of things and takes pride in "being what he must have been by laws Infrangible and for no kind of cause," a man who looks with his "mechanic eyes" at an "accidental universe" but is not disturbed because he cannot conceive of the world without him.

In the eighth verse paragraph, beginning "Whatever the dark road he may have taken," Robinson sums up the several types he has presented and comments on them and on life in general: "His way was even as ours." Now the center of his interest is revealed: not the types dramatically conceived but the ideas he has assigned to them. From this point on in the poem, the opening figure of the man against the sky is lost from sight; he has served his purpose as a starting point for philosophic speculation and he never reappears.

This third and purely abstract part of the poem presents Robinson's conclusions. That it does so with neither poetic richness nor prose clarity or emphasis is hardly surprising in view of the structure of the poem as I have noted it so far. First the poet mentions and rejects various current justifications of life—the capitalist and communist variants of the notion of progress, scientific humanism, evolution. Then he asks if we shall no more hear the Word. One cannot be sure from the poem which variety of religious enlightenment the Word represents, nor does external evidence help very much to clarify this rather literal but at the same time vague symbol. One thinks, of course, of Christ as the Word, but one of Robinson's clearest prose statements on Christianity was made in 1896 when he wrote to his friend Arthur Gledhill, "I have been slowly getting rid of materialism for the past year or two, but I fear I haven't the stamina to be a Christian, accepting Christ as either human or divine"; with which we may compare his statement in a letter to Laura Richards written a year before his death: "Christian theology has so thoroughly crumbled that I do not think of any non-Roman acquaintance to whom it means anything—and I doubt if you do." If Christianity then is out, could the Word be just any comforting faith, any "religion" which would supply the missing sense of purpose? Presumably so; yet it is clear that some of the faiths which the poem has already rejected, notably communism, serve their followers in much the same way that Christianity serves Christians, supplying an orientation and a sense of purpose. It is significant of the confusion in the poem that it rejects various religions on grounds which it does not specify and then calls for a new religion of unspecified nature. What Robinson probably had in mind in writing of the Word which we might or might not hear again is somewhat more clearly indicated by another of his statements in his late letter to Mrs. Richards: "There's a non-theological religion on the way, probably to be revealed by science when science comes definitely to the jumping-off place." How such a "non-theological" religion—which is to say nonrational, uninterpreted, unphilosophical, and in the last analysis undefinable —would differ from Robinson's own religious sentiment, which he found so inadequate to his needs, is not clear.[6]

[6] With this statement of Robinson's it is interesting to compare one made by Thomas Mann in 1941: "Unmistakably the spirit is today in readiness to enter upon a moral epoch, an epoch of new religious and moral knowledge and distinction of good and evil." ("Thought and Life," *The American Scholar*, Vol. X, No. 4 [Autumn, 1941], 414). The insight common to the two statements seems to me in process of being justified, but it is notable that whereas Mann predicts a genuine religious revival, with articulated "knowledge" at its core, Robinson sees the possibility only of a revival of religious emotion.

Robinson read many of the works of the philosophical scientists in his last years, and what he probably had in mind when he hoped that science would come to the rescue of intuitions no longer adequately supported by religion was something similar to the idea expressed by the famous scientist Herman Weyl several years after Robinson's death, an idea wholly typical of the newer interpretations of science at that time: "The connections between that abstract world beyond [the world studied by physics] and the one which I perceive is necessarily of a statistical nature. This fact, together with the new insight which

The poem ends with a passage which is clearer prose than most of the earlier portions, though it is probably weaker poetry. It might perhaps be called a negative affirmation: since none of the five attitudes reviewed in the second part of the poem, nor any of the several "faiths" presented in the third part, can be accepted, and since no one today has "ever heard or ever spelt" the Word without experiencing the "fears and old surrenderings and terrors" that beset us, the conclusion can only be considered negative in fact, despite its apparent intention of affirming some kind of faith:

> If after all that we have lived and thought
> All comes to Nought,—
> If there be nothing after Now,
> And we be nothing anyhow,
> And we know that,—why live?
> 'Twere sure but weaklings' vain distress
> To suffer dungeons where so many doors
> Will open on the cold eternal shores
> That look sheer down
> To the dark tideless floods of Nothingness
> Where all who know may drown.

No answer to the climactic question has been presented, or even clearly suggested, within the poem; on the contrary, the poem leaves one with the clear impression that science has certainly made it clear that there is nothing after now and that all will indeed come to nought. So one is left echoing the question, why live? It does not modify one's impression of the poem as a poem nor clarify its actual structure to learn that Robinson explained in a letter written shortly after its appearance that it was intended as "a protest against a material explanation of the universe."

---

modern physics affords us into the relation between subject and object, opens several ways of reconciling personal freedom with natural law . . . . We must await the further developments of science . . . before we can design a true and detailed picture of the interwoven texture of Matter, Life, and Soul. But the old classical determinism of Hobbes need not oppress us any longer." (*The Open World* [New Haven, Conn., 1932], 55.) More recently Lecomte du Nouy in his *Human Destiny* (New York, 1947) has continued a tradition now at least twenty years old by arguing from the evidence of the new physics and from the statistical nature of scientific law that a true understanding of science leads to an outlook which he calls *telefinalism,* which in turn is found to be consistent with the religious doctrines of the existence of God, of free will, of original sin, and so on.

Since it is not my purpose here to attempt a complete critique of the poem, I have omitted specific comment on the verse as such. But it is not only the logical structure—or lack of it—which makes the poem a significant revelation of the effect of the cosmic chill. Consider, for example, the ending from the point of view of its language and figures. Three rhyme words are capitalized in the last eleven lines; because they are both rhyme words and capitalized, they receive the chief emphasis in the climax of the poem. They are *Nought, Now,* and *Nothingness.* Generalized diction seems to me appropriate to certain kinds of poetry, but the effect here of the vague abstractions is surely to suggest the collapse of both poetic technique and controlled feeling. Even the *Nothingness* which receives the final emphasis has not been imaginatively felt, it has only been vaguely feared. Its alternative has not even been conceived. Compare the "nothing at all" that concludes MacLeish's "End of the World," where nothingness becomes a felt quality.

Even those three figures in the last eleven lines which are not wholly abstract are highly generalized; lacking precision, the "dungeons," "cold eternal shores," and "dark tideless floods" can have only a vague emotional import. They are evidences not only that Robinson too often availed himself of worn nineteenth-century language, but also that he did not really quite know, so far as he expressed himself in this poem, what it was he feared and what it was he hoped. Such was the effect of the cosmic chill on a poet who for other reasons and other poems deserves to rank as one of the chief modern American poets.[7]

4. THE EFFECT OF THE REVELATIONS

"The springs of philosophical thought," Susanne K. Langer has written, "have run dry once more. For fifty years at least, we have witnessed all the characteristic symptoms that mark the end of an epoch. . . . We have arrived once more at that counsel of despair, to find a reasoned faith." [8] Robinson's attempt to find such a faith was fruitless, as perhaps any such attempt, pursued in the

[7] It seems to me that the best case for Robinson's importance as a poet has been made by Yvor Winters in his excellent little book, *Edwin Arlington Robinson* in the New Directions Makers of Modern Literature Series (Norfolk, Conn., 1946). [An extract entitled "The Shorter Poems" is included in this collection.]

[8] *Philosophy in a New Key: A Study in the Symbolism of Reason, Rite, and Art* (Cambridge, Mass., 1942), 13.

way he pursued it, must have been. Science was the antagonist he feared; philosophy, which might have helped him to understand the significance of science as a part of man's experience and one of his ways of using his intelligence, he distrusted. For Robinson, as for the average literate man today, philosophy had become academic, unimportant, as the philosophy of the Schoolmen had become to the literate man of the Renaissance. In his published letters, there is no evidence that he profited from the revolutionary thought of Bergson and Whitehead or cared to become fully acquainted with the traditional pragmatic positivism of Dewey. True, he read Herbert Spencer with enthusiasm, Nietzsche and Schopenhauer with partial approval, and William James and Royce with disapproval during and just after his college days; yet for a philosophic poet he strikes one as rather innocent of philosophy. Like his own Miniver Cheevy, he "thought, and thought, and thought, and thought about it," but with no apparent results. "Was ever an insect flying between two flowers Told less than we are told of what we are?" He could find no starting place and he had no method. All thinking, including the thinking involved in science, starts from unproved assumptions, but Robinson could assume nothing, not even the reality of his own experience. When he assserted that the universe "must" be purposive, he meant only that unless it is, suicide is logically called for; and he could never be sure that suicide was not called for.

In an age when the rational disciplines no longer commanded respect—his low opinions of logic and theology are cases in point—and when the implications of Newtonian science seemed to indicate that life, mind, purpose, and value were irrelevant to an estimate of the nature of reality, Robinson could not conceive that the method of observation and experiment so successfully followed by the older sciences could be right for the subject matter of those sciences without being the only valid method of inquiry in all areas. He could not conceive of any valid criticism of that "bifurcation of nature" which, as Whitehead has shown,[9] arose partly as a historical accident and partly as a response to a practical need. He felt that there must be something that science was leaving out; he

[9] *Science and the Modern World* (New York, 1925). My indebtedness to all of Whitehead's work that I am capable of following without advanced mathematical training is so profound that I shall ordinarily be unable to acknowledge specific points of indebtedness, since I am no longer always aware of which of my ideas come from Whitehead and which do not.

did deny scientific positivism; but he could not articulate his feeling or offer grounds for his denial. He was wholly unacquainted with the thought of one of the greatest ages of reason Western culture has known, the age of Aquinas. With the proper New Englander's amused contempt for Popery, he was more inclined to judge the validity of Christianity by Christian Science than by Catholicism. Though he sorely missed the lost faith, though he enjoyed his own variety of religious experience, he felt in his youth that William James was no match for Herbert Spencer, and his last letters and poems suggest that he at least half agreed with John Burroughs' somewhat fatuous pronouncement that "Natural knowledge is in the ascendant. The sun of science has actually risen . . . and the things proper to the twilight or half-knowledge of a few centuries ago flee away, or are seen to be shadows and illusions."

He did not enjoy the new sunlight. He missed the shadows and wished that he were not compelled to recognize the illusions as such. "Is there a God. . . . Is there a Purpose or a Law?" he made his characters cry. But despite the urgency of his need for faith, all that he could confidently assert from within the Spencerian system was that if the world was really constituted as modern knowledge said it was, then life was not worth while. No wonder that his "religious" and "philosophic" poetry is mostly verbose, tedious, and vague. All the words, all the thinking, come to so little! Without Frost's tough-mindedness or Eliot's instinct for the nourishing elements in traditional culture, he could find no way of answering Lord Russell's rhetorical question. In the "alien and inhuman world" in which he thought he found himself, he could discover no way to keep his aspirations untarnished.

Like Hawthorne at the end of his life, he suffered from a sense of discouragement so profound that he could neither express it nor wholly repress it. Like Hawthorne's attempts in the late romances, his attempts at affirmation sound the more hollow the oftener they are repeated. Like Hawthorne again, he had in early and middle life found the symbols he needed to express a sensibility still sufficiently unified to permit artistic symbolization. Like Hawthorne, finally, he shivered in a frozen world until the cosmic chill congealed the artistic powers that had once been his.

Robinson's Modernity

by J. C. Levenson

E. A. Robinson made an easy peace, though qualified by irony, with the poetic conventions among which he grew up, and so the Robert Frost epigram on his having taken the "old-fashioned way to be new" has usually been repeated with hardly any stress on the *new*. Though his traditionalism is no longer dismissed as out-of-date, the epigram still makes a difficulty. By *old-fashioned,* Frost meant to call attention to such timeless virtues as only the new-fashioned might miss. "Plain excellence and stubborn skill," qualities which Robinson ascribed to George Crabbe and hoped that his own work would show, have never been modish—nor can they be called modern, either. Yet the traditional and the timeless in his work do not mean that he is a poet for the ages only. Looking to tradition is his cultural habit and generalization is his characteristic mode of speech, but he is also a full-fledged citizen of the twentieth century. When he defines the present in relation to the past, he is trying to fix a particular present. And when he generalizes most broadly, he still is giving expression to a particular historical moment. Thus, in "The Man against the Sky," he meditates on a grandly isolated man, seen looming against the sunset, who goes down a distant hill as if to death. General though the subject is, it places the poem historically. Even without explicit mention of world war, this is a poem of 1916: an ode on the very faint intimations of immortality that remained a century after Wordsworth. The man who descends to darkness contrasts with Wordsworth's child who stands in an aura of cascading light and cosmic reassurance. In the flame-lit gloom of Robinson's poem, an inward steadiness exists without evident bulwarks of spirit outside oneself—or

"Robinson's Modernity" by J. C. Levenson. From *The Virginia Quarterly Review,* XLIV, number 4 (Autumn, 1968), 590–610.

even within. Except for one brief positive statement, faith is tentatively expressed in questions, or else it is implicitly affirmed by elaborate conditional sentences of which only the negative side is worked out. Now I do not mean to deny that Robinson in his later years had the poetic vice of liking to go the long way round, but in this case the method of tentativeness and implication is right for the poem. In the poet's meditative process as in his represented subject, darkness almost envelops the scene and the source of light is below the horizon of consciousness. There is an unfortunate touch of Dumas in his concluding dungeon image, but he could justly assert that his terrors are not of Monte Cristo but of the soul:

> If after all that we have lived and thought,
> All comes to Nought,—
> If there be nothing after Now,
> And we be nothing anyhow,
> And we know that,—why live?
> 'Twere sure but weaklings' vain distress
> To suffer dungeons where so many doors
> Will open on the cold eternal shores
> That look sheer down
> To the dark tideless floods of Nothingness
> Where all who know may drown.

Doubt is certain, disbelief plausible, despair sympathetic, and hope obscure. These are the first principles of Robinson's imaginative world. That they have also been primary facts of twentieth-century life accounts, in my view, for the continuing modernity of his work. My argument is that he derived these principles not only from temperament and the circumstances of his private experience, but also from the cultural situation of his time. I believe that by fitting him into his milieu, we can recover something of his historicity and of our proper relation to one of the early masters of twentieth-century American literature.

The quality of Robinson's newness has almost always been a subject for argument. But by the time of his "Man against the Sky" volume, he had fairly outlasted rejection by his elders, who genteelly deprecated his work for its prosiness and inglorious realism. Almost at once the tables were turned, and he found himself classed as obsolete by young men who denounced him as genteel and conventional. With his long look back to Wordsworth and the language and form in which he cast his latter-day Immortality Ode, he was identified with the nineteenth-century world whose passing he tried to measure. His juniors were tempted to think that Prufrock's evening "spread out against the sky like a patient etherized upon a table" reduced to triteness the old-fashioned sunset which, early and late, was a controlling symbol in the older poet's work. Within five years, Eliot was dismissing Robinson as "negligible," and all the disdainful young men joined in. Readers who were arrested by the highly dramatic language of Eliot's monologues felt themselves merely deterred by Robinson's slow-paced reflectiveness. His grave manner did not call attention to itself in any case, but when minds were tuning to the flashing wit of a brilliant modernism, his subtlety and strength were easy to miss. His being formal was misunderstood by those who were reacting against the politeness of polite letters. His tone of consideration and reconsideration led them rashly to conclude that he was stolid. Formality, thoughtfulness, and reticence concealed his emotional depth—though not from everyone. I would suggest that the most notable and interesting witness to the immediate usability of Robinson's art is John Crowe Ransom, who, in his development from "Poems about God" (1919) to "Chills and Fever" (1924), learned what one could make of a native bent for formality, thoughtfulness, and reticence. In his verse Mr. Ransom more than half mocked the qualities of scholar and gentleman which as a critic he could professedly admire—when the distance was right. His model *seventeenth-century* poets were, in words he might have spoken of Robinson too, "weighty yet idiomatic; polite conversationalists perhaps, who do not have to make speeches in order to offer important observations." Mr. Ransom has, of course, spoken up for Robinson directly, but the indirections are what best illustrate his acute reading and deep absorption of the older poet's art. And as different from Mr. Ransom as from each other, Yvor Winters, Winfield Scott, and Louis Coxe have also shown—by profession and by practice—how much there is to build on in this perennially unfashionable and valuable poet.[1] But the fact remains that for about thirty years the surest way to praise a poet was to claim for him qualities that could first be attributed to a seventeenth-century poet, and

[1] [See the essays by Yvor Winters and Louis Coxe reprinted in this volume; one of Winfield Scott's best discussions of Robinson may be found in *Exiles and Fabrications* (New York: Doubleday, 1961), pp. 154–69.]

idiomatic weightiness was not likeness enough. Harking back to Wordsworth rather than to Donne seemed to place Robinson, for many a young avant-gardist, as a creature of academic taste and presumptive gentility.

When gentility is a pejorative term, I suppose that it means being insensitive to experience and incurious about truth and not simply being well-mannered or well-educated. In that case, Robinson transcended the Genteel Tradition in the simplest way, by being immune to it. Notoriously not a revolutionary, he drew great benefits from the standing order of society and culture, and he discriminated accurately between benefits and liabilities. When we attempt a like discrimination, we can understand how he stood with the old America, middle-class, republican, and confident of an unchanging domestic tranquility. His father, who first shifted the family from the artisan to the business class, no doubt helped instill in the boy an obsession for demonstrably—that is to say, economically—making something of himself; but Edward Robinson also read with his son through "Bryant's Library of Poetry and Song" and other books of his ample collection. Gardiner, Maine, reinforced the boy's small-town economic ethic and his guilty sense that poetry was not a decent calling nor art an acceptable success; yet Gardiner also provided him with a first-rate high-school education (including a little Latin and less Greek) among friends who were intellectually serious. The town, in his later view, hardly could number half a dozen people who cared for poetry. But among those few were the gifted amateurs, a homeopathic physician and a spinster schoolteacher, who welcomed the boy into their literary conversation and taught him the intricacies of verse; with their encouragement, he became the virtuoso of villanelles whose scorn for mere technicians had the authority of a master. And among the old and well-established families of the town were discerning, generous people who were quick to value him: after seeing "The Torrent and the Night Before," which he had printed at his own expense in 1896, they sought out his company, they tactfully underwrote his next books at the publisher, and offered more direct support, they knew how to find him a job in Cambridge, they put him in touch with other writers when he went to New York. The well-known story of his rescue from demoralizing poverty by Theodore Roosevelt in 1905 recapitulates on a national scale the intelligent and practical openness of late-Victorian America at its best—just as Taft's new broom, which swept him out of his custom house in 1909, may stand for another kind of reality which was never far from Robinson.

Circumstance encouraged the poet to stay on good terms with the official culture, but temperament accounts still better for his apparent submissiveness. His youthful discovery of Whitman heartened him in his calling, but almost as soon as he understood the radically anti-traditional meaning of Whitman's work, he decided that his own way must be different. His was a nature that chose discipline, and through discipline he gained the freedom to speak in his own voice. Any other kind of self-reliance might have been disastrous, for it would have left him prey to his normal uncertainty of taste. For example, he seriously thought of ranking James Lane Allen next to Hawthorne, and he read "Stand Fast, Craig-Royston" and "Jude the Obscure" with the same reverent enthusiasm. He could easily have lapsed into mute inglorious provincialism if the prevalent culture of small-town America had not offered solid nourishment to the critical intelligence. As it was, he became an exacting reader of poetry by training his judgment on Tennyson and Arnold, Wordsworth, Milton, and Shakespeare, and beyond them on the classic writers of Greece and Rome. His literary education was simple, academic, and in some respects even meager. But it disclosed standards by which a young man could take the measure of his time.

As he proceeded to do just that, Robinson acted for the absolute inconvenience of those literary historians who like to divide the American scene between radicals and traditionalists, new men on the one hand and decadent respectables on the other. In the first place, he set himself ironically apart from the great national tendency to sing of fresh dawn and crow lustily over prospects. Even in his twenties, he was not young enough to find much to brag about. His early sonnet "Oh for a poet—for a beacon bright" announces that he can find no beacon among the flickering versifiers of his time. "To rift this changeless glimmer of dead gray," a true poet would "wrench one banner from the western skies" and take to himself the one available glory—of sunset. But while he rather undercut the chanticleer strain in American letters, he gave no comfort to timid conventionality in this sonnet in dispraise of "little sonnet-men." Having declined to cheer with American dreamers of unlimited possibility, he equally kept himself from the more temperate optimism of proper classicists. He had a little chill for either side, as he showed in his quatrain—

> Drink to the splendor of the unfulfilled,
>   Nor shudder for the revels that are done:
> The wines that flushed Lucullus are all spilled,
>   The strings that Nero fingered are all gone.

We may legitimately suspect that he enjoyed playing Banquo's ghost at the national barbecue. He had noticed of himself that the smoothest part of his face was around the mouth "where the only wrinkles of youth rightfully belong." But the quick wry grin has its own place in a nation of legendary roarers, and that place was not necessarily at the Saturday Club. As one who neither gave way easily to laughter nor ever altogether tamed his sense of humor, he managed from the beginning of his career to look before and after with equal eye. He splendidly chose as the epigraph of his first book: *"Qui pourrais-je imiter pour être original?"*

Given a critical acceptance of the past, Robinson proved that the supposed conflict between received tradition and direct experience need never occur. He simply assumed that one major use of culture was that it enabled a man to confront his destiny with more than his single strength. The tradition that gave him Hawthorne and Hardy scarcely led him to think that culture spared a man anything. On the other hand, he could not swallow the past indiscriminately. He gave up his early admiration for Browning's poetry because, he said, "its easy optimism is a reflection of temperament rather than of experience and observation." His own experience and observation led to a more somber view. The lifelong chronic earache which hurt so acutely and constantly that he sometimes feared it would drive him insane; the early, utter crack-up of his promising older brothers, one caught by drugs, the other by drink; his father's slow dying, accompanied by the spiritualist manifestations with which he managed to haunt his own house, and his mother's horrible death by black diphtheria, when neither doctor nor minister nor undertaker would cross the Robinson threshold for fear of infection; the alcoholism that fastened on him when artistic failure seemed as final as his poverty, and the heat and racket of his job as time-checker for a construction-gang in the New York subway—the list of ordeals could be extended, but length is not its proper measure. The quality of his experience depended on his making a discipline of suffering. As he fathomed his own powers of survival, he came to see in men's capacity to endure the mysterious touchstone of dignity and in their going down an equal mystery, "too far beyond the scope of our poor piddling censure to require of our ignorance anything less kind than silence." The habit of regarding human life *in extremis* conditioned his idea of reality in the literature of the past as well as the presented reality of his own poems.

Robinson's sense of the absoluteness of things has its complex origins in experience, temperament, and culture, but though such perception is old as tragedy, his mode of seeing was new. Before our own time men had been able readily enough to conceive a world in which "everything is to be endured," but they had been unwilling to reconstruct their idea of the tragic accordingly. It is very much of the twentieth century that Robert Frost should have adapted a phrase of Matthew Arnold's and declared that Robinson sang of "immedicable woes," meaning something like eternal truths. In a century of total violence, actual and threatened, poets have explored new regions of the unshakable once-and-once-only world where "nothing is to be done," and Robinson for one came to believe that endurance might stand out against the waste of life even when more practical affirmations could not. But not even survival was an unquestioned value with him. Exploring the last of doubts, at a point where he was literally engaged in the criticism of life, he found that he could not make meager joy balance out enormous pain, positing nothing beyond them. For one of his experience, he decided that for life to be worth living he must posit both idealism and immortality. He never became so much a philosopher as to argue his beliefs or so much a visionary as to elaborate their content; but the need not simply to believe, but to think through the meaning of his experience made him a meditative poet. Experience, not faith, was his subject; thought, not faith, was his way of handling it. That the resulting work should have coherent form, furthermore, was not an accident of genius merely, but the most important instance of Robinson's instinctively making the most of his academic education. And in this case, his debts were not so much to the past as to the liveliest and most advanced of contemporary thinkers. For Robinson's cast of mind was critically affected by his two years at Harvard, and by the great philosophic dialogue of William James and Josiah Royce to which he was eyewitness for a time. They, more than any others, provided him with the intellectual equipment for handling the irreducible facts of his experience.

Of course, Robinson was utterly candid when he said that he was not a philosophical poet to be read for his philosophy. He never wanted to be a philosopher, never developed the skill or talent to become one, never even fully understood how much his own thought depended on their speculative achievements. As a student he would happily have settled for the apostle of gentility, Charles Eliot Norton, whom he regarded as the greatest man on the Harvard faculty or in America for that matter. As a young man, during his Cambridge years and after, he was supercilious about the greatest collection of philosophers that has ever been gathered in America: he gave Royce's lectures second priority below Friday afternoon symphony, and he wrote of James as a "metaphysical funny man." Yet I believe that the arguments of Estelle Kaplan (in "Philosophy in the Poetry of Edwin Arlington Robinson") and Robert Stevick (in "Robinson and William James") set us on the right track with respect to the philosophers who made Harvard resound with the clash of ideas. For James and Royce technical proficiency and even profound originality were not the only ends of their speculative careers. Their philosophies, as James once said, were like "so many religions, ways of fronting life, and worth fighting for." In their Thirty Years War of the intellect, they could not help setting the issues for young men and forcing, at some level of consciousness, a choice of sides. Young Robinson responded out of his constitutional need to compose the facts of experience for thought and to proceed only on a rational path toward supernatural belief. James' questions and Royce's answers affected him for life. The ideas with which they equipped him for his own reflections account for the largeness and the structural strength of his imaginative world.

James' energy usually set the direction of intellectual controversy in Cambridge, and his warmth kept the discussion focused on elemental human concerns. Two of his addresses of the nineties, "On a Certain Blindness in Human Beings" [Talks to Teachers (1899)] and "Is Life Worth Living?" [The Will to Believe (1896)], specify topics to which he constantly recurred. His themes, taken up by Royce, were translated from what he gaily called "my crass pluralism" to terms out of the Hegelian idealist vocabulary. But

James recognized what was different about Royce among the idealists when he spoke of his colleague's "voluntaristic-pluralistic monism." James did not hide his satisfaction that monistic Hegel should have been pluralized in the Harvard environment, but he never claimed influence. He generously granted, rather, how much Royce nourished his own mind, and he indulged himself in the notion that they might go through eternity locked "in one last death-grapple of an embrace." Something like that wish is fulfilled, I believe, in the way their ghostly presences survive in the imaginative world of E. A. Robinson.

In his essay "On a Certain Blindness," James defined our imaginative need to recognize human claims which usually escape perception in our myopic habit-crusted lives. He said what the poet was ready to hear, since Robinson had early decided that "widening the sympathies" was one effect of his personal isolation which could become in turn the moral aim of his poetry. What James did for him was clarify the theme and give it intellectual standing. The philosopher spoke of "how soaked and shot-through life is with values and meanings which we fail to realize because of our external and insensible point of view." But it is not James' rich sense of life shot through with values that comes through in the poet who worked towards the same general proposition from a base in deprivation and hardship. James' more negative formulation is closer in tone: "The subject judged knows a part of the world of reality which the judging spectator fails to see. . . ." Thus, the shallow business-like "dear friends" of the poet who kept asking him what he was going to *do* appear not only in his letters but in his poems. They become the typical witnesses to the stories he told, the chorus of townspeople who ironically miss the meaning of the tales they tell. The chorus envy Richard Cory, seeing his glitter rather than his humanity. They think they tell all when they give the outsider's view of unrequited love in "Eros Turannos" or of unmerited love in "The Gift of God." The irony is often compounded, furthermore, by the chorus being called "we" or "I," for then the reader's illusion of reality and his moral involvement in this human blindness are most immediate. Yet Robinson carries his dramatic manipulation only so far: the unreliable "I" of such poems does not entirely control what readers may learn, for the chorus with a limited point of view blends into a narrator who quietly presides over the story, not as a technical makeshift for passing information, but somehow to let us see both our common insensitivity and what it misses. But his departure from the dramatic mode reminds us that James affected the poet more by his expression of a common truth than by the metaphysical application he made of it. When we turn from the relative knowledge of the dramatized chorus to the narrator's quest for stable meaning, we see how James' influence is interlocked with that of Royce.

While James may be thought of as proposing the theme of moral blindness, it was Royce who provided the poet with a conception of what it is that the "judging spectator" fails to see. Challenged by James' reverence for individuality, and by James' charge that Hegelian idealists let everyone in particular be swallowed up in the all-inclusive Absolute, Royce devised the "pluralistic monism" which his colleague saw as complementary to his own philosophy. Royce's innovation rested on his idealist analysis of individuality itself. His argument runs that our minds know an object only as it fits general categories that are common to other objects, and so we cannot be said to know anything that is truly unique; the unique can be known only to an all-inclusive Mind that transcends the human need for categories; so the idea of uniqueness implies both unknowability to human minds and the logical necessity of Absolute Mind. When the argument is reduced from metaphysics to plain poetry, we have the individuality of a Robinson subject coming through to us from an unknowing chorus who cannot see and an omniscient narrator who does not tell. The poet's problem is how, without saying more than he can know, he may convey an apprehension of his subject that is greater than the sum of what the spectators in the poem may see. This is one aspect of Robinson's effort to make, as he said, "a language that tells us, through a more or less emotional reaction, something that cannot be said." His starting-point is a conviction about individuality. His fictional Hamilton says of the Washington he admittedly cannot fathom:

> It seems to me the mystery that is in him
> That makes him only more to me a man
> Than any other I have known.

Assuming that he faced a challenging difficulty but not an impossibility, Robinson proceeded to set his subject in traditional categories and to keep us aware that our conventional ways of knowing give only partial truths. He thus presents Eben Flood as a Down East Roland, silhouetted with his jug as if he were winding a silent horn, and he requires that we discern both the mockery and the fitness of the heroic image. Such judgments on our part imply a larger context than the "time-born" categories of literary convention. So the poet has prepared us for the ending in which conventions and ironies are discarded; as Ellsworth Barnard put it, "the humor and the glamour go, and the world of unadorned fact is left." Yet when he gives us this sense of unadorned fact, he presents his subject not simply as discreet, isolated, and fragmentary, but as unique and somehow fulfilled by being part of a world where its existence and meaning can be apprehended justly. The loneliness of Eben Flood, though it transcends both his gross absurdity and his pathetic dignity, is less lonely in that its meaning is known. The organic wholeness of the poem, while our minds dwell in that context, stands for the wholeness of the world.

Context gives us the ideal whole, but poetic representation has to stay with the ordinary human world in which we encounter the blindness of most people and the impenetrability of the individual. "Richard Cory" is a useful example since the poem conceals its powerful particularity by appearing almost tritely conventional. But since the surprise ending of Cory's suicide does not, after a first reading, surprise anyone but the "we" of the poem, it is worth looking for deeper causes of its hold on readers. On the one hand, there is Robinson's tact in presenting the title figure. By his scheme, moral blindness is overcome, not by factitious insight into another mind, but by respectful recognition of another person. So he avoids the nineteenth-century, common-sense method of realistic characterization and gives us nothing of his subject's motives or feelings. He sketches in Cory's gentlemanliness and his wealth, but not his despondency, and he lets the suicide seal the identity of the man forever beyond our knowing or judging. On the other hand, he can characterize the chorus just because they lack individuality, and he invites us to judge their blindness on pain of missing the one sure meaning of the poem:

> So on we worked, and waited for the light,
> And went without the meat, and cursed the bread;
> And Richard Cory, one calm summer night,
> Went home and put a bullet through his head.

They do not serve who only work and wait. Those who count

over what they lack and fail to bless the good before their eyes are truly desperate. The blind see only what they can covet or envy. With their mean complaining, they are right enough about their being in darkness, and their dead-gray triviality illuminates by contrast Cory's absolute commitment to despair.

"Richard Cory" is but one instance of Robinson's handling the question "Is Life Worth Living?" On that topic, he would have agreed with James that "The nightmare view of life has plenty of organic sources, but its great reflective source in these days, and at all times, has been the contradiction between the phenomena of Nature and the craving of the heart to believe that behind Nature there is a spirit whose expression Nature is." But James went on to recommend that we by-pass the tragic contradictions of natural theology; think of nature just as background like *weather,* "doing and undoing without end"; accept a pluralistic world in which spirit may express itself as a force for good among other forces, contending for mastery and calling on us to join battle on its side. Whatever the cosmic weather, then, we ought to exercise our right to believe and take sides with the power of good. Given the problem of evil in a God-ruled universe, what James prescribed for the theologically distressed was a radical change of metaphysics. To Robinson, who could no more become a pluralist than he could change his genes, James seemed to treat the human symptom but not to touch the tragic problem, and what is more, the Jamesian hypothesis seemed to him a fiction, a mere placebo. An unshakable monist, he could satisfy his own religious craving only under a system which dealt with all being as a unified whole. Royce's idealism fitted his need. Furthermore, Royce's temperament harmonized with his own, for the idealist had a tragic philosophy which made endurance rather than moral exertion the ultimate ethical value. Just as Mind was affirmed in the recognition of individuality, so Spirit was affirmed in the recognition of woe. Acceptance and courage rather than more strenuous virtues were called for by Royce's psychological approach to the problem of evil. What suited Robinson best, however, with his will to believe so nearly overmatched by his capacity for doubt, was that Royce founded his idealism on the very fact of doubting: his most famous contribution to philosophy was his proving the existence of his "Absolute" from "The Possibility of Error." This modern version of the ontological proof argued that the conception of error logically implied a standard of truth and a knowing mind to discriminate truth from error. Instead of assuming a world shot through with values waiting to be intuited, Royce began with a world in which nothing was sure but doubt and then, by the effort of logical speculation rather than the seeming-easy way of private insight, reasoned his way from doubt to faith. Assuming only the very opposite of what one wanted to believe, trusting neither perceptions nor feelings, one might still work his cautious way to affirmation encompassing all.

Royce's logic authorized Robinson to work out his own dark-side religious psychology, a kind of negativist revision of James. Where James set up the healthy-minded once-born and the sick soul as stages towards conversion of the twice-born, Robinson developed somber parallels: he identified the once-born with the morally unborn, insensitive and egoistic; he emphasized that moral awakening might be the cause of soul-sickness, for sensitivity must principally be sensitivity to grief, of which the most likely consequence was all-consuming doubt; and having thus divided most people into the "comfortably blind or wretchedly astray," he put into his third and ultimate category "The Man Who *Died* Twice," once to complacency and once to despair. The hero of "The Man Who Died Twice" arrives at a dreadfully simple, though carefully respected, assurance that he has been born anew, but Robinson usually stops with presenting the inadequacy of un-faith. Illusion and despondency are his frequent subjects because they predominate among men; whatever else there may be he leaves to ironic implication. "The faith within the fear," Robinson declares, is what "holds us to the life we curse." What could transform his "Children of the Night" into "Children of the Light" would be the ability to cast off illusion without falling into belief that chaos rules the world: the task of declaring the tragic truth without being unmanned by it is symbolized in his injunction to "put off the cloak that hides the scar." And since truth-finding rather than conversion experience is the end he has in view, Royce's dialectic is even more important to him than James' dynamic psychology. The symbolic movement from false light through darkness to genuine light, however faintly perceived, does not occur dramatically through revelation scenes, but meditatively through taking thought.

Sometimes Robinson pursues his reflections to the point of philosophical abstraction, and then the poetry shows its intellectual workings more explicitly. Thus Merlin's special wisdom lies in a capacity for seeing the world from the vangtage of Roycean idealism; he can perceive

> In each bewildered man who dots the earth
> A moment with his days a groping thought
> Of an eternal will. . . .

The malady of the race and of the time he sums up in a formulation which covers both the failure of belief and the moral blindness of human beings: though men objectively are parts of an ideal universal scheme, subjectively they seldom even reach the stage of doubts, for they are

> strangely endowed
> With merciful illusions whereby self
> Becomes the will itself and each man swells
> In fond accordance with his agency.

The illusions of self, while they mercifully keep a man from the awful qualms of theological anxiety, can wreck the world. The assertive will may keep men out of a psychological darkness, but the ensuing works of powerful men, each fondly thinking his partial cause to be the highest, brings down historical darkness over Camelot. But the philosophizing within Robinson's poems is usually turgid and ineffective; the benefit of Royce's influence is to be found, rather, in the generalizing which grows out of the represented action. The poet rightly concentrated on the world of experience; the function of philosophical ideas, as of literary culture, was to help him find order and meaning in the lives of men.

Robinson's speculative education affected the shape of reality as it is represented in his poems, and it affected the form of the poems as well. His preference for narrative over dramatizing techniques, so that immediacy is less with the event than with the thinking over; his concern for the organic unity of each poem, so that context might give poetic effect to even the plainest words; the dialectical progression that leads us past egoistic blindness and fond illusions till we confront even the most dismal truths, and confront them with acceptance and courage; the irony that affirms by indirection—these hallmarks of his poetry all testify that his thought helps account for the form as well as the substance of his work. All the technical elements converge in the poet's handling of symbols with such subtle casualness that they seem to operate almost below the level of consciousness. The emergent symbol has its cumulative effect without coming into focus in a climactic epiphany. It discloses its meaning, not in a single blazing moment, but through slow reflection; and as that meaning comes home, plain words and unpoetic subjects turn out to have been poetry after all. The basic anecdote of "Isaac and Archibald," for example, does not seem far removed from its prosy origin in the coincidence that two of Robinson's older friends each confided in him that he thought the other was slipping into dotage. The poet gave the incident a country setting and made it over as a boyhood episode, recollected in tranquility by a reflective story-teller. The boy goes with old Isaac to see whether Archibald, lamed by years, needs help in harvesting his oats; they find the oat field harvested smooth, they visit for a while, and after the old men have played cards in the shade, they eat supper and come home. Changing things thus, Robinson seemed to do little more than shape his material in accordance with century-old Wordsworthian conventions. His strength appears to lie simply in old-fashioned qualities like just representation and tactful humor. But the changes make the difference between an odd coincidence and an event in which the simplest facts may become symbolic. Walking, in the revised plot, becomes a constant underlying movement in the narration. The walking is unobtrusive "stage-business," a touch of realism; but in one local context after another the fact takes on meaning. The pace that Isaac sets is not explicitly heroic, but the boy sees the old man as striding along "like something out of Homer." In his short-legged, never-quite-surrendering struggle to keep up, there are emulation and respect that bespeak a kind of greatness. Again, when Isaac muses on the sadness of "being left behind . . . when the best friend of your life goes down," the language is so nearly trite that we may hardly notice the imagery of movement; but after the next pause on their road, the boy lets us see that the figure, far from being vague, is accurate, just, and intrinsic to the context:

> Isaac had a desert somewhere in him,
> And at the pump he thanked God for all things
> That He had put on earth for men to drink,
> And he drank well,—so well that I proposed
> That we go slowly lest I learn too soon
> The bitterness of being left behind,
> And all those other things. That was a joke

To Isaac, and it pleased him very much;
And that pleased me—for I was twelve years old.

Woven in with the old man's blessing what he has to drink, even if it be only water, and the young boy's unconscious aping of his companion's solicitousness, even if it be unneeded, is the remark about being left behind which casually and lightly proves the earlier image to have been exact, though lightly handled. Life goes towards death, and the living are characterized by their relation to dying. The relation of boy to man and of both to life and death comes through forcibly on reflection, even though each separate touch that contributed to the picture has little intensity by itself.

The most vivid moment in "Isaac and Archibald" occurs when Isaac and the boy, after their long hot walk, go down to the cellar to refresh themselves with some of Archibald's fine cider. From the glare of the August sun, they enter the dark, and with that movement into the dark, a new and special sensitivity to minute details affects the narration:

Down we went,
Out of the fiery sunshine to the gloom,
Grateful and half sepulchral, where we found
The barrels, like eight potent sentinels,
Close ranged along the wall. From one of them
A bright pine spile stuck out alluringly,
And on the black flat stone, just under it,
Glimmered a late-spilled proof that Archibald
Had spoken from unfeigned experience.
There was a fluted antique water-glass
Close by, and in it, prisoned, or at rest,
There was a cricket, of the brown soft sort
That feeds on darkness. Isaac turned him out,
And touched him with his thumb to make him jump,
And then composedly pulled out the plug
With such a practised hand that scarce a drop
Did even touch his fingers. Then he drank
And smacked his lips with a slow patronage
And looked along the line of barrels there
With a pride that may have been forgetfulness
That they were Archibald's and not his own.
"I never twist a spigot nowadays,"
He said, and raised the glass up to the light,
"But I thank God for orchards." And that glass

Was filled repeatedly for the same hand
Before I thought it worth while to discern
Again that I was young, and that old age,
With all his woes, had some advantages.

Isaac is not a Down-East Ulysses making his descent to the underworld; the cider-cellar remains just that. The scene stays in memory because it is the graphic center of the story. Its significance is not to be intuited by classical analogy, but comes out through Archibald's rational discourse. When Archibald in his turn has the boy's ear, the old farmer discreetly states his worry that Isaac is losing his acuteness; but he has something else on his mind, which transcends that dismal partial truth and keeps weaving into his talk:

Remember, boy,
That we are old. . . .
You look before you and we look behind,
And we are playing life out in the shadow—
But that's not all of it. The sunshine lights
A good road yet before us if we look, . . .
The shadow calls us, and it frightens us—
We think; but there's a light behind the stars
And we old fellows who have dared to live,
We see it. . . .
I'm in the shadow, but I don't forget
The light, my boy,—the light behind the stars.

Archibald lacks the heroics, we learn, to be figured as a Greek hero out of Flaxman's Homer quite so easily as Isaac. He has, of course, harvested the oats that Isaac thought he had lost the skill and strength to do, and so in the world of supposed fact, he has proved himself a man on just as large a scale as the friend he loves. But in the context of the poem, he is lame and Isaac walks, and talking as he does of light and shadow, he seems to ramble more than the friend whose mind he thinks is aging. Yet he speaks a faith that Isaac has acted out:

"I never twist a spigot nowadays,"
He said, and raised the glass up to the light,
"But I thank God for orchards."

In his casual talk he illuminates, after the fact, a casual gesture that almost escaped notice.

By the end of the poem, the several images come together in a unified vision of life. The tired boy, resting in the orchard shade, has the sensation that all time is summed up at once, that the whole of existence may be comprehended as a unity. His fancy, filled with the landscape and the day's incidents, catches now and then

> A flying glimpse of a good life beyond—
> Something of ships and sunlight, streets and singing,
> Troy falling, and the ages coming back,
> And ages coming forward. . . .

And the "flying glimpse of a good life beyond" is not merely subjective in the boy's half-dreaming mind, for walking home with Isaac in the twilight, he sees the flaming sunset beyond the boundary of the forest horizon. Nature herself seems to confirm the image that Isaac acted out, that Archibald expounded, that the boy dreamed. The "flame beyond the boundary" is as much a reality as the man and boy walking altogether naturally together towards the night.

The genius by which Robinson made such simple, telling poems was his own. But if we wish not to be self-deceived in the face of his simplicity, it is worth an effort to see him in his historical context. Before we can do full justice to his particularity, we would do well to understand what he made of the literary conventions and philosophical conceptions that came to him ready for use. Like every major artist, he changed in using them the methods and ideas which were a part of his culture, and at this distance in time, we should be able to discern his originality as well as his traditionalism. Informal in tone, he could match any modern formalist in the care with which he made a poem. Realistic in manner, he developed a complex symbolic technique. He was a man of doubt who could not finally get round the absurdity of unbelief. And as one who knew what deprivations could do to a man, he hated sniveling and he honored honest praise. Apart from temperament and experience which made him responsive to the leading themes of William James, he saw life according to the conceptions of Josiah Royce. In his imitation of life so conceived, he had his originality.

Chronology of Important Dates

1869	Robinson born on December 22 in Head Tide, Maine.
1891–93	Attends Harvard as a special student.
1892	Robinson's father dies.
1893	Returns to Gardiner, Maine.
1893–97	Completes the contents of *The Torrent and the Night Before* and *The Children of the Night.*
1896	*The Torrent and the Night Before* privately printed. Robinson's mother dies.
1897	Robinson moves to New York. *The Children of the Night* published in Boston.
1899	Employed at Harvard College until death of Dean Robinson. Permanent return to New York.
1902	*Captain Craig* published, the expenses guaranteed by Mrs. Laura Richards and Hays Gardiner.
1903–04	Timekeeper in New York subway construction.
1905–09	Employed in New York Customs House through the offices of President Theodore Roosevelt.
1905	*Children of the Night* published by Scribner's through pressure exerted by the President.
1909	Herman Robinson dies.
1910	*The Town Down the River.*
1910–13	Robinson turns to writing plays and novels.
1911	First visit to the MacDowell Colony in New Hampshire. Robinson spends the rest of his summers there.
1916	*The Man Against the Sky.*
1917	*Merlin.*
1920	*Lancelot. The Three Taverns.*
1921	*Avon's Harvest. Collected Poems* awarded the Pulitzer Prize.

1922 Honorary degree from Yale.

1923 *Roman Bartholow.* Robinson visits England.

1924 *The Man Who Died Twice.* Robinson receives his second Pulitzer Prize.

1927 *Tristram.* Robinson wins his third Pulitzer Prize.

1929 *Cavender's House.*

1930 *The Glory of the Nightingale.*

1931 *Matthias at the Door.*

1932 *Nicodemus.*

1933 *Talifer.*

1934 *Amaranth.*

1935 *King Jasper.* Robinson dies in New York Hospital on April 6.

Notes on the Editor and Contributors

FRANCIS MURPHY is the editor of the Penguin Critical Anthology *Walt Whitman* (1969) and Associate Professor of English at Smith College.

CONRAD AIKEN'S *Collected Poems* were published in 1953; his *Collected Novels* appeared in 1964.

WARNER BERTHOFF is Professor of English at Harvard University. He is the author of *Example of Herman Melville* (1962).

LOUIS O. COXE is Professor of English at Bowdoin College.

JAMES DICKEY is a former Consultant in Poetry in English at the Library of Congress.

ROBERT FROST'S further observations on Robinson may be found in his *Selected Letters* (1964).

EDWIN S. FUSSELL is Professor of English at the University of California, San Diego and the author of *Frontier: American Literature and the American West* (1965).

J. C. LEVENSON is Professor of English at the University of Virginia and the author of *The Mind and Art of Henry Adams* (1957).

JOSEPHINE MILES' most recent volume of poetry is *Kinds of Affection* (1967). She is Professor of English at the University of California, Berkeley.

W. R. ROBINSON is Associate Professor of English at the University of Florida.

HYATT H. WAGGONER is Professor of English at Brown University and the author of *American Poets* (1968).

YVOR WINTERS' collection of essays, *Forms of Discovery* (1967), appeared shortly before his death. He taught for many years at Stanford University.

MORTON DAUWEN ZABEL completed his *Selected Poems of Edwin Arlington Robinson* shortly before his death in 1964.

Selected Bibliography

STANDARD EDITIONS

Collected Poems of Edwin Arlington Robinson (New York: The Macmillan Company, 1937).

Selected Early Poems and Letters of Edwin Arlington Robinson, ed. Charles T. Davis (New York: Holt, Rinehart & Winston, Inc., 1960).

LETTERS

Edwin Arlington Robinson's Letters to Edith Brower, ed. Richard Cary (Cambridge, Mass.: Harvard University Press, 1968).

Selected Letters of Edwin Arlington Robinson, Introduction by Ridgely Torrence (New York: The Macmillan Company, 1940).

Untriangulated Stars: Letters of Edwin Arlington Robinson to Harry de Forest Smith, 1890–1905, ed. Denham Sutcliffe (Cambridge, Mass.: Harvard University Press, 1947).

BIOGRAPHICAL AND CRITICAL STUDIES

Barnard, Ellsworth, *Edwin Arlington Robinson* (New York: The Macmillan Company, 1952).

Coxe, Louis O., "E. A. Robinson," *University of Minnesota Pamphlets on American Writers,* No. 17 (Minneapolis: The University of Minnesota Press, 1962).

Coxe, Louis O., *Edwin Arlington Robinson: The Life of Poetry* (New York: Pegasus, 1969).

Crowder, Richard, "The Emergence of Edwin Arlington Robinson," *South Atlantic Quarterly,* XLV (January, 1946), 89–98.

Donoghue, Denis, "Edwin Arlington Robinson, J. V. Cunningham, Robert Lowell," *Connoisseurs of Chaos* (New York: The Macmillan Company, 1965).

Hagedorn, Hermann, *Edwin Arlington Robinson* (New York: The Macmillan Company, 1938).

Kaplan, Estelle, *Philosophy in the Poetry of Edwin Arlington Robinson* (New York: Columbia University Press, 1940).

Neff, Emery, *Edwin Arlington Robinson* (New York: William Sloan Associates, 1948).

Scott, Winfield Townley, "To See Robinson," *Exiles and Fabrications* (New York: Doubleday & Company, Inc., 1961), pp. 154–69.

Smith, Chard Powers, *Where the Light Falls* (New York: The Macmillan Company, 1965).

Tate, Allen, "Edwin Arlington Robinson," *Collected Essays* (Denver: Alan Swallow, 1959), pp. 358–64.

Winters, Yvor, "Religious and Social Ideas in the Didactic Poetry of Edwin Arlington Robinson," *Arizona Quarterly,* I (Spring, 1945), 70–85.

Contrivances

John Wilkinson

PUBLISHED BY SALT PUBLISHING
PO Box 202, Applecross, Western Australia 6153
PO Box 937, Great Wilbraham, Cambridge PDO CB1 5JX United Kingdom

First published 2003

Printed and bound in the United Kingdom by Lightning Source

Typeset in Swift 9.5 / 13

ISBN 1 876857 60 9 paperback

SP

1 3 5 7 9 8 6 4 2

Contents

Acknowledgments

Signs of an Intruder was first published by Parataxis Editions, Cambridge, in 2001.

Earlier versions of some poems were published in *big allis*, *The Gig*, *Jacket*, *Parataxis*, *Poetry Salzburg Review*, and *QUID*.

Saccades

First Run

Sunlight seeps component hours therefore forbear to set.
One only accompanist, it twanged
the white fingers will embraid then shake their tally open
like tap sticks; & the fob of the guardians
kicks in to chatter, balance wheel spin, escapement clutch,
but are not what they angled for,
attraction/repulsion reaped the light these would uphold.

Gaps narrow, fingers sweep their sensory weft according
to what shade jumps hyperactive,
like a loom clanks silently they oil the nodding kiss grove.
Waive the near approach of
silk slip, hessian scour, velvet might hold back but slopes
damaged for the thought of it.
Behind, a lozenge licks out the sun. Light no more seeps

its automatic crop. By shortfall only though it cottons on
egg-ridden like a moist pad
chewed following precedent, in double twist wound tight:
what could be more hurtful
than this event foreshortened? Mechanisms start to whirr,
the heliograph to jerk & sputter,
lengthening at verticals but flits down treads & banisters.

Collateral fire pins down but they wobble loose, the recoil
knocks them back. To listen out
swells up like the backflow is consistent with listening in
springs which are double-leaf
or breach, for stretched ahead of reason or at time's diktat
pinged into its anacoustic case,
the required fistful is impending through a shaft of light.

Compiled inside the sheets where a fire-belt discouraged
pain from crossing, little shits
manage & rehearse that their sheared pivots rock against,
then mesh together guard-like.
Face it if my scarf was doubled over, the sheaf it proffers
stood, just held its lining
flapping like the fires nearby its belt consummately shirk,

once again forgetting & oblivious birds sing out of cover.
Part to heal all parting I lapse.
Rejoice to find the break which suppurates in ugly burns.
A last enticement coming up
to take breath demurs against the guard rail & overhears
what living shadows shadow,
stacked, loaded, saturated, stoves in the inter-entity brief.

Empty envelopes shake drowsily, wrinkle as on deflating,
        never mind that they balloon
at any thinking twinge, a method of least squares prevails;
        they scope by such false modesty
even as they are lost to view will prick through their folds
                The magnet turf is charged,
lets no sprig of forget-me-not or pennyroyal underpierce.

Eyes wide as saucers asking more, ears splayed as dishes
        swirl with aggressive birdsong,
no metal nor contact plates are stunning the rubber ticks,
        nor a funnel for ants siphons.
Banded muscle peaks the tent should headroom fluctuate
                in mimicry of the sky
reports a thunder-clap, concussed into being repetitively.

Intact though its underside will stay, inflating to the high
        mission of its nervous barrage,
twittering receptors switching all for output torch in eyes
        peeled from their treads, background
pins & nipples staunch this lampblack sighs to riddance.
                Succumb, be drawn
two-timing, two-faced, flash in its synapses sensationally.

This is a fast train, no stopping
at Farningham Road; the paper mills'
castellated stack is edgily withdrawn
to where I hung about, no key
on a bare concrete landing,
prepared to be measured up.
Slogans at the nearside bring forward

lank neglected grass, pierce instantly
the stare of indifference,
How shall their rustling fliers pin?
Attention spoils attentiveness, & pains
taken little relieve pain,
the categorical is like an undiagnosed
pain in the chest

which like a stovepipe, a cross-section
metaphor with its gap closed
There's only a sheet of
Paper's width in it
threaded with sharps.
That's black paper, sugar paper,
how needles always came

to be opened out on a dressing-table,
buttoned within the slice
they were charged. Interruptedly
they learn sticking.
Behind the flats is scrub ground,
boys kicking about as usual
treading the uncut
down to a winter's-long mire, & frost

compels a certain decorum, so I feel,
but the near side is snatched
& let leave.
Ghosts slot between the floorboards
dreadfully traced.

They have been filed there
by my heart's despondence

sinks towards the floor, won't be fixed
Though fluttering with pinned-on
half-moon collars,
is ribboned with ghost sleeves.
There is a price-
tag knotted into the double shielding.

Stubbed with poker-work a fret line has for business end
a Jacob's anvil, fold-together fist
retains a hook connects with negative blur, so will redden.
Was that masked by the gouged-
away event which up till now had been its spoiler, a ruse
found out in its dazzle halo
overcomes in overcoming to be incised onto brutal space?

Though jarred by its scaffolding a forearm pestle grinds,
clenched round a furled helix
hardly glimpsed before intelligence slows output, a scam
to put the brakes on productively,
throwing tendrils or roots but no pathway it might grip.
The ascenders were broken off,
rib shears, pain's locks, its cast of mind for dilucid burial.

Eyes fill with stone. Presently the sediment lingers down,
smoothes away the pits &
pores disfigure this block of mourning glints covariantly.
What shimmered above was no less
great to feel, despite the controvertibles of touch & trust
thicken in fat soot below;
every take calcified by hand which on every count scored.

Dragged half-conscious through its slats, sent reminders
        heard as cries off dropped water,
scuff in a finger-bundle knotted to keep what is assessed
        incorrigible; come in the skimpy ones
who gave heart for derivatives, spotlit at stipendiary bay.
                Cuckoo-pain or such froth
demonstrate what cried empire out of their translucence.

But every soft forgotten feigns indifference to that finger
        looks upon it. The scallop
may be prised open, letting the astral fragment fly above;
        pick up what flutters back
sliced as if for a barbecue, in defeated pads gobstopping.
                To be a pilgrim
means open & shut will lie snapping in its starry harness.

Immanence leaps its own wand mentally it hops & scoffs
        unsatisfied its foam hinterland –
that's where the playground signage went, some existent
        partner carries a torch
whose pollen trespasses the chalked no-go. The half-face
                affronts half a face.
Then to sleep together calmly & impassively were shingle.

Shall thundersheets baffle their tents be they fly or furled,
conditional between the shit-faces
cantilever winds; shall this portent strip the sour washing
Human Capital Programme
flaking or disjointed, grip childishly throughout the night?
Think were going to step-
fail, penduline on air which strips them rigidly distraught –

that was their stuff, insects. When triangulated, set down
for a caution, for a mercy
bedded in their fold entitles show-through to its fools cap,
they shall mark edge, exiguous.
Undertow of shadow was to be what swung for weighing.
Slots within the false fruit
bolstered & guyed like a tent dissembling to full capacity.

Their mount of folly mounts yet further with a false peak
bears the table rock-silent, on
the altar lies a conventional knife. Rend the tautened cloth,
cut its guy ropes so to think a hill
downrightly, plumed in thunder will it nursed in thought
free of the shame in folds –
bring off a bolder stroke, deposit the winged ants instead?

The house of cards then falls
the opposite way, to circadian order.
Curtains slump on shagged mattresses,
rerun
lost to view, jolting automatically
the way they fold,
the way they stack beside sleep

& after entertaining daylight
crease on the runnels ants patrol.
Shall they smother their disturber
moaning after who'd forgive,
blowing his ring
blowing his eye-stalls by episode,

jiggles his bunch of fingers
splits his keys:
How shall he render odds, get even
& give nothing out?
but spew a trail of infected fat
will soften drains & lay
prairie plumbing. On their trigger
legionaries of Mara shall drop

owl-like with their stone-age
machine-guns
prominent from their ruffs, firing
tumble-weed, the termite
columns picked off in spats of dust
untether & reorganise.

What does he need to act right?
their moving wick
his tallow will then sheathe,
some thread like a vicarious nerve
inside its tubular bed?
At a pinch the illusionists monkey with

his lump by brilliant tremor
Reciprocal when an arch

oubliette each eye
is shuttered inside, the cherry-petal
pads of trapped alacrity
leaking what I had lent & want myself
however they fall, fall
aporetic on what pillow.

At heart the light slows down,
kick-starts his fluttering organs
throb
Wrapped in a coherent aura.

Embargoed bring to tie up the loose ends squall & buffet.
        Some day this artillery
scuds their palm will not unfurl its aperture is gridlocked
        Some day a body dragged out
bequeaths its painful atmospheres that incubate like gas
                bars collect the scraps of energy,
each flame above each wound fluttering in ignorant light.

The eye, the teeth of a storm snatch to flower the diadem,
        flame petals rip but reassemble.
Droplets hiss between wraiths interlace for another heart
        of touch going by construal
held up, stuck down. The ingots clamped on the horizon
                float as if their ballast
buoyed by the scrubbed air had been juiced & now afloat

assert their coverage & ponderously circle. The fiery boss
        pivots with new confidence,
lashed to a twisted throat its bucking bars, no a threshold
        should vibrate Aeolian,
mount it as the gnomon's vegetable heel shall order light.
                Dividers court possession,
swivelling in on after-draughts, keeping like for each end.

Snap those optic fibres had been styles for their shell-like
        bear the stigma break to glow in
perinatal flux. Carbon & the dream of it were ring-sealed
        dreams defend their coil,
aligning the idea of a dream to a step of high quadrature.
                Stuff & real stuff
wax its fog distortion by resist then turns out on a drum.

Clip it opaque upliftingly, though its leading parts screw
        over the catchment area
force but can't influence, their pandemonium ticks reflex
        off by numbers like a devil's claw,
those they pollinate will furl down in paralysis will please
                their wanting-to-be-captive,
suck them into the hopper, sacrificed sleepy side forward.

They just seemed to click. Quite how its stiff new thumb
        got lodged into the chimney
stalls a dream of the day's finery, mummified in backlash
        shadow wrestles point by point
the dragonfly to offer you its thorax: like ever the relative
                does all gloved in ruby
welted shake, grab its wisp recoil, scrunch its deathshead.

The perianth now its windbreak if they stump: Walk off.
        Teach them once the jump-leads
wake a sealed unit, feed them into a taking white formula
        drools wide open – this example
claps the ears, will box its mouth in turn, the photocopier
                leafs the forest pennant
out of shingle, to command its lines of pith with one pass

hauls their shadows inwardly, the naked fork where falls
        a crinoline of through-light,
hypertrophic on blowback fences handsful of wet leaves.
        It is known drawing focus
from their opposite continue to prospect in skeletal pods.
                Head to head were scratched.
Then what was left when a face between like a slug duels

in cutaway were bracketing shots, contacts off their body
        laced at index length secure.
They go as sky in a new slouch might reveal them wholly
        faithful to such things
obvolved in memory were sheaves of duplicate stiff parts,
                accepting what is made of them,
have to yield their first idea like moisture is drawn by salt.

Steep enchantment stacks up to crown a throat instructor
        vertical, joining canters hectic,
for staring in retrospect joy was but such gaseous clouds
        gorging in advance by taste,
the more truly imitative the more varied what they threw.
                Diffusely bump along
Reaching for the stars but they lose buoyancy, piss & shit

the same & not the same shall interweave for ripple-effect
        then separate like curds & whey –
skies bulging with mythology, scarf a wake of dead yeast.
        Truth-timing was the simple lever.
More analogies salute like cuckoos that drawn backward
                ply slots the gods deserted –
none was meant to widen, but hooting down so urgently

gapes in flagrant purity, a free-range egg is date-stamped
        before through a sign-stimulus
curls inside ectopic when grip fails, that shameless throat
        shook ears like they want it,
o they couldn't but accommodate its strain. Vapours pass
                representing, no agenda
stood down their stand-in, hugging knees, cough, fidget

fire unremittingly the receptor site set far squint. Inquire
        which way the wind blows,
the lie of the land already 'yields' in a shameless caricature
        unfit to plead. The screw-fits
ruckle as did the lever-with-a-coin's, the palm's crossing
                clanks, squeaks & batters
on the forecourt over the ciborium, the scooped-out tank,

a funnel gummed with sperm & a carafe of sticky residue.
        What came first, the skinflint
or the squander? First & last smudge open, slot inspired
        into the constant with a goldfinch,

a dew-cup, a petal-crusted portrait-frame, anterior lights
                    inwardly thought to mean
plump gods bob & dip exulting over the stunned catalyst.

Here is a slice the shutter took now curls on aching gloss
like damask off its opening
kneels clumsily, & the maker's mark is indistinguishable.
Light replies like stiff oil
staggers a whisk. Curls of butter, brandy-snaps, turbans
of spun sugar soften out
nevertheless, the seamstresses reward their own creatures.

They don't deserve the homage. If do table-work & strip
the mattering pathways
strangle that they wrap self-curing, the dull brain retards
about a trophy it persists with,
being in its mental coil as obdurate as it gets. Its angle of
declivity deflects a stone edge,
trembling on withdrawal rips through the tensed drapes.

So send a set of duplicates by courier & meet the damage.
        My Sanjay too, but smiling . . .
No skin off my face is grazed against boxed-in banisters,
        or lurches up a narrowing spiral
called a bonnet, till the single wall has me by both elbows.
                Is the wall warm or chill?
Is its impulse fundamental decency, or a reflex I chalk up?

How else should it carry? Through straits anticlockwise
        like a shell e.g. a biconic
open newel stops the urgent throat, or a clenched cowrie
        unexpectedly spills or retracts –
cannot be separate from or for its shadow it might slough
                ever turns upon & loves
with all the emptiness a heart can muster, was generosity.

Second Run

At the Photocopy Machine

These were tenements which host to too great integrities
called nothing to stoop. Fair copies
having been taken, inferences talliable went close-packed,
crisply as at first. A coin or chip
by contrast, for all that world withheld is chiding & feels:
rant & rave then, weary out
a sugary lump, pluck their entourage stints for approval.

Snatches reel out flimflam, how farsightedly make use of
birdsong for their taunt. Its tack
of disposition, such as set a master to perm chip by chip,
teeters as if abseiling or
put back, orchards & rabbits throng concomitantly true.
What they circle round?
some wodge a set-face PA taps & bends to load, alleviate

the urge to cut loose: always the facade must stay bright!
This was the gateway as bulkhead.
Fingers twine their shadow friends but will elicit no help
reinstates a fluffed or two-faced
harbinger or flaw their desirous scene was eventful from,
tasking each other's joinery
despite the fly heat or cormorant chill, dead dazzle proof –

too close to build the model, jolts its elbow or will skimp
on the material, fabricate askew.
Over-prevalence brought its lump to the tip of a tongue's
industry; on these tin islands
tenements or rabbits get inverted but to congruent scale.
Rant & rave then, weary out
beside a washbasin, nothing grows but it was equivalent.

Square-set the master lowers down the stairwell, glooms
        treaclish in a cloistered sky,
mouthing coin like the sun's disk illumines spicks of dirt
        odds had been predictable,
will wrap its fruit in tissue even as the object self-abjures:
                its fruit which shall pay
inside a fixed aperture, aligned to an inert double crown.

Just how long will that pay their rent for? Or free radical
        technique by girth or fingermark,
in cutting quality, storage, powder burns from its feeling
        automatic, the splicing of stock film
is keyed to an original, but the project's custom windows
                replicate as a lump dissolves,
flicked in coins below the escape to rust, pip & coagulate.

Eye Trouble

Flat against the rhythm track the unified theory advances,
each sentence starts 'and', & spurious
connectives reconcile: all are migrant, the whole resource
scarred by this pathology. Place
each face down, will memorize each long enough to copy,
slipping between rollers, through
horizontal gates to slide into Tray B unruffled, creaseless:

hissing copies scrawl walls in tick plumets of feuillemorte.
Favour them, their outgo squares
flesh with stone, the chiselled profile lining up its shadow
claps-to like a door hangs light,
& fruit trees will rotate rotting cherries & bletted updates –
plush below their shared-office
accumulation, ghosts on the walkway tiptoe their canopy.

So what is this catches in the throat? Like a cistern rattles
rightly, complete, fit-for-purpose –
like a physical remnant tugs or overblown insipid melody
circulates the wilful stalk:
stops in its tracks, blushes white, it can't keep up; thumb-
marks complicate such sound,
glittering like quartz will restructure the operating system.

Out of a pit below their ramp, scraped metal may release;
up in the shelving arrays
pneumatic grunts discharge, a thought regulator kicks in;
on the back of a trailer bike
a CV in its pizza box; skies imperial whisk & chronology
spirals through the air, a reading
across domains ties down functions wish to blow, period,

drives exchange by one for one occludes the rip blow-out.
This device chokes any interference
received: the hand snakes its needle & thread or spanner
stubs against invisible little jets –

that windy scamp would transfix the marshalled muscles
along their file-paths,
wish-merriment throbs error messages, pulsing in hippus.

A Word in Your Shell-like

Quiet was the square itself, so intracted in its inner glow,
        held in brittle underdeveloped
pods divided by each spring, that a figure blinks violence
        (implacable its latest fold)
backing off collapses, squints the OK to a sharp-shooter
                picks a particular fruit,
trains shadows, trains masks, pins down with highlights,

& intimacy relies on distance to pull its true image. What
        need to unfold it further?
This dawn seems the dawn spread across their wall-eyes
        took the distance, but yet
in withdrawal realises its full spread, the old hit-the-spot
                hoist was disengaged,
fumbled as the blusher in the makeup suite's near-truth.

Threw off restraint, but the launcher flops piece by piece,
        lets go & clunks wearily. Finches
dot the staves like a pomander in cloves, see a fuchsia red
        crease to dazzle from,
while thistledown administration makes float away before
                pleat invention, flickering
cloud-shadow wilts on the heather, bunches over granite.

Too neat a fit. It stops down as netting stiff with creosote,
        as a jelly-bag udders with
pips & mauve skin, wrung ischaemic in the blonde array,
        evidence its faces in the lees.
Pull-backs couldn't ease blood or slip bonds generously,
                between lips was dead space,
the beats of pitch-&-toss in its shrunk pulp were pitiless.

Clay pigeons, bags of water shatter & explode, a prompt
        will spill its meant outcome:
seeing is what seeing does & the tongue furls like a tulip
        odourless as white goods

plied against expanses whose dead cells have been locked
                in radiant, folded sheets,
& gurgling crawl his back was silenced in knurled shells.

When touch stops up at fingers to protect what touching
        hooks & tears, skin being held
negligible, will their depths too be cauterised, contained?
        The sun sighs like a pillow,
earth rashes in a longed-for sward. A stealthy marksman
                chinks his sight on glasses;
all collapsing in devolves into these shells that quietly lap.

Obelisk

The universals race, pushing aside presets, the full heart
        launched off involuntarily,
hold filled with fine skins, cowries, gems which were eyes.
        Raise the new capital & chorus.
Its dizzy shown frontage marble-clad, is a Potemkin wild
                with ghosts, admits nobody:
no report is current but that which shivers the tin islands.

Where disks had jiggered out for counters I spread news
        through the vacant boardroom,
breathing on mirror surfaces. A scheme is by such token
        not a person (or vice versa).
A stone is not a stone but a hot hearth capping emptiness
                had squandered their titanium
rib-stuffed vertebrae. Curtains behind them jacket lustre,

in key bunches bear results, indexes & standing in public,
        the compensatory voices hang
are shed in four-decker tape is spirals onto the shiny rug.
        They burn there, their secretary
wipes the tape between her ears & fingers Shall this fizzy
                die-for-it discriminate
in the medium term, dredge one message for its director?

Non-stock voices shake aspirin boughs, resentful overlap
        & flapping coats will see bulk.
How faulty was their take-up (both ways) would cover it;
        a full course of stone is laid
against absconsion held to cost. Full-pelt a bracelet flexes
                the nervous cord, so help you
part implies; stones rattle surrogate, Assisted Conception.

'Open' is their gauge who would master the presentation
        skates dazzling surfaces.
A marble headboard blinks over a bed of algedonic gravel.
        Fire-ants raise like scabies

rights of the so-signed in their runes, a long flame yearns
                    to skitter from its funerary,
a will-o-the-wisp dancing over the marshes behind sings.

The Blink of an Eye

Click or snap or so the rifle seeding on all fronts its hydra
 mayhem over drear, spitting smoke
from its puckered bay, fomenting what it had needs must,
 the sun streams still, particles
will irritate a voided chamber: But sun can never compile
  its expression & will fizzle out.
White fingers carry this less glimmer & snap sorrily fault.

The indulged fault by its lower quay could uplift distress.
 A high fault locates & kissing dark
resigned the self-slipped skull to treat its difference, sum:
 skin of a rapt servility
swelled so taut anticipates one round can pierce, burn or
  burst soul recoil on through,
derogates to watch, trembling admires a mensual routine,

bolts out universally to circle & pin down with fiery seed.
 The sun suggests there are worked,
gone terrifying reasons underlay such incandescent trace
 outlives the mouth. One single shot
or sheaf had set its more conniving course, one small dab
  post-hoc would shrink
to a mascle sported like a pendant in the eye, a set comma

blinks brushed with webs to contain the reaction, caustic
 threads of spit were a cream's horn.
Here a spice engobbed disports a breath sheathed within
 & invites one sidelong foil.
Nutmeg bloats the mace, slicks into the rasp o imperious
  mentor kneaded out of shreds
beats within its col of salt, a reef below this burning floor

throws rubbery stalks like a devil lobs their tracer-shells,
 finding work for the hard saps
wrung & rubbed & budded whenever a tear might swell
 offshoots out from it, ruining

its particulate world was its band never brought to proof,
never was previously disturbed.
Save where the kiss is thickening fiery on a cocked finger.

Folding a Scarf

In the room where secretaries sat the old workings yawn.
        But it was a calm arrival
held laptop, gave dictation, against the door leant hooded.
        Rays would coil & beat. Here a woman
squats on the earth before the threshold, kept for trophy
                with proud nipples, useful hips,
raising fallout bruises glow like emblematic snails crest.

Spoked flanks quickly get wheeled on to stop the mouth,
        reconnect a limb dangles
through its shutters so an outline hauls out fully-fledged.
        Who longs to collapse flushes orange
princess. Aggrieved spirit giddies & perms & rebuilds,
                tearing off a long, clear
sweat-thick plastic bag, bicuspid like a cherry dumps on

twined favours' soft-landing, spread where stintless rays
        put about them gallantly,
that cluster sparking off the lymph nodes re-inter as one.
        Gendered with carnations
fisted bundles unclench, these too voluntarily consumed
                vectorize point-to-point,
making love with an eye to love-making. Now won over,

filled & capped when a man's eyes slot down to interface,
        glow sullenly, discharging brown
rubber invertebrates pull off a stroke with no seam whirr
        furious in the imago, cockchafers.
Suffice this progeny of their threesome straddles the pit.
                A carriage return slams
heavily in the strap-lingam pupae o his mouth is pursing.

Mainstream entertainment. Loop. As a tip-malingerer's
        brute calliper seems chased
with stock vision, jabs & pulls to clinch the rays' turban
        Tucked into the up-&-over

fire flickers above the curling carpet tiles, hooks tendrils.
                    Has to be firm compliance
among parties inch away from the pit would ask their all.

Internal Audit

No compensation forward, nor edging-tape, nor button
        thought went ever so far
as ground itself reflective makes lighthearted use of bay
        espaliers, mounted on each pole
its clef of starlings, signed above a bruise's spiral recess:
                saw it coming always,
attached to a bud outgrowth relaying as two might graft

like a tree there, a biomass, the coupling of nub & spiral
        strews the sweating shiny leaves
with imp devices teetering on footprints, gaily improvise.
        Downwardly they bevel,
hanker for the pit spews out these complimentary pairs,
                blight sent its burning
premise was the floppy hooks are catching at their roots:

A door shuts. A desk partition topples. Now a day temp
        with trembling resolution lit
shifts the gearing off its spindle: now the cassette of fire
        will feed its rink to resurrect
the same nodding bunched cherries: animals which tick
                rub up against a glass bowl
Spot-on Adam spreads his palm to mirror back to earth.

His fingers lately frozen up, the console that withstands
        the force of such a rebound.
Pollen, gravel chips or a dead tape hold the contribution
        swilling round a cup's brim
in calls unfolding poisonously. Shot a look were shafted,
                waited on its pleasure but
still nothing more or less extends a row of clashing noise

went gap-to-gap with the trellises, theirs a peg prototype
        a totem god might forward
likenesses hung out to dry hope to emulate, – close to him
        they should be tickled pink –,

stemmed in quickening shades interrogate feet, a curling
            structured bruise lures
by its thin piping, chats of courtship woken with the lark.

Duplicity to structure emptiness now retorts where back
      fell indeed at the epicentre
pumping the embargoed one might scrape its living just:
      shall it prompt fury or a making
compensated projects thrown out with bluster, summon
            up their full height:
Earth crackles, waves spit, there they burnt out draughts.

Paint It Black

Obstructed in the inner costume of its violences this rock
  was pudding stone, the genius
an upsurge of analgesics will beat against but not resolve;
  so pavement light must swerve –
but bring no cheer to those who hate its vaunting & lope
    next to it like a loose wolf,
blow on blow entreat as in wounds they could remember.

Investigate the ivy ripped from walls, whose bristly scabs
  will crown the pan-pipe shit-
stirrer, hands-off down had shoved his metered followers
  onto a scruffy dog-shit patch,
kicking about a stone where their details are held in store.
    Downwardly causative,
wedged between a rock & no place is the so-abject pillow.

Spirals in the concrete which they called Sarajevo flowers
  sheet-bombarded, corrugate the
gabbles of a hectic lip that fridge-vacant still must satisfy
  its thick & repugnant moss.
Water! Water! Fetch me my chips! Let the infirmities fill
    my dreamt hollow: they shall en-
crust over an electronic billboard as dreamt in contraflow.

What is their crackling purse so empty with? Candelabra
  rookeries raise up their cups
triple-decked in squabble, spurts of gravel see them soar
  in their communities, ancient dialling
redress settles two nights forward flat like a palette-knife
    slides into some bedroom
as a squint square blackening on the spread, for this was

their matter for choice, intense to overtrick such sombre
  premonition yolked. Endorphins
rush to neutralize the bright-rimmed cloud, frail warmth
  a tense earth strains against,

left to work out shoots had eked light had begged a crust
                    from lipped bowls of effluent,
cradled by the disconnected & superb darkness mossing.

Try a black baize door closes yawns 'open' in its defence.
          Moss dries to a mangy crust,
a lunging chisel clatters before the draught-swung gates
          Then will you see this visitor
towards the hearth, no, go upstairs, to the lump of stone
                    won't you? Arterial blood
soaks his blonde pelt, it is a stab in the dark, a phosphene.

Ant Barrows

You who seen ash trickle through transparent bone
but that it was notified, fills what walked ahead, casting
off its cloak slumps like a garland of jellyfish:
whose fingers shadow a wardrobe, make a bird or clown:
their I-love pendant gathers into what was meant by heart,
these trinkets & these flashes-in-a-pan.

Whether in lunch-break or took time at the stoker's place,
they scatter & hullabaloo before the idea of a shed –
a makeshift store or dying in spirals, either of, but both
hospitable to tumult. Ants draw a lintel, ants a thin bolster,
or marching a rubberised strip monitor traffic rates.
Screens blister, driverless rapid transit tatters the skin.

As beehives & graveheads are indistinguishable at side,
you have to be a contortionist to walk in the narrows,
their roof so high, the hooped ladders spidering.
A figure drags the bay & writes one name only freezes
'forever', 'never change', tugging its emblems
from their pits, twisting ankles & releasing them to scatter.

Melt the panel scrap to figureheads in the receiving yard,
who will be let drop, self-murdered while a hand construes
by utmost generosity, falling foul of the simple lines
blistering & scorching, lamming home like rivets.
Such a degenerate spiral into what bruises deep:
no don't stare in the well or will be giddily reformed.

Straighten not like an illness but best you approximate,
wrapped up in a necessity, upheld by frail double cords.
In the fullness of rising over the world to reach,
impersonally as the full need always freshens the arc-en-cièle
divisible as a sky freed from earth shudders,
the hitherto durable earth heaps up in vague statements.

Drifting walls serve for costume by a stony marsh
of gunpowder works, embers then in turn are medicine,
shift themselves & go on what was potassium-
clear, leaving their pile to be packed into repeatedly.
It beautifully ferments but the warmth becomes caustic.
The preachiness, the adages, the welter of tongues licks.

In this rubbish the pilot leaps up & will burn fiercely.
Come looking to identify; man as the invention
of the matter in hand will dwell on his individual lump, lord
on its inertness. Never proof. A shed to exclude draughts.
Now I'd pay tribute on the stuffed meridian
to an empty crisp packet a trickle of ants shall colonise.

You pinched, pursed creature of lids & covers
whose nostrils are so sensitive someone will feed the cannula
for you, whose attributes have been leased out.
All suchlike wish to see is perfect call-off.
Speak silently like the nerves. 'I served my purposes'
inches across the marsh & pontificates as an ignis fatuus.

Following the Grain

Brought to its device embossed there, though if germinal
a watching spike, a beard
blazing russet, paper whose whiteness despoils the heaps,
the vegetative maze crawls
engulfing detail So lunge to claim it or to catch its laden
trailer, to grab that ear
too for a husk flaring at its edge but coherent at the germ

as though mummified in baltic amber or the black gunge
stuck with quills was like it.
To pleat is more human was eyelet having come to term
latches onto the fiery flank
musing over wormholes had been patented, another side
was grossly overweight,
the fat of disappointed possession. Who'd have the nerve

asking for returns on this, swapping bauxite for oil? how
could its weight be forgone?
In the Special Economic Zone chew hungry behind-faces,
products in their trough.
Their consciousnesses race in mirror cars & the personal
financial products go belly-up,
or does money breed money? They drill the passageways,

collapse the paper chairs & icecream masks to an address
encoded in the germ. Only
spare parts can't be found, but spray-paint its mausoleum –
This tiny grain of rice
suffices for the mirror of recursive love, but sows a doubt
engraved on its surface.
The yelp of zips & disconcerted cries of children answer.

Then scatter grain on the sole-hard earth with hits of sun,
of patchouli, of sewage.
A cartload of cable will be wheeled across to be put to use
flat between dabs of scent.

I want my car & the burning speakers can never stop me:
whether the twist be amniotic,
or its leads be of aspherical glass: unlatching eyelets ached.

Third Run

Spraying & feathering toner, rainbowing into shutdown:
    as if the carbon watch-cloak
manoeuvres slant to draught, pursues an object will shift
    glamour to what it fancies, –
but coin of the realm from a tinny horn still can propose
        chucking more, the windpipe
lifts its song from the dark, back where it yearns to shut.

The least vapour became droplets. Placate in sap velocity
    off the block lips cuneiform.
Amongst collapsed stars amino acids coil matter venting.
    The hellhole, the tough shit,
chill or scorching as the crosscurrents flayed their shred
        colourful spectra, ground noise
for which there had been no foreglance but a metre taped

lifts compatibly, from her bag is someone incriminating
    swirling out in bias cut –
chewing a bumflap, inturning in darts, the hobbledehoy
    of dip, of breath thermals rise
in red lines & gilts cross-revetting their punched leather
        stiffens under notice.
Armoured contour in line, peering past a modular set-to,

that's how she lost her rags & found them, wafting stack
    castoffs like as next of kin
harvest & barter lucid pain to restore pain to steep dark.
    The collapsed brightness
broods like an eye sucks out the socket, smirched clouds'
        shadows confiscate a wink
or some derogatory spark, its skintight accent fluttered

no more than is deliberate, cap. Wriggle its scud piping
    deep where the unsingable
cannot be swallowed or hoisted to straddle attendant air,
    catches nothing but self-consumes

in panting, bronchial flames billow were sent randomly,
continually sounding off
unimpeded that might breath & velleity block or impart.

Fold here down the storied line weighs as blandishments
        said only to withhold,
aspiring for the cast of it should admit no other purpose
        warmed again that dough
proffered moist in california shag-pile, a smirk don juan
                tingling to the back teeth
asks only it draw apart, spasming such lethargy as serves

coolly to fritter out his pearl bead into the braids of four
        continuously alongside, under
their trick of weight buckling intensities of vibration-free
        fold-down tables awkward with food.
To stay cool, keep balance while their shears grind softly
                pinking oddments, all that
cloud decks & alters: no yielding pirouette, fond flounce –

yank them open so his hydroscope's drip by drip sperm
        pads out the frame in 3-D
hair-upholstered like a parent, celled like a risen brioche.
        What's the muffled clank, three
who unclinch the scaffolding first thing would brush up
                consummate life-skills:
padding down the soft roll of the aisle with its easements.

Select but with but one thought grabs the skinny steward
        bearing its ingredients, chill-
cooked for low & average levels of intimacy, their flavour
        has been processed, dreck of
Quality Adjusted Life Years. Squash the roll as a puffball
                correlates negatively
with whiteout stare a silvery snap had shrunk back before,

leaving a thought of depth scooped from a nacreous shell,
        their naked pulp back-flipping
spilt not one drop. The depth line is urgent in black seed,
        locally cowering & the fruit falls
overripe, too late the plucking hand but it shall desiccate
                remotely, a time-release capsule
wadded in this vacant sphere, puffs in slow-motion. Who

will its fruitfulness be bestowed on? The range might list
        as home-made, as hand-milled,
the finger-rolls rising corpulent, poppy-strewn, attractive.
        Then tape in vulcanised carpet
Soak at the moorings. Wiggle free the sterilised fine tube
                will probe this aneurysm
homed-to, dump its load, reflected in a tray when stacked.

They'd meant to extract in caoutchouc, embryos, gelatine,
tucked-to make a spasm cornet
matched for their skin friend a graft won't reinstate ever –
Square-regress, their bell & cup
snuff like harebells over flame withered into rings of soot.
Between the backup lights
a delegate of hearts will palm deftly, nods each smoky joe

tulip through the pink diaphragm will shunt *in media res*
his sainted latchkey child
to stacks accessible in memory. So they were backing up
like ground elder in their network.
Keck into that vase as would a thrush have tuned its note
quivering the lily-earnest
filled with tears holds a room-key firm in amber or aspic.

Down the aisle's fairway he putts the rubber to a gaping
pocket to suspend the nervous
ground of being. Squares of sweetmeats. Arranging fluff
into as fast-disappearing haloes
fledge among the girders squawking clangorously: I I
seek foothold on the saved tower,
president over a napkin sure the residues are scooped up.

When the psychic system fails its subordinate shall think,
lengthening out of no-way-
disowning, rides the brilliant lanyard given its head, slots
the whole into the first place,
busying though it slacken. A spindle hauls its puny scope
circled by hygienic blossom:
this way reports, measures the light saturation underfoot.

Its inventory upholds the stained glass when motes fizzle
through the atrium dominates
the HQ building. Chunky steel-frame chairs were drawn
away by servants white-clad.
Inside an access tunnel, children doze with scorched feet.
Don't neglect the edifice
whose nearness to collapse has an organism waiting on it;

over its splashed granite floor some are fucking by intent,
they let everything else go hang
crumpling like a tin, spindling like a plastic box! Because
of staring at the glass too long,
not its transcriptions burnt across an endless foyer stuck,
but acts of perverse inference –
on the backs of children, flattened saints & martyrs glow.

A smile stretching out peg to peg to supervene on trauma.
They stood about the buffet
fixing their sallow dials, touched off cheeks off-handedly
picked needles from the welting.
The dead bones of what they loved shall lift their mouths
spat at filleted ghosts
once they had been rebound. Rattling up the missed eyes

lip hookers bruise their correlates who frozen to the skin
squat behind in soot, in worldwide
cavernous sheds there echo too much hurtfully & thump
like graders sort at flower trestles.
Such dying flickers gave them heart, such hemline shiver
pout, tongue-lash behind
lips that on one glimpse would brush o flange imperious –

They are more feeling now when constructively forgetful.
In dailyness their hanging flaps
go interested. With my body I thee hybrid we did & died.
Hover. Paw for its openings.
They are too fit to purse against the blinds in the lapsing
ceremony of what touches.
Looks to harrow the unnoticed in grooves of faded smiles.

Hook out those bones jiggling in the stockpot sling-it-all
        antecedents, paint the yellow shield
polyunsaturate, sloughing like a scratch-card or his skull!
        The graders groan internally,
wrench the sooted windows & the skylights lime-daubed,
                rub the glass for a little warmth
soothing the circumference, a styptic web to lay on cuts.

What separates us spreads the sheet on which we couple.
        What unites draws its strength
from what stays unlinked. What is shared divorces. Such
        is my integument is yours,
swirling in its bias cut clings & falls, a veil hides & gapes
                responsively. Pinned-up hair
flies to unguarded gears engage, tugging tightly to reveal

a shaved map, a bone-ridge scalp, its seething glue eyeful
        in cuerpo had been latticed
by hot numbers, misaligned but fascinated held the stare
        raps their sentence boned out,
rechokes the engine where a thunder sheet of corrugated
                limbo represents the ground,
a floral clock blows, an arum lily stinks, the pitcher wells.

Glazed in heat then quickly frozen, glistening in cohorts,
fat of the land knuckles them:
although a controlled, selective judgment strategy looped
peg to peg latches ever tighter
puncturing a roofless shed in stabbing crocuses, lengthens
a dream bridge to here,
freeze & burn & set in snowy fat their axles freewheeling.

Each validates his own imperious shade, proxy who more
flexible scouts his inveterate
chaser after his own flesh self-employed will cut its aliases:
reflexes may dangle loose
like old sash-cords or like paper streamers bear no weight,
but one clot is heart-rending
truly to the way things have turned out, kick its hubcaps.

Frail flesh a personal ramp be if though sun blots the sun
stuffed in bracket cheeks bracket
will by degrees hollow out a change in orientation, cheek
eclipsed for heavy plugs
Enough exactly, that heart may feel. One side or its other
cruciated, beats out time:
the hand dangles freely to be gloved now & held to point.

Flop – a pan of ashes trenches its way through the rancid
        educated fat, is seething down
to pockmark, to stud for growth. Every fillet hinges back
        as invited, & the exposed spine
ratchets out the gangway a heaven squit arrogantly walks,
                while dropping away above
the ripped-free forfeits venture in hierarchical regression.

Planets break orbit, comets plunge, sun-dogs either side
        glower at their run-off
trickling down the slot to cool, enamelled trough for this
        fiery milk. & still in the feeder
tributary the heat discharged fizzes in a tray of clinker ice.
                Semble like sherbet. Pack-ice
flakes as though stripped of words, shattered so a toneless

phrase spells it once more in bloodshot eyes pan vacantly,
        pausing on an ankle ramp,
stare where the subject flaps away. If ropes could tempt:
        they wouldn't climb but tug
routinely, ash & sperm daubed on bales of cotton waste.
                They hug their inflatable jackets,
cold creeps up their shins. Safe as they are beyond feeling.

Inside-out each lining then goes visible, despair & smiles
honeycombed throughout
the rich lesions. At the tip of a poking tongue the woolly
eucharist, a midget carpet tile
sits half-dissolved. Construct a bud, tight tooth amalgam
at the face ensepulchres,
rots hourly to the nerve, spills pain by reference & beside

itself with non-productive pain it brings the blossom out
from soft tile, from furry cheek
each subject had for backing, by glue or starch or syrup:
these caught expression like a
peel-off X-ray, stuck like irradiated spores over cardboard.
Drag across their lightness.
Then all you must compliantly as flywheels nodded down

embed in brow or finger where it corrugates, their traffic
calming corpse of a baby
dragged from the beside park, mauled by flashlight dogs;
encode it for its delicate smock
in finger pads, falls to seed which fell on weak & dazzled
ground could not be said, neither
stammer, tasting lip-gloss, *'I I I? Was I cut out for all this?'*

No dispute a burning wreck contrives a tolerable outcome:
        some spatchcock retainer
padding about on a grille above puts two & two adjacent.
        A lovers' knot churned spectral
any fletch of eyelashes, scalloped lips too moist to launch –
                vestiges of the loved one
digested for namely farce, ash into the humours of the eye.

Had it rolled out of my head like wheeling from an atelier,
        if from my heart a fluke
togetherness, fires of the damned rise up to diffuse what's
        held at the core tightly furled,
fire burns through all activity moves on the same account.
                Napped with low blue fire,
flagged with a wild yellow, pitch was buttered near & far.

It fluctuates & thus I made my foothold though my edge-
legislator stills that trumpet
troublingly, echoically fixed bounce; contoured resonance
quelled a night's revolving
heedlessly might churn it first, mess that disposition goes
to hinder its dilapidating
into radiance, heaping carbon dust will print a toposcope.

Forgiveness has stretched across its flat roof more like tar,
black & void of feature.
& what is the curtilage of such a capped inferno, product,
how much does a tree draw
for its life's water, or volume does a flame void of oxygen?

Eyes opt for kissing babes they can train on, resolving lost
    breath of surgical spirit. Smile.
Don't disturb that cousin, your gaze will empty her purse
    rummaged in gauche warmth
like a puffball a look would rip did straining lips not hold.
        Touch anemones were minded.
You cannot kiss me that well you are carrying something.

We are too particular against snow & sand & fat. Or else
        (repeat, repeat to vapour.
    You don't have to touch any to order.

White turf covers the handholds, fog blisters seal the lark
        configured from chirps in a box:
the centrifuge or the ammonite clock which believes itself
        to muster its own smoke, *is it*.
How do I get rid of mildew grows on a lens? Take its blur.
                Walk in / Dance out.
Not stoop but climb: convince the down at heel till sheer.

Glass cabinets crack about a haul they put a good face on,
                prop a rainbow as prettily
diffracting such borrowings, a child skips from my corpse.

Pause

Structure

What snakes autumnal but alert under the fire blanket,
scourges as in jeopardy the innocent leaves lain there
have lain long in an envelope of contrived inaction rather –
let them rot if contrivedly, wear through to the lace
like thumb-nails in the image bank show their structure,
dispensing with structure for what it counteracted
so to pique direction, to tire into the accident that saves.

The bristle clump abrades their envelope, in relief
makes the bones ache & eyes blink dryly. Self knowledge
then is self seal. Invisible pyjamas, so accommodating!
They will arrive ready-opened; used, but being used,
much safer. Can this be what they will settle for? Fortune
in its car will notch down as they struggle to make tense.
To think that flesh too once was called ephemeral.

Silence browns the bloom from the fields, pipe turnings
have been stopped with icy trucks. So all limits curl –
waste cooking oil libates on the patch to shale white
emulsified like abdominal frost, glues the flap
flutter of every desirable thing, shut. Turnip tops also
would be beautiful. If the emphasis were on design,
best to take any at face value. To see its face & scrub hard.

Even the stinking leftover of brussel sprouts on poignant
shares of earth. The tightness of rye bread. Time
passes over the cheek with its shiny trail on. Only those
who have never felt pain could wish to know the structure
of their food or their muscles' concert. Keep in a scratch
file, on the slate. Was it to think or to take thought
away, scratched into the bone task, could lend opacity

to the brilliantly hoared ground, on every crumb of
loaf an advertisement, obliterating into full presence?
Then they retract, they believe almost any old shit
will empower them, but that doesn't mean it's beautiful.
O to be so bound up that the blood is only the gnats'
whine as it makes the surrounding silence an evidence,
or was that the tinnitus which attends to itself at the roots?

Manners

Have you heard? If what had been heard kept a scrap
in its involutions, it was then for hearing to be deceived,
& it has been more than half deceived. Flame licks
the tiltable chair, the most organised of workstations
browns & starts to blister, & does that nylon mesh really
wrap a woman's tongue? Why fear the familiarity so
that it is evident only where it snuggles into closure, –

clingfilm on a previous book or bubblewrap for beakers?
A wedge of mud hiccups from the cleft & then flows
thick with perambulators, mangles & typewriters. Is
this as near the heart as can be acknowledged? What
of its new release, its transfer, its appliqué laid over
the inscrutable whose unmoved pieces soak up movement
like springs? Preferable is the keyboard if its characters

half-rubbed-out, a dirt road, the thorns – on the face of it
in any event, gives them shine. Valves yawn & perish,
every leading lady had caught her look somehow but
she does infrequently, head down in the tin islands.
Mitigate the path with flickering light. Water paddles
lift upon their spindle & are caught up in the mud slide,
do they urge it forward or are they just carried away?

Someone who died recently, a little anachronistic, a bit
repetitive. Did you hear that news? She was for sure,
like propping the sky up over the mud, like holding
covers up over the mattress as though a tent were a laugh.
Like her perished lungs leave voice behind pages
gone in the libraries; who is stopped stays always & what
circulates becomes indifferent, wrapped & stickered.

Swivel to endure the flames loud in their commentary.
Blacken margins, spill on the hot marble like day's
running shadows have been exposed & are perdurable,
the dead set inclines. Here the flapping heard has bound
my head like martens are returning despite the cool
remembrancers of the last minute, their personal jordan
pissing upon their feet as they unwind, interminably.

Darkness in a Gold Frame

Estrangement now is the daily bread, the defamiliarised
for clothing – so as orectics we tease, smirk & scatter
through carnal ordinances. Pressing round us watch
on drains thick & soft with fat those grasping at entirety,
the torture in a metaphysical sense we long cast adrift.
Who shipwrecked retrieve their spars, the brands
we'll expunge, a grille knuckles cross-wise to their ribs,

but our arms, ours, are fastened the other way round,
outstretching digits will go root through scarless skin,
a plastic, a material spirit at bidding heals & self-builds –
rearrange the skyline, come to think. We orectics bestow
on these mounted in our gold frame – employment;
what binds tight to their succession is weary as what
clothes labels call the authentic & genuine, the original.

But how they blunder about. Coherence is their snack,
entireties which would be worth having, but what's this –
clasp the chest, eat the food, talk the tongue, food has lost
savour & whose words are hobbled, shoes clumped
with earth can't fleet through interstices a city allows?
Clumsily they would forge whilst we scribble light.
Their violent politics would forge so to make the link

adamantine, their bulk is a residue they carry like a cross.
Idempotency – great stuff, kids. The stamp is a float:
what is skin-deep if not the structure? In sight of stacks
protected by their net warp, they look & chunter on.
That is a pivot poised by wrinkle & tug long-sightedly
Can't be caught so doing. Better the devil you don't know
in the midstream will arrest those who serve for a time.

We the orectics squeeze our organs through their purse
& feel something give. That is ripeness like dropsy
whose mini-explosions spit spores to the end of the earth –
not earth, not ends, but a glistening sphere. Why, the
filaments cover the globe out of one naked lightbulb.
Then these are ordained, the only way anyone might live,
3 million migrant workers are ordered home at a flicker.

Zwitschermaschine

To be put through to another, distance must be kept –
as on the phone, how else can you engage one without
the distraction of shallow skin or motive so contingent
it becomes amusing, or distress itself gets patterned?
But the call comes from the stranger who cries suddenly,
asking you do anything but stupid love stops you.
The world it presides over buckles & your forename

becomes a surname for one who stakes your humanity
on a broken voice. The webs shrivel to grains of dirt,
but how their structures haunt! As gibberish they
worry your lover during the night but fully reassemble
when you clock in, & into them you burrow to be
delivered to a committee room as previously appointed.
The car seat adjusts automatically & heats your back.

The swivel chair is angled & sight lines fully cleared.
Ills & unhappiness have been thrown in a room together,
& on the storeroom window-ledge are the empty cans
of Special Brew, the syringes & discarded roaches.
What climbs out to ask for love & gets it like a spiritual
hernia, piercing the folds of the administered world?
Going the opposite way, wrapped hands mess about

corrupted organs, masts on unspoiled heights – no scar.
Shake a stick at one, there you go. Milk the corridor or
fertilize the glass partitions: neither *does* but *disposes*.
Spectacles slide off, earstuds & earphones are visible
on slumped heads like zips left gaping. A mobile
means being always in the same place, contactable at
all time by the winged flights of hormones, the pineal

seed exchange like glittering salt is crystallised on fat –
& what falters makes this bequest, microprocessors
operate a withered arm through known structures, pull
low-hanging fruit to be digested in a plastic self-seal.
The caller states that she is touched badly by the men,
they all have sex with her, & despite medication
she feels fire from the waste-paper bin. She will set it.

The Blown Rose

Revisit her in her bedsit in Sheffield, concrete eyebrows
        on an incline, fire in the
rubbish bin, paper handkerchiefs, tampons, cotton buds
        crackled by her stare alights:
then to resist. *Asi. Asi.* Burning away the combed stubble
        outside Royston. Circa when.
Or underfoot under massiveness, beneath Godre'r-graig

history on rumour breaking forward the correct tongues
        like a wrap of polythene
tongue-lashing while the arm hands in, the heel grinds.
        Can love make it wholly useless –
like those beauties that though crumpled persist in name –
                soup or a scalp treatment
fished out then add water, sops like rehydrated croutons?

Will you double or quit? Those old grounds will reassert,
        moonshine on a dark hill,
nominal fat will clutch & clamp your head. Either paths
        go right through you,
or you will tread down anyone. Maybe it was Cairo zoo –
                the ostriches, the dust –
or in Bradgate Park the pulpits, no the bins opening fire

as though pain would lend its tongues for a processional.
        Treatment left her scalped.
The unadopted street she paces, gratings thick with hair
        caught the cinders chattering.
Asi. Asi. Were you ready to tuck the shyest, the most lacy
                of blankets, beaten out
of thick serge; a shiny patch of having been elbowed out –

I'd know that fedora! You're some pimp, you're François
Mitterand, you're a real love –
who lavishing like a joint stripped of fat appears authentic
under Sainsbury spotlights.
Sure you have some room left? What does a name matter?
Tuck the trailing end
up behind your ear & lay for a fuse. *Asi*. Shut up & deal.

Signs of an Intruder

From a Terrace in Tuscany

Clearly but this cartouche,
was it an exhaustive bitter train
                    flares from the seed –
even such geometry as
shakes its ventured flower out?

Why not prefer that orb whose
unreflective case
        empties
hot rubbish in the remembrance,
a long time
        past to this canonist
hybridizing bleached songs.

Section one, section forever,
        & the interminate
length of sentence was the germ
        in repair, unrolls,
rubs within the capsule
protecting it.

Diligent or contrary? Re-
pollinate strip or thirsty spike
                    engineer
snap chemical clock
also known as
        have the best bits for mine.

But you must buy a key next year,
                    they last one season.
Light must be shed
through the definitive leaves,
        & a particular case
stabilize their flickering

makeup like the positional
winged ants
mote by mote plume as completely.
                    Is it nothing
rasps, raps, the chisel-
plumpnesses bursting to stick,

all slow dredge enzyme?
            Their chewing-gum
parades, the starch, the sperm
                    rip iridescence
down to the tasked traffic, edging-

blade honeycomb run by the mill,
will thicken sky, dispose of
            flights of cellophane.
Their filthy light
sings through any such delivery:

scar taste was the only distance
unrolls
            Cut the brilliant flower.
Fade.

Irrigation

Whatever I did does well enough,
        but I was done
        over in bits,
& what is the voice I use
but their transposition,
        a carry-over,
a show-through,
shining through our shingled
heap of estrangement at the out.

A measure of care & spoken to
        has sedimented
down in the way
the powerful will applaud.
I clap myself,
creating a world for the untenable
        or flail
about for the general good or to
stay abreast. The free voice

has been cut off & its side-suckers
grow like withies all round
        exhaust their stock.
Inside the acoustic hood
unanswered
calls to the hotline bristle –
        this is the only
shelter from the fluorescent light
& slack fungi bunch there also.

I want you to hear my answer
mounted on its thick
        dampening cartilage
only you get through.
Read it through the layers
emblematically

like a bleeding heart on
flowered wallpaper
sinks into the brick
made porous beneath its influence.

The Evidence Base

Hitch up those glasses,
            rotate the knurled ring.
Here is that preponderant light,
grin the surgeons & barristers
helped to a portion,

needs no instruction from the set-
at-nothing,
                    of-little-account
beside the welded water-jet,
the secured TV,

independent of the fixed focus
            scud & whose delivery
systems fly between rows.
Dabbing each closed face
   it steals innocently,

stealing off them nevertheless
the facepacks of new
evidence, the pimple record
strummed subliminally
   tucks up,

racks up the tension one twist.
            Transom bars lock
into their jaws, the foaming bit is
holding them on-
message, rising share.

Confident to fill the
bed will lie on them like steel
posts configure
palms & soles for their flush
                    ball-&-socket

keeping mouths occupied,
fully kept to place to convince

how like tension lifts to alleviate
the locked stone will be
schistose, battery plates –

what of the welt
lines then lock *pietra dura*?
The outside lights lessen.
They're fireflies
They're stuck

flaring
oncidia

glue-ear
property

scab oil
witnessing of bonds.

In Seclusion

Possessions were that honeyed &
            unctuous in its case
example when brought home,
worked
perfectly in rank.
            What it held it wanted.

Any allowance would be lessened
chance of pay-out,
            any dampening
might as well mark down,
depreciating with ordinary use.
Leave the toy in its fresh
  bubble pack.

We could allow some remission
            silk against the grain,
the high-yield surface is our
chiasm-
metred object –
even pumice, even on a matt finish
as neurone sand mixed-in makes.

We visit her at our initiative,
            four-page spread.
Now over the seclusion room
lumps of light play catch-
as-catch-can & splinters
of light shower sponsored details.

Couturiers
rip their copies up, disillusioned
            confetti stock.
            She could wear
those too had she been minded,
layered above a coir

mattress lain on paper waste.
   Their shreds want entirely,

she would extrapolate herself
in loops,
            phase entrainment
trips the catwalk convoy.
Thumb this other out,
            it circles & sings mellifluously
round her cell of flat brilliance.

London Fields From Afar

Whether market forces
or upsurge in confidence
picks up their heels,
the drop-shadow slope makes
a grounded look
before the tilting windows.
Why then scurry
over the fens like crazy hearts
dressed in sun-
shine or moon-allowance.

Windows open so far.
Misery belts out the sunken vowel
stupid in its pot of
Now Jump
as legislation or style altogether
state their own state.
Jump & land in shadow
breaks their legs
then flounder like clouds stop
over the Amazon.

Watch out for skin texture.
At ground level light goes turbid
on the young thick wheat.
Where did the allergen
spray rise,
over no advance?
This is to burn, a spy glass
kindles & will blister
to admire or even pluck.

But stay.
Affluence in a capsule
will trump the next hand.
Moonshine has less

going for its fisty shafts,
its spill
of antic vowels
than the canter of such chains
the sun against the skin is locked into –

phase transition. Dust rises
beside the mauve ledge & marble
hits liquidity. Striate
over the mineral hills
plumes of vapour
blot down, their lustre
swiped between the legs' withdrawal

or as glamour counts,
but fruits weight & the granaries
shut your gob or gape
resequenced to be sterile
shall not, can never detain.
Run with the refugees
along Mare Street
to London Fields, Elysium:
Ensoulment is an instant's work
The ears pop
The eyes water.

Better the Fence

Better the fence
            than the even blink
of green corn with wilderness

Better the fence
            than the squawking
wrist advising the certain cave
'be careful now'.

In the compound
we can do much as we like

but in the simple orbit
lorries drain & dribble out,
            yellow suffuses the eye.

Better the fence
            than daisy-ball
stipple that judges your attempt
ahead of you

Better the fence
            than all the frames unbe-
knownst holsters lock open

gluten allergy
alabaster fever,
bales of the humming invisible
            make mutinous its curtate.

Within this shield
we skip as though also-ran

ran to an unrehearsed track
of saturated white

tight as fruit but less penetrable
triggers violently.

Better the fence
          than wild oats, poppies
or ergot that will spoil the crop

Better the fence
          than the pinwheel
disturbances that grind obvious
dark/dazzle lenses

or their interface:
          twist the Etruscan device
against the bank, set it spinning.

Time Enough

You will be stabilized for a period
without limit of time
without term.
                    Period.
The electronic curtains sense
the dawn & evening,
            day starts, night starts.
Where are the folds? The little apples
rattle like shot in some other corridor.

This is the loop, the pole
bread travels along.
We have these mouths
damage stretches.
                    Who you are
condemns you, what befell
we can bring down to a precipitating
pitter-patter in a high room elsewhere.

Call rape for all you like
No crisis, no trigger.
Long twilight interferes
            dusk molests,
but it's the scratch, the spit
in the caring lenses, the false blouse
opening its sympathetic box, drawing
shadows from the daybook to ground.

Savage & disdainful
is this unceasing care
            catches & rips at the hearts'
co-ordination,
preparing new life
identical to the life they switch about.
            This will work differently.

No dance, no dope, a swell of praise
pulled into the loop then shaken out.

When will be our release date?
Early, the tobacco air,
scattered rice specials,
                        window
dressing that we acknowledge
deep down, trust in their
xanthic creepers
break the sun as it too
is on the up & up, cloud-ruches fall
like guarantees rattle in the plastic tot.

See the larks. See the swallows.
                        Burnt sienna
shadows are their exponents.

Answering Back

Take cones out of your fit pockets
to be rolled
out singularity –
a slouch or way of looking
skance eyes up issue –
a curvature,
deviousness, an
answer
for anything.
Now answer straight
should stand as the engineered crop.

Pre-set is the play of a fountain
alongside factory playing-fields
What dithers
is instructed so, or polarized
applying to perch.
Await the call
to the squash court, thunder rolls
out disparity,
piles of leaves
consolidate like solids
held no light & like light
had no body.
Peaks & troughs
wake the monitor as after droplets
ear-bashing, *coup d'œil*
rip down the figure.

Coastal trace by pallometry its fire
peach-curl at the edge,
asphalt
blankets tugged away
at the corner by a grass handle,
fuse into the rock-
port in nested heat pockets.

Show
Hold out insolently,
ricochet-positioned to one metre
over the human harvest,
crystal in the air like digital tuning
shocks the hills to lava.
They spread out.

Crickets phase-bracket & this place
you occupy is bounce:
Slam your fist
down to say so much
& fitted
body is dispersal, is expansive
Lower back or
ear ache/
gut or
heart rot
broadcast down the assertive slopes
sunflowers face haphazardly,
breaking drill.
Now for forage, now for oil,
for fertility
no more tropic than sun.
The fungus cloud masses
red on the forest floor
It drifts off.

I Looked Up

Within its gorge an interleaf refinery took hold,
    but the voice grain
rescues what little whizzes where they might be
    counted arbitrary
like fire-flies really torch, or it flicks like a knife
    woke those individuals,
       struck dumb
       allowed but one minute,
       butterflies
       ephemerids
flock like spicks of turbulence on the Han Sen
or a slow-dawning point a father tries to make
    assembles. Let go.
The executive flies in on a fixed-term contract
    from HQ in The Hague.
Intelligence needs locals, glance-photoanalysis
    like midges figure.

He'll know what colour shifts like light sieves
    through the leafy
shingles of the sycamore, the acacia, mullein or
    so many foster-
parents' hands admonish, calm, love, interfere
    across due kisses.
We all know do we not in that luminous hour
sadly worn.
A little wind gossips the plastic on the trunks
       wrap about & strangulate
rings before they have anything to put towards.
We know this from the performance of cattle
    grazing in Eritrea.

Set it against meteorology or to world markets
    break a vertical section
lights the ranks of processors, the living roofs,
    a spider drops

from the canopy on casenotes & it is psychosis
read off one exchange.
Horizontals stay well-lit,
steps shadowed, depth of field pulls off-stride.
So zigzag wanderer how will you stand for C3,
zinc, a pinch of salt?
Where is the deference as you look straight on,
too much like a child
fending with light which must be picked down
in nonsensical bits?

Air turbulence has combed the flowering nettles
alongside the runway.
Hooded are the changes he introduced but this
glare however distinct
touches base in a green nap, hits the very spot
like mildew
stiffens material beneath an impenetrable shield.
The song-
skein has been jammed that held a flotilla true,
the cast
of decision among the swallows sags to earth.
The hands pass through hair & are interpreted
by CCTV
according to a behavioural databank – woman,
white, mid-forties, not a suspect.

Look up, no shadows.
Overhead, the lawn he smiles under.
Above us the audiometric panels.

Growth Potential

Beyond the walls the kine graze, that otherwise
would stray confused & optional.
The different levels skew to each other,
supposed to stop free fall –
but click like a wrist or straighten round the
black snaky lance.

The panels fall away like beetle husks, the sign
revealed is what
the wing flaunted
dominance over, the embossed
wound for it became an innocent polyp, they say.

Deep costume gags on the camera like a called-on
stand-by, it was a star-
finder found the palace, oyster-
shell encrusted, gaudy, all evaginated
surface. I understand the rococo flaps & dewlaps,

growths defying function flourish
against the water-tight bulkhead lamps but can't
get a grip with plastic cutlery
or shift normally in
riveted chairs, break out over the place.

Why can't you return me to Viet-
namese, Ethiopian cafés, sisters on Mare Street
trinketing the pavement,
you don't walk on the pavement, you
walk down the thin concrete reservation to avoid
late falls of glass

but deep insignia will not be enclosed, they hatch
& from their mouths, from mortar scooped
fly the newsbearers
scattering leaves,

smudging that underfoot reproduce mosquito-like.
Or miniature wolves
I'd call them in their ranks, their parallel arrays.

As out of water the imperious came like chain-
drive vehicles & sand shifts organically,
skews one tessera & these are Europe's
concrete citadels in collars.
God is little.
An ever-tinier arc constrained by self protein.

Consequences

Blue to enhance
titanium chalkings,
          malachite to learn
in the high dark.
Polychromists hug their bells
          & on the concrete
beach will manage breakers,
either sealed in
          glass or understand the
phrased predictability
of their force while
          keeping back. O let me
                sandpaper, cut
                glass position,
                travel the larynx
          self-deferred, drizzle therefore
trust my comprehensiveness,
voice that clips
          friends & family stuff
off the Kingsland Road,
soothe this irritability,
          smuggle nothing through
the electric fleece,
do not suborn the guards yet.
          Some go
like the clappers but I muffle
tongue was coated
double barleysugar curse,
          it had to
          crack on hearing.

Now fallen travertine
thumps softly because the sky
          Living death
propolis for verticals
full of talk.

The screech-owl owing to its piece
        the ant drags,
yellow dominates
irrespective of saturation,
        pipistrelles
light the path, the fat black bees
check & in commotion
        fertile dust. Here
              cloistered in the
              next-generation
              cell, a cool
              hydrophane re-
        stapled to the
Milk it for this account
this disregard
this exception
organises multispectral watch-lists.

  I have a hunch.
I contemplate this sleeve & prompt
the music, no intermediary
 spins & spools
the pod of intercepts,
        variegate in
              pink quartz
              custodial jade
adds up to but
drains out its core function
come to that to
        distinguished
        carbon-grey
fringed & wattled
over-runs or excess stock
  Ornamented
Coxcombed, tufted with
        sinkholes whirligig & crest
pouched in waves spin & gurgle
        ripping the skin

            regraft,
            in every chimney
dust elates, the chimney
convolutes, now sheath, now pith.
   Bribe the receptionist
glosso-laryngeal.
            Stop between security doors,
stop & drain out,
   the mud-mat delays
urgently as more elaborate life,
            spiky capsules
   the suckers,
tubeworms cluster for
            their hydrogen sulphide.

Soft spawn of light
splots
through the canopy,
the kicked-in
nest reassembles,
plein de jour is the coeffect
showing its organisation.
            O rasp off
                    the pornographic
                    glaze, everything shown,
                    the diagnostic
                    territory, the thoughts
            break & ring stintlessly
Spiked rolls of thunder
motivate
the tempera blue haze, tickle
a sticky disembogue.

Emphatic Caprices

To govern means choke off
at screaming valves,
to regulate the energy, don't cry.
            Compass conflict.

To govern wards all conflict
to proximity then deflects:
  Do not meet
  Do not attend or
cross the child curfew orders,
            scoop compartments
from camper vans, nor disturb.

Then the face was all my crop
done from life.
            My sock stock
put in a swaggy heat

crossed under a baldachin,
the fret babe dispensing
            perfect English instantly.
Bundled free.

To govern means at root
light grows turbulent, on thick
hand & foot,
            hums with no apparent
            security, no keys or bars.

You may think it, that
  doesn't mean you say it.
Deponent fox tamp down,

withholding any cry that more
heartless demands the bun
            would better

have been cindery
than with its fullness split.
I need sesame but can't hack it.

To govern fills with pity
& swallows hard. Then let slack
enough bridle.
My pattie's glaze will shake
off its allure,
dust accelerator
full throttle.

Let dust then come to standstill
bamboo & buddleia
about a garden cell
cut & dried. Do not assemble.
Do not move in packs.

To govern means to keep
on the right side. No hidey-holes.
No burrows.

Patch the links with burnt hands,
now fetch the wirecutters.
Trade shall not
be impeded but the sweet moans
are hobbled,
do we buy that?
Or skip & dance & follow teams.
Trespass childishly.

Glory Hole

Say what you must with sweet commission,
          feed-forward imprint
takes place on earth
rolled out in her polkadot trousers.
          Steep the bloodstain out,
take soundings from the pumice,
          carbon meteorite, the
costume of showers fizzes across the sector.

When Mary and Susan and Emily stop out
past their bedtime,
   a heart-wrenching cry
calls them to the faces they
hung before they pulsed their love of
   the long night forward,
every move self-replicating, every move unknown before they wore its naked purpose.

Go back now where is
thanks for use, cascading through a foliage
as I mean to say,
          go towards the public pump
humming but a 200 times a second cycle
breaks renewal violently
          like light riddles
leaves seemed once plastered or marcellised.
          For such suffering there is suffering
                    dock to dock
          sat in glory.
          For damage
          hold your course.

You were approved as new-laundered, non-
absorbent sack,
carrying bits we never wanted
          tightened hygienically,

installed from a list I never knew I was the
grass
weevil biscuit.
Repeat her, embossed,
rolled out
with rocks & stones & trees. Unconcentrate.

Out & Out

Minion hold active sucker frame,
a prie-dieu
cupboard's heat was ice as it befell,
            inspected
but heard he rules the Ivory Coast.
Bend in your time.

Smattering in defence but musical
like-so I'll put this pencil,
            put the eraser there.
I wore your head.
Words weren't bounds before yet
housed in boundaries.

Light fillets the lice-filled hair,
punishment
is what we give the punished,
            lucid moments
signalling a failure to comply, a lovely
open texture,

pressure-chambers to keep afloat.
            Plush safe, he think,
but it's a shocked quartz
fringe shows where the main event
impacted
into abstract own-own body.

A steel shadow saw-tooths a wall.
There-there.
Their-their.
I have been mad these last months:
nothing could distract me.

Transpiring

You have this other skin or so you
were with burnt lines in the untidiest
slough or new growth.
          Your flame-red
suit dazzles out folds,
  & you are invariable now
watching all this stir. How do the
falling leaves remedy distinction
bar the seasonal need, let alone the gift,

how does spring tendril the shifty cut,
          marginate
with early foliage springing
from discarded
watery silk as it does you,
          eager to cordon nakedness,
holding off like a halo all-over
  sanguine or ruffled,
can be lodged inside a mixed media

envelope but where is the mouth
for its delivery,
          fading firmly, no aside or smile?
The stock thoughts congeal.
What flutter may best tangle
with a transit
vine or take distinction by the horns,
ravenous for eternity
lodged in the afterimage

fading so distinctly as never lip or flirt?
          If you love
you don't put up with what
avails but use a material shader
to simulate the environment. Call out
or protrude,

but send the sharp message
never to maul or dissect or chew over,
            won't fur piecemeal –

filling the dying interval by drawing
more matter,
            waking my ignorant
skin with pocks of admiration.
So I am raw & covered
inside my only skin,
  rucked & sequined
in snow, pearlised in hailstones,
ageing in the leafy poultice aggravates.

Sideways Looks

The sun hops sideways
          off its pedestal, remaining low.
Women & boys sit on boulders
in the river, or in the leaf-
  detritus, the cosseting mud.
In their notice
a mute crease flexes & shows
          by one glimmer –
where the brilliance is, through hiding
openly, on the surface not the level
          laying out a screen.

The day is the right age for all.
                    Stones
mark out territory as the eyes wander –
  here's one looks worked. Foot-
balls boys volley
are dented in their catch-&-catch.
It's over now & stained
in cross-section, glinting
          with disorders of memory,
                         old
preoccupations seize
or dilate in flexing from that pinch.
          Over & further out.

Hold the picture where the pebbles
curb tectonically.
          The crease in my
eye's corner heals but it still stings,
embedded in your level gaze
about-faces sick of itself.
                    You give more away
by not accepting.

Meet my look but don't flicker once.
  The sun too
sets out to help not catch,

overlaying the paintwork & boulders
with craquelure,
            pre-vandalised, weathered,
ferns throng at the inlets & vents.
  All invecked bracteoles,
the river's pile
controlled by creases in a half-screen
holding this release –
            I want to
fuck water but the water is an
island in water that is more of stone.

Refine the mesh now black and white
checkered. Apply a flag.
  How western the sun is! How
not an orb!
            How not long a character!
The split, the open
grain soon runs out of stone,
  the mending, meaning
integument & integer,
            will pass off what I mark
lest it persist, being arrogant
            snag, snatch,
tighten the churning rainbow knot.

Belly the split reed up towards it,
look aside.
            Charged with purple,
saturated
  grapes split, the plums exude,
yes hold the sighting reed
at full length
against the continental stones.

The only shadow
walks off down a finger
of jasmine scent.
The only source of light
chides not opening the way through

a sliver, a healing yawn, a flint's
soft absolute other
signing lewd mid-day.
Heat rises & distends
into lowering clouds,
heat lies,
caressing women crouched in mud.
Mud wrinkles.
Eyes are stopped upstream at a
rocky dam. The lobes crease,
receiving it for the whole
delta but with clipped dendrites.
So any moment stops,
ricochets, repeats,
imprinted on the colloid stream.

Some Marking & Yellow Highlighting

I carried a forkload which was warm
& not heavy –
wispy as candyfloss.
          & said This is the very best
I can lay my hands on.
If a gold dab were to hand
I could
          go in now, let this slide off
& be on fire without ignition.
I could take you at your unsaid word.

But I had to use that particular word.
At once the pitchfork
          grabs a pill went down
the wrong way. Whichever.
          About sixteen years
she can expect in the circumstances.
Keep your bit of kindle
          to yourself, maybe chew
for a retaining mess
          Like horsehair
bonding plaster. Up to you, to drivel,

weep maybe or squeeze a blob of
cadmium. The high sky
sends to shelter, weather will change,
clouds reconfigure
black, red & gold over Davos,
          blown by an ill wind
sharper figuratively than any wind.
  Substance
may function as a transmitter of pain,
          dream
flush the overstock. Whichever.

I'll take food when it crosses your lips,
  not the rack
lain across the horizon,
      a great deal absolutely
gags where a forkful reunites.
     This is the only
place left for us, a relative freedom
in its encircling walls,
crackles like straw behind that chicken
wire left over. How golden it is.
     How freely it burns.

Gate Fever

Food amplifies the funicular bundle, so
intent though still inventive,
          wiggling up its
carbon sleeve, the open tuft at the top
  splayed as a tube-worm, rootlets
hiking the canopy higher
Glazed, urgent, self-regulatory,
          scanning for distant

blood & noting the grillwork covers another sphere,
          showering keys,
adjusting table water,
profligacy its response to
stunted palings, those pencil-thin
  invisible beams criss-cross/
read the rain penumbra
like core code to a cool flame. Tempt

reticular were the senses which give over,
tearing tusk
from pillar acanthus, dropping
lank outmoded birds,
          scattering
remnant bones. Where nothing feels
diversified, where leaves
die & a cage of branches

will not be placated, busily definitive is
left still to swing,
          a filter gathers darkness,
a chimney chokes
  City container port
  Suspension files
  The order of this panel's
fruitlessness in one inhesion

not hold but entertain
prisons light which heel slips & shocks.

The most condensed do serve
time swagger athwart the holding door
If at the point all's held
detailed but whose tissue of conception
never could raise a crown/
Grandiose
thought-tree,
an electronic routing-slip
shakes down like foil,
responding up the yolky splats
to its aboveside, a high rug
spikes in roving cross-contours.

Light will signal through a flap
left to swing
uncontaining, budge obstinate heels
Arrest fails Wedges slide
Brimming sockets
mounted on balloons, bladders, jellyfish
pulsing in the loftspace
stream behind a flap,
trailing flex & shocks & sparks.

Restringing

The strings have to be pulled tight,
to the hilt the agile moves
          Like a cello
          a squash racket/
break-beams for the intruder,
security gates unfolding outward
knew who this beguiles
          by temperament.
Girls laughing along quays
below hills drawn spontaneously
          to echo them,
are penned in together.

Happiness tugged at loose knots.
If summarily I trailed,
          thought-through almost
before knowing my own thoughts
          Almost tripped
          Almost guided
into the echoing undervaults,
still gentian
still the green shot strung on vines
insisted on a responsiveness.

Coal sets the limits against clover.
Sculpture however clumsy.
The jackal & the wolf
forsake their god-speed, float
above my head as though swatting
giant ears,
& the boom out of quarries
searching for antiphony.
Give it time. Give it
          necessary distance.
          Case star core
languidly sings between girls,

permeant if not original,
halting, but continue
passing over the loved face,
the highly strung which tangled,
husked or shaped bits
feel, tasting
            each's near-capitulation –
scraps of song known well,
these were known in circles
becoming mazy disputatious roots.

Off the terrace the diapente rings
Off the terrace a blue note
curves the flight
magnetically to its interval
            So too resin
            coltran or cobalt
draws behind a chador on
the flat-out, on the main drag/
                        erratic & purposive,
hotspotting the limbic waste, burns
what will be memory
through coarse stuff,

by rote becomes by heart,
            the catch, the glint
against the contrast medium: Who
this might be I croon to myself.

The Still-Piercing Air

The still-piercing air / that sings with piercing

Argument

Conserve is to retrace. Then tread
the audit trail, wanton heat
stalls calculation, capture this

in the rock-face of record, pit
hopes to become trinkets
turned for use as hand-tools

glow & are dropped. Defiant
heat raises hopes. Just as you
can't know before its choke point,

devising your accident. Step/
slip. Foaming with redundancy.
Always to be caught up with,

        in the beginning
        was the rub
        radiating gently,

exactly as abandon had held out.

The Line of Resistance

If even the best known twist & hang,
concatenate like magpies, the import
of a missed call snags to a different
neck of the woods & with its voice
the clew to what this has been, residual –

if assignation flocks & swoops from
its volleyball pitch, day's idlers, dealers
suddenly gone to belong somewhere –
the beach has been suspended overnight
on my account or yours was this –

a page is flicked, the confident follow
this up marked, a pill taken assuredly,
soap lathers, all clicks on as day does
lift what's left coagulated, hear the
news if you must & you must, try

taking the conscious line from consciousness –
its tarry lump doesn't lessen but
pays out a line too workaday after
one engrossed tight as a knot of trees
snares piebald birds & did they sing.

The Line of Definition

What love dominates my abstract deal
position, more now satellite revenant
canoe or oak pew, warmth is target-
virtuous, accords with the high blot
stands above. To be authority so
far kindle in dry intersected streams,
love must not be answered but established.

Answer peels, unbinds the fool, fond
frittering throughput Mint-pole for an
answering current shorted in too-swift
rejoinder. Any heatspot closes up
fontanel – to polish the taps in the
closed-off, boomingly stagger the guest –

who won't be helped. Right you are
has been highest strip & so depressive
tests for accent, interrupt, respect
for her bootstraps. No-one stops upright.
Under that horizon are fish to fry.
The geography is never a brutal enough

fact for the sand in sheets to shake
amounting to an embodied deal. Rig
new shoes then deck them out historically
fish or fowl left to flap at signposts,
alienated only from what would touch
with a full hand, for fear it might extend.
Love self-tests & fêtes the empty bed.

The Line of Reinforcement

Catch it again pluck, sounded flat.
        The skeining soon repairs
melodically strewing rosy parts
        uncaught, uneventfully.
Central demands stay viable but
        neatly disposed of.
O falter, o buy a fatter duvet
        not to put too fine a catch.

Apple-bobbing I kept my head.
        Riding the king's
highway came no cropper, relay
        yards of silk, calmly.
So wherefore the hair in the tooth
        flexes the tongue or
dull down waves of sun-spasm
        vary the all-in-all?

That's the catch catches nothing
        remotely. Cries may sound
dissociated, thick pond
        grant no wish, then in a flash
a crowd forms for a fire-eater,
        & over stainless surfaces
accompanied song skids
        straight to the heart's clutches.

The Line of Conviction

Their leavings glow on the plate
before risk business. The apple
sticker, the rind stamp – these discards
having been said for grace, swound
in fatty troughs, indistinct.
Their leavings are a typical basket

tending towards the fabulous. Pure
obsequies of the gut. Down this road
conference objects, counted off
beyond number treat a longed-for kiss
as immaterial now, the silence
pressing on that episode

not pregnant or exhausted but set aside.
The fire freighter tests its hydrants'
spider crouch, pounce, originating
The Thames. They finish up fast
before the next raid will amerce
rejected scraps into a killing.

Take the noviciate. How shall their life's
cover freckle new scope varlet
hold, repeat, for the same
index pokes down the appealing tips
safely queued. This atypical
movement hits like a harbour wave.

The Line of Betrayal

Union is the first port of call, on
going break. Once visited the arch
back clamber quells happily
gulls prodding vocally & shuts
up the sounding cliff. Perhaps this
completes the end of the thumb,
fisticuffs it comes to. Stand on the
newly unknown & take birth.

Muscle is crowding shoulders
via natural light. Motility the light
seizes for archetypes, jesters
& such, their glow enamels not
animates. About that far the normal
walls retire, for a repeated
buy confirms the dim pathos
shades immutability facetted,

the polished well-worn thumb
glows in the carrier bag & if it
starts to hurt that would be more
gratification. Yes perhaps it hurts
& can depress the mountain.
Yes the gulls shriek as devising
ever-new intricacies they reunite
about the clot of air conjectured.

Interlinear

Love that knot. The cascade
indivisible, teasing
curls for false treasure, rout

green ogive window park,
the lances beribboned.
How darkening would be true

deliberates in open arms
allowing these fly up, may
confound stacks of livery

set at odds, a naked ruse.
We're there. There's nowhere
else tied up less despotically

the one full colour. Feed
slippery satin, play
into its most generous billows

complete as a night rainbow.

The Trail of Scent

Meanwhile by my own voice on a chubby arm
stood guarantor, stood ground, this grinding

activity supports a no-action state cut down,
rotting in synecdoche. Its covers end to end

shift onto the boards. What human referend
scales airy fencing to fill its air pockets –

speechlessness lets loose speech's ties
pile intemperately; outbursts that scent-fixed

monologize a baker's shovel, like falling snow
placing one tongue turns covers, opens arms,

then replace the tongue. Let it talk out,
all of the cockshy dwindle to a type species,

meanwhile feints & fluency modify the voice,
prepositional fear unhinges a little spot

affixing joy, the loved one was that certain
globe, the one component sent out on a limb.

Wash off, swill behind the ear. If rapacious
breaks for thaw might release the furious reels,

brakes off, how sustain the rate of narrative,
silent pivot feeding off dirty source materials –

what goes unsaid still pitches for leader strip
flipflop in a hinterland close to home.

That voice which faltered on awaking, lights
out on its distracting voyage, casts round

like a dinghy on a slack hawser risks pull
to snap adrift with certitude, old love's recall

off-shoulder skims the spating current –
beacons, scented pools, shoals of untold length.

The Trail of Evidence

Cloaked in light's binding without a hitch
forgettingly attends, the pressed thrall
glows purple, swells, so combative
lies, warps & makes instruction over-full
buckled against its unmarked mounts –

Light shows are encroaching to bombard.
Billboards contribute what stays bluntly
undercover, don't bother agent to unseal
your orders but deliver nonetheless
body-sensors checking the grassy pillow

love subtends. There must be someone else.
Bravely positioning those fly rejuvenated
gods on the off-true shaft, laying
about it fretfully, the apple of disclosure
setting to rights where it sunk inwards.

Here the razor grass stiffens after bedding,
cutting sheets to ribbons. Their mount
brave affectation, some maypole dream
directs a tatty, twisted flag signal
to repatch them that a lawn assimilates for

they go compound. But the spaces persist;
mark you, all conveys, a dog's bearing
answers to the moving freight beneath
a supermarket carpark, the falling lights
have the points of contact picked for them.

The Trailing Sash Cord

Small help the furious blinds slam their frame
encumbered by their apparatus – just so
an offer of the long-sought collapses
steady pull through weeks into muscle ache

defencelessly flat. Chinese painting, a spray
revives or makes obvious a behaviour pattern –
Egyptian blue chain or cool choker too cheap
pools in a palm in its paltry summary.

Line them up picking heads & rotating caps.
Pad the rolled surfaces & the flat glass.
That's enough about you before you open your
mouth accepting earlier scenes like bonbons.

Why trouble to call? Blinds hang provokingly
skew, palms fan against the kidneys,
the very table irks. They bunch together again
then rattle down clumsily to close in display.

Tracking the Perihelion

The spoken-to unbinds & fans,
revetment blocks off-face
peacock lampoons. A chat-up line
fake to the core but knock-off

skids painted toes, a side-slung
breast below dough lips. The smile
across the tracks, the smile
in the crossed eyes, flinch-

bestowed to disappear
meticulously, how shall it anchor-
strip the bruited tambourine?
Tomorrow the wrestling is,

sire's address hung on a spindle
in her doublet, succours
insupportable unity,
couriers through childless streets.

The Trail of Withdrawals

On the nail held tone refaces with a light-
weight mounting tissue. Grass-stalks, if
his boasted hummock, crouch in a half-scoop
bunker or a car by his required presence –

as though presence held, not to feint or blur,
downcast or lift sights, he'd preferably be
thrust aside, taken up with, otherwise
but to be filmed. The spade flattens a face,

succeeds in showing its flag. Forced objects
hold a line for the beloved, feast jealously
followed regardless of standing. Badges
put what might have praised, but convoys

said I have no order to unburden, high-tone
on implausible stilts. Now devil drape
memorial, kiss the absorbent brow, seedy
nap buried repeat as panels in my breast

disperse & thumb their telephones, down-
load from their closed box. Much as a
shrugging earth in place for heart levies
hooded doors blank the colonnade they list.

Tracks of Cultivation

Where it filters distractedly to its routine home
are many types & some wear armour. Geraniums
reckoned by geraniums in their strip, re-forced
in ranks, in gas-burners, steady flame in tufts
feed out what was input to disrespect the porch,
let them carry, opening that valve subsequently.

The roll is one note wrapped about a question
swan-neck adjusted to its harness, automotive
fixed eyes, computing the flow. Face it for a
raised concrete causeway, that but for constancy
might well be loved, constantly will never turn,
smiling shyly; habit checks a flood in long adieu,

but the night auditor names & will be followed
by new growth. Paper supply sprains the wrist,
the fife back-blasts, a barrister says Cast your
mind forward, that reddening diode she appraises
thanks a bunch intensifies on top of the bar, give
more thanks it will mete out its combustive sap.

Lines by the Referee

Will a dial now take the shine? Affidavits
scrunch in distant bolt-holes, fastening
warm sleep about them, & the trouble
leaves one face less marked: alongside
in the alleyway voices take their tumble
rough with the smooth; all the cringing

magazines reset. So discharges fill time,
though shot about to the loneliest place,
where whatever approaches reabsorbs
into its mobile, broken & human sleep.
Congested those marks seem available
to scrutiny, flawless at my ringside that is,

dial flattened to the face of a safe duress
hooked where some clapboard theme
suspended but his brief went ballistic
off unprovoked. Voices had been spent
in focusing a gumshield, a fingerplate.
Rather take the call, press the soft switch.

Gethsemane

Construct or convolute
full point copula,
joins what tries to hold out

taking one more turn,
denies a windowbox
full of brightness,

collecting brightness,
giving out brightness,
held in its turn immanently.

It is a desired icon.
Brightness blackens
shadows, blots out itself

unendurably bright.

Case in Point

§

Little question point will revisit, countersunk
mark I accept I palm, tongue-kiss
migrant but ensconced point, which

way you cut, proportionately, cross-
rolls its specification
keeping something back: Fly not their button

prompts to act like mistletoe,
not the membrane dot provides access,
neither remembrance would, its aphid crowd

sticking thirsted to the point
occludes any pore or the skin water-repellent:
the question ripcords from its POV

but is the same spangled entreaty
        placoid to light,
the same deflector so much its own, re-frames

roots. Hide their tracks, shred paper, captions
        devastate the pile:
                is myriad singleton

behind the face, not as if sewn
up or styptic where its lopped branch, its knot
of mistletoe is a back-formation yes?

§

Little question point I'd wish to make fluidly
might nod its stem, stem
the displaced point, edging-tool

as sawtooth or scallop went about the houses
Shrink your open hang-
trap your hang pudenda, daffodil

or double trumpet News in oxide-
red desert up to the neck plant matter stuck
before it skids over Then at that point

Why does am I bloom standard madly bolts?
        /greet this small cheer
Little question

stuffed inside the bag before the throat clears
        /here goes, shall it tackle
subset to those smash & grab

prate of socket violinists, floppy-necked rims.
On the loosened, broader field,
on an interminable lawn clamped

So help me, little gone to earth, little
resistant point, the infill
dark uncontainer, dark lantern. Take it away.

§

Such screens pan out veins as day's eye closes;
like an unbroken clickclack
toils through the horizon ring, feeds

filature to its underside, diverted, bled across,
opalescent when focus pulls. Flowers
like taken by the off-centre

sidetracking necked or stitched like swarming
mandarin ducks, wear blatant
fanfares for their patches, polarised,

all resort levered in by the dull spot shone up
point to point, cross-threaded. Blank
bleeding hearts, primroses can-

not anticipate, roses make the fist
that will not blurt, pout
or gulp after a show of resistance – the daisies

scatter much hereabouts, bossing
out yellow sex centres were they to make bold
whites in pink blush, a signet

          were anti-daisies, aliased, in
their own points reticulated. These they were.
These is. Rolled neatly.

§

Leather gauntlet or water-ice in a frosted bowl
Whether the bowl's pearly bloom
by chill night or through cereal/

plunge back to daub on starch &
shall stock response sleep-walk,
slouch up from behind, then inwardly freeze

lest following, wouldn't their starts or finches
seed payload? Enough that buckles
then break, one-time accomplices

mock them by flashing the over-valued image
plunged in & out repeatedly:
what leverage tugs it from the bag?

Goods delivered up that animals would skate
sleep rationally, formidable children
found to dream. The young

for security burped, scratched, doze. Gobs of
finger falling healthy, flex,
rummage in a vat of starch or varnish:

that bran-tub will glove each
fork jarring on its sweetheart, or if the plunge
won't connect, shivers in a long call.

§

Ingratiating sleep, sleep carrying out,
thumbed its sandstone but its well-loved face
in piles, in barbs of millet –

Sleep-rolled buttons, bleeding heart
vibrates for its limited best
retention for to smooth, or if venturing down

look the stonechats hull lickety-split –
Indigestible rosaries of
pips annoy these dream scavengers, laid-back

pioneers skid awake. Apply my hopeless pads
but wager none, give package flowers,
a stereo print of deep forest

replicates as life-long or where sleep,
either collapsed, either perfect,
cahooting over the blocked hopper, stressful,

wrecked on a cheek shore this mild Odysseus,
holds of grain have burst,
carpeting the way to a shed of caresses.

Shuffle their point ribcage! Dream
dahlia-spread like one ribbed echographically
from birth. Husk smack.

§

Back conventionally blue. Skies flourish blue,
for *trial* read *tuck in*. The half-crushed
reach to strap-hang the vault,

mouths like Boreas puff redeeming breakfast
bowls of cornmeal cooling rigid –
Did their asides lip, jut, sheet

southerly to ball their weave confute
like a self-governing squirrel, their frustrated
squall of fury, so one seizure

crabbed to make for bestrewing, draws a line
beneath see-through pleats? –
those guard, those wash, groom

in a dream of activity. How the point
folds into the point
What's the difference, hunger for this or that

rejoicing in an uninverted bowl,
        a stemless bowl,
was that a different hunger, blue wash above?

Employ the pipe. Reeve the blue
& ring-bind inwards, oppilate or choke what
gluey mess sets its cap to, baggy point.

§

A bag is what you sneak your hand in, gloved
with fat but a box would have been useless;
for example a foreman sidles up,

adipose by half. He strives for that consistent
yellow will coat the wall Phooey:
Better it was wrinkled & flaking,

was held in a bag, a bag that never resentful
fetches or festoons. Holds grain.
Holds money. Holds the shopping. Sooth

to handle, shopping grows a skinny hem
scrunched on one side transfixes. Dream stuff
hung from ragged lips will tempt

autumnal bags. Air itself seems never enough
insurance on its own, save if
plastic-coated, bidding fair to hold.

A bag belongs, the bag to carry its bag carries
the fat of the whole intent. What boxes
do, comparatively? Echo the point:

Fragile: what you want is best
avoided & in avoidance shines whole intent.
Your bag was sealed with a side hasp.

§

Worshipful, its crawl-plank shaken violently,
its pasty things now derelict
tile a light-flooded entry, deep allure,

the well dressed in slippery orange
layers, touching massive trunks & slabs
should hoist their horizontals, but horizons

set tombstones to belief or bellied
canvases were vent-plural
floodlit clickclack: God's message to an over-

ride shed, shit billet... seize it in its wellhead
pleochroic blind spot,
the pivot whatever nonentity speaks.

There the thick reeds will shear,
on that side, where a condensed blue lagoon
breaks whose fall: where sluices

on the other glimmer, trickle
inauspiciously, so to not breathe even
tangles a first writing. Eyes what kites unfurl,

& bucking blue high light up
escape a well whose grinders throw heaven's
weight round. Churn the cylinder.

§

Thinks: because of a cloud buffer
view or search or archive, or when a stripped
skull on a glass sill, free to say

Think many shrunk in glassy collars, swollen
in their positioned vapour scarfs,
free to say. A moveable pump

at the plantation gate wreathes their baggage
with light mist. The depths are atomised
like upward dowsers, injury

settles beneath the cope:
a sustainable microclimate covers in bruises
every branch. Providential body-art,

lip-tattoos. 'Theirs' the hanging buckle
secures, theirs the goatskin
grain enhanced, a shawl shook for the count

cloud storage recapitulates, a whip of vapour
dashing the high tip over,
gave its stem clarity. Swags of cloud

smelling of jacaranda flowers, cartoon a god
short of breath, make swell.
To be dragged through the pinhole.

§

In the rainy car-
park with the wind-
        screen wipers going;
shall it be a pool,
the rising & falling
        chest & thorn
blossom puffs down
urinous & does the spate
        stick fliers
on the unswept
glassy papule glass? The rain's
        machinery
keeps at it, fen
stripes shatter, spray pumps its
        curves over
a stand of homes, trees,
expanding in a thick strip.
        Putting it about
Relaying pollen
Strewing thousands &
        for the field trials,
absurdly signposts
most of that expanse.
        Truing & fairing
Driving them past,
differential wafts
wipe the campaign.

§

How make them out if in crates? Deep-laid
orders stack below, elected
forward without saying, lips sealed,

pace their jitters round miscellaneous goods,
grind the root, expansion
joints lettered in Somali, truck-

dry was the powder stirred & wet for manioc
beside the field road. Orders
multiply for onion sets, eyeballs swell

on tall poles & catch these moving
O slash some open quick, scoop their dollop,
cut the bag down, fill charity

cones that were fumbled voids, gangmasters
tread cash from their blisters,
restaurants that buy in a pillow

countenance race forth having orders to kill
rib pamphlets tiling end to end
minority languages. But these

ones boxed with sweated produce lay strewn
about by sorting shelves,
dialect spilling there like root powder.

§

A veal calf wobbles about its point
More please. Nor would the carrion feeders
wipe their mouths then fall to.

Herds lumbering in, their enclosing breath
drags crow surveillance. Pocket-
shucked wheat sprouts,

blankets shrink like spider-flax, one
seemed to care but came over more exacting:
shall I intubate? shall I drop-

lip his mouth with meal or with crystal dust,
from block polystyrene shape
his warm successor, carving out

the profile acanthus-wreathed, its dog-eared
label flops in moist deference.
Draw being laid as though to scale

next to game the mobile hot breath reveals,
a thick veil conceals, betrays –
unites objects with voraciousness.

Moist-eyed outside the crate
having made the replica they breathed alive,
eat dirt while installing its heart.

§ *(after Don Judd)*

Merchants perched on boxes accept the decor
laying lustre snail tracks,
ribbon lymph pathways, bi-coloured

smeared gold Broken shed offers an overlook
expanse of ocean Made in Macao
        made in China

– fancywork. So many candle power
teardrops golden appliqué or ivory silhouette,
scattering a one they would as one

swing up the light blue girder they divaricate
their mucous track. Serrate/
Infill/Rasp/Restuff, admitting crest

portmanteau with snitch pollen, lay potential
step-change behind the sheds
smoulder, their ripe boxes advertise

a neon wake. The warehouse shell could wear
that fire, that mould, what say you
        sidequarters, hindrances

Blasting guano to infill
beaded candyfloss, chickenwire, rough
finish would contrast. Thinks through decor.

§

Take this. Raise the competitive bowl. Chew
the official gum of unconditional love
Delicious/ Humming across

silken points into the meadow of frequencies
combed through yellow, coaxed
by twittering runabouts, branch-

conditioned, entices further to sleep,
ruffled, each retires to its point
diminished, aside, which sparkles indefinitely.

Save porridge for after the funeral,
corm not desiccated entirely or stem snapped,
bowl replenished in neon

cocktails, bursting like a little car spreads happiness, & its delighted passengers
roll down their windows, breathe

success, raising glasses of fizz to the wide blue.
Soft, soft the glaucous bloom
that love & dear affection contrive,

the peach fuzz is whispering, the elderflowers
vibrate on moth frequencies:
See you soon. Beat you into the ground.

§

Stoop to the bowl then lower lost for words.
Rubble steeps in some gumbo,
rubble falling from a skyscape. Its organisers
grappling for a stand-off/
lean bankers, skinny kids swinging lanterns
gang to launch
winning stranglehold
will pepper-pot,
Wormhole-shafted, taken
triple rake
hogshair or vaccine or rigid
designer value pack is rubbing plaster down.
Cakehole brought to book at last scoffs
message fine meal will drift
singing numbers make the stack of bowls
anchored on the glass & marbled mill-pond
violently skid off.
Take a punt on them, unwind
scarfs of algae & pond-weed,
scarfs of cloud
pierced with flying ants & mosquito larvae,
plagued with 24-hour total coverage,
such expanses deadlines cross.
Orders in council pushing through the sieve
arrowroot, cassava paste on the
swollen oval,
wipe the breath from the oval *en papillote.*

§

Open avowal drains the mouth so keep yours
shut best thing. Boxes keep counsel.
Nerves writhe in mounts, an opoid

numbs them: screw you & yours, newspapers
blown across a garden, ragged mere,
rubbish for cooking fires piles

waves densely-packed: pillow fuel flambeaux
on each pathway. Shelter
spills or mere opens, haybox for a moist

warmth, a near miss catches, thrives, crackles.
Gardeners feed with snipped spurs.
Votaries of this or that mystique,

loss adjusters screwing about tap-roots
heedless of skip-beacons,
claim loss fills their mouths, replaces mouths

with bare earth. Minus stood for surplus
holdings. As: who'd mistake
you for you Screw you/ Keep it shut. Ragged

mere. Multiply it into the box. In case of fire
        tamperpoof. Access mere
dot dot dot mere, tongue lolling useless.

§

The inmost track was least reliable,
shearing the whole thing in abeyance brought
                    tongue-tied
to a tender rasp
          underfloor where bonds had sunk –

a packet concealed under his tongue,
wrapped inside a blindfold cloud his evidence
Like bangs/sticky mass, the upswing

vapour-locks the director beneath his canopy,
flat against wall-scumble, circling
insect choirs trail as the day's

hard-copy, its deformed topiary
shook in commotion hard whip-willow skirt
magnetically nudges up & under Woa!

at just the angle, just inside inside:
save where a blue sky banks, swerves & spills,
save its scrape to moony scrape
          Everything buckle-tight

groove to a tongue grew sentiment flickering
for this metal
          The day he was run off
          Rotated, tails & heads.

§

The point stands like a portrait does or it did.
The point cut intaglio, a belly-button.
The point flush. Point near-prolapsed

refusing to take the point, so spread & dazzle
pen or pinprick or finger, prise
open a dialogue whose every line fattens

to apex, does this make a box? Untitled 1987,
mourns the box its forgotten corner
Yours, was yours your cobalt face

riveted in brilliant aluminium? Inasmuch it
will never shear or wobble, because
it is display & is that vehement

spread like sunshine travels, as a riptide does,
exactly it is the general
waste wants not what had been shed.

If the point or reference doesn't call expressly
enterovirus (that's what it looks like)
You are one of 197 people

complex or bagged mess. Did you wear black
cargo pants? Bypass, cut, degenerate
colourfully, multiple slit letterbox.

§

Setting lotion. Mass of orders laid to order
blue skies amass/ like triangulate/ like
get it in one at the porter's desk

shrinkage, a to-scale vehicular puck
nudges through preformed concrete
stooks rose. Where everything-to-hand went,

everything-in-one-box, magnets
drive the analogue circuit, rough-
cast, scrambled egg, did you ask for porridge

walls in birdshit warehouses, drill
DIY relief, riddle answerphone
pronounced as a straw doll stripped & cleated

pressing against glass. Incur
that set of primed days, the darkly brooding
forethought Get it in one whose rills

lock the unruffled image pool
Retrace the clipping paths, like here
oblanceolate in blue book compliance packs

rings round the saucer of shadow burst open
sodden grain. Pretend to miss its
lay-figure propping stiff but airy bales.

§

A boxy frame right tangled, a left elevation
loosened by the furious stick
A sail or blade cranks up & floats,

a vacuum cleaner sips at the vacuum: Come!
if locked within its matrix, glaze
lifts the newcomer, so turgid glaze

consolidates the base, a lily pus-filled,
a stoneware bowl joins its stack, the windmill
showing-off a punch corrects.

But light needs fatten, skin must needs thick
down O such expansive point
convinced the ordering, the may-it

self-impediment I batten on I lip-reposition
till the axis tercet pulls together.
Does the sun delight in shallows

wafering to full extent a flagstone from flare-
point dissolves the padded
baseline in combination? One point

boxed numerically, immunocomplex
wire gets more I lip-reposition/
if required for the rhomboid sail floating off.

§

Semolina, call it frogspawn,
jellied gravy is the only
connective there
congeals as it overhangs,
aquariums sea wrack wall-
paste swags of organic
strop blossom. Clear
brooks, sort the vellum
in-tray, shuffle packs
performatively
squat in task group in real-life
stamp achieved
outcomes as meal drying off
shivers its redundant
bulk; best value powder fire
blasts just the heart
of the producer. No longer
slowing down, fat
builds on its rendition,
incinerator catches
the concerned branch & net
disregards blow out a
thrush's egg, glutinous
rich mass. There you go,
compact. There the forename
sticks
inaudible as a rule, nor merely the first gob of phlegm I spat.
Therefore the surname becomes the billet I must post to with
full dispatch, heel of the sound which exposes as in flower
the curls at an otherwise inarticulate nape. That's as may be
an expression of love pulled off with a flourish & stowed. O
go boil your head. When hair is a shellac helmet, what are the
other globes unturning, undishevelled, which what you were
pleased to call zooms in on, wagging brightly? What you say
boils
fenced-off bones & a short

        hop, hung in sticky
sacs from the design
        exported to the Philippines
exported from the Philippines
slumps.
Let them have our babies.
        Such gloop is not
the note to thwack against
        steel knuckles, pressed
increasing discomfort,
        contemplating pain's
mission, contemplating
        These augment.
        These are the permitted.
This is not the note to strike
sticks.
Should it swing, see advance
        cylinder the curly-head
impression. Those creases keep,
        stripes are operatic
vengeance as the face glugs
        from its jar in one
cogent spiral shaken out. Shall
I tell sorghum
seed both & syrup? Or
        deform a unit interlace
inbuilt like an egg; she
        soundly engineered,
hammerhead at soft wood
        shock-absorbing, roll
like shrunk Mars metal nails,
        let it vibrate the bar
sticks/
build & then lock the wave.
Amalgamate like sago.
Hammer gelatine veneer.
Who our is I ween but we don't.
Who is I womb

by gum or by the eel stall
        long stressed-out
ties affectless, stood
        offspring not relatives –
scent of smoke & chyle –
        poking like the pickets
once displaced, resin
        of an unnamed tree
exported to the Philippines
exported from the Philippines.
Connectives go weak,
        the great shoulder
slumps,
counterfeit
incused until a blurred version
looked on & struck
        another from that mould –
        we thought I was our
man in the street, taphephobic:
nothing hits the spot, only
microns shallow
bas-relief
        choked like hair a plughole.
Therefore take this point
        like a green plastic
baby in a cracker, like a baby.
What if the point
were to burst out/
        the innards' new sex?

It's in the bag recoil-less.
Potato face on a wire frame.

§

Little question pays out thumping snakelike,
tangles & confounds a false self
with elements of truth, twists the cap

on potential, blowing gum
gums up the carding stacks spew vermicelli;
little question trounce by 3, by 4

the flatworm that
presumably brace-claims our front, segments,
then rolls up & gives over. Shirt pile.

Little question, pleased with itself
gets it in the can, in memory,
unspooling crosscut scenes of Irish folkdance,

rocking boats, snatch passion, Tuscan villas,
wriggling transparent sandworms,
pop-tenant foreshore, the burst

spread pulse illimitable, fanning
vistas corneal, ancient spurs.
They countenance, *my my*, in endless lividity

combs wave crests, rakes them low
for all the world devise
what prompted them lying on our bed coiled.

§

Waves bunch below turf, the meadow shrugs.
Waves readjust their order,
send a billet, combing out outliers

sustained by their statics, what if
wave power strips stick-ons through its tines
    Our ranks carry all before,

a nematode republic in spasm/
picks through as see attached, turmoiling
the flat lawn to shroud spider roots & rocks.

Tinny birdsong & autumn crocuses
penetrate the brush, deer's hot
breath against the copper beech, the brachet

petit-point in silver on a flat ground.
Ensure nothing takes place or from the place
none depart: tightly stitched,

held hard, until some spread divert
fails to acknowledge or respond to command,
twittering in judgment, unflappable.

But every local sampler, every song
knotted with a man orchid or a slip of a girl,
staples the homely earth. Nip & tuck.

§

Little question stay on hold, scaffolded
stays upright on the flats,
receives, plays over a responding voice, keeps

on the console in a holding pattern.
    Proof ruffles
stream off the fiery spectacle, waves of sound

transmitted through scaffolding, & millet 30
pecks shall it dance on the
ground-map lattice. Conscious hum

we tend to distract on approach. The curlew
estuary a convulsion of sand
makes nervous, calls in its flights.

Retrieve a red jewel-case Don't look.
Listening at one remove
so kickes the curl'd heads of conspiring stars,

of jewel-like buds & buttons
lit to measure, lit to advertise a false runway,
coax them through salvo on salvo.

Hopeless salience plots out
one gem per high order block, each descends
up the spout, flight box unretrieved.

§

So like any civilian, point. Your box contains
grape samples or amphetamine, it holds
expiring breath & faded air,

colour will bring them out. Seriously that box
is a treeless forest, sighing
away its wood. Trees are but decorative

torsade, for the box a colour readout disloyally
has laid bare, so fill its clearing
with calm questioning in dark blue.

Across the bowl-curved analogue, vine tendrils
stretch a colourful chord
to twang & pollen flies inventively,

clogging wind apparatus, bestows its touch, a
fingertip erotics. The sharpest rind
the tongue anticipates, rind

about a space voluteless, scarcely can compete
with the blue of a box, the rind only,
previewing a display of displays.

Such blue tablets, such black box decodes, air
racked on affirmatives, these
the vine disrupts with lightest fingers.

§

A DJ puts that groove down in a private club.
A scratch held apart so as to incubate.
A vigilante takes his heat. Hotshot.

Feet compress the forest trail, its underthatch
        /horsehair sags aloof desirable
Where's the pocket. Ripped out.

That's to provoke not some resigned attitude
uniformly strikes
lash for eyelash, feedback in the cubicle

detects its always front makeready thin stock,
soaks in saliva,
soaks in acid, in urea
        Soft-shoe
        plantation

rowan splash, photoperiod burst,
        fingering a blunder mass installed
base in that booth sucks the silt back & forth

        mending & re-mending what
lemon spare part So let flatten
                So a regular pulse
locks & re-dilates,
sweeps the sand now marked out for runway.

§ *(after Richard Crashaw)*

Wound gape. Mistletoe fix the sweetest sweat
to a pearl's purity, scar asides
puckered through its beading-work/

their residues of ultraviolet
show where the snapped-off nourished
schools of leeches, most refine a false fluency.

Seed had yet to take, wounds to transit
flank to flank, floor hung or Yoruba hanging
engineered for the richest yield:

box dries the pulp, squishes berries
harboured in its craw till vinegar brought out
caked mud to opal splendour.

        Push the little dials
        in the mud, fertilize.
        Pass them, martyrs, minions
until reduced to greatness, ground for
        death's life/
wreath-like the ritual implement click-shunts

availing them of door after door,
blood consisting the trail
panic filters into, drilling their green mounts.
This agent flushes down the cannula.

§

It is the palate connoisseur, skinless,
priming his clicking locks. Love transliterates
in child's talk, such loaves

mashed to breadcrumb, the waves & railings
decomposing, wooden leg knocked
down to matchsticks, reconstructs

higgledy-piggledy, broken the infernal grove –
nothing turns its tumblers, white lead
seizes, won't allow their voice,

won't unite the needle with its groove.
Look, no scratches.
Checked it out, not one puncture.
    Not one scratch or footfall or one mortal

thing crumbled, making shift or scraping by
default so each vowel
brought to their hearing, test soak,

sticks as a crocodile clip
plated in gold microns-thin sets up a supply,

a choke whose broadcast rises. Broken voices
unite, ascending like a pad
of phlegm above the infant boughs.

§

Cascade then or float as maturing fit to burst
break the stem, break the cassette
        Or to have yielded up.

Autumn crocus, aconite, naked shoots colour
fleshes out, the far-
flung spores gasping, a let-rip of spores,

the air a velvet stole which by what operators
cramp, crop & crimp, this puffball
        poised on its metal tips
in reliable firing order, soon outgrew –
few shunts
of a now receptive hurt. The believable motes
force our eyes to weep. Tree-mould
stings. Locked
on a fussy ordinal, on its permission,

a tight version knowing its strength weakens,
puffs & heaves, exhales,
            fed on multiple
data-streams will re-launch
        Its pleasurable
slack capsules float ripe to rot, so ballooning

rise over an innumerate marsh
        clicking safety catches. Float. Disbanded.

§

There must be that point from which one
does the peony's pink horn spring capable –
behind the earth's frock. Deeply motile
any garden, even a not referenced bronze
or ignored, the cylinder's big idea trails
too light cursive. The point warms, shone
earth from heaters underground, a mush
protecting the tropicals, over-competent
a label were to wound its quantum hook,
this indifferent sort of plant. But stumbles.

Anyway it wouldn't serve. Howso-eminent
the peony still crashes, some heavy bubble
aeroplane brought down, gross, mundane-
ly squandering its airy rash on thinnest
slipknot streams yet it will make vacant
harbouring eyes; delinquent or unlettered
is the drone it fell behind the flat garden.
That was the journey's point or heart
would the lakes be, or highlands, tundra.
Flat the heart with no greedy point amidst.

Roll bearings, pull impressions flawlessly,
allow warmth's outputting, but votive
leave still a speck, a seed, a grain cradle,
a light cherry blossom wind-spat smudge.
There will harbour's expanse lie precluded.

§

Miss the point was the point's own course,
red-lined through proximities, remedying
every miss with closeness. Fine off-course,
what falls out regardless to extend the line
unspecified coordinates. Call that by name
on each almost-appearing, for a near miss
thickens the horizon comb if not in sight,
so to call it beckons undislodgeable trace.
What is complete cannot be named. Spice
islands with no landing stage, on no chart,
waft their trumpet fullness flop ragged.
Miss the point. Miss the point, have mercy
when I tack too close. Rather be the shell
holomorphic, listened in, than stop point.

Evacuate the void fills the void, least said
soon complete will clear the decks. Singly.
But then yank the door, turn the handle,
terminate on this rim. Do not impatiently
unpick the lock. The way out as signalled
is the way to the concourse only, no stairs,
concourse where whomever shall get lost,
canter point to point in fierce avoidance,
winnow the halt, voluntary heart avowed.
          Tilt. Ellipsis.
The point they miss will configure the off-
plan, the instead exposition in their midst.

§

Stem it close to the earth. Then key
branch consentient, joins in harness, octopus
behaves with emotion, wriggles

periodic/fully, what was hammered
spreads *my my* Watch how you go!
wireless router. One turns to face serpiginous,

tautening & clustered muscle, juddery fleshes,
tentacles recoiling at an almost
bunch of keys, redden, assert a grip

tending their tri-dominion hole. Yammer put
along straik, whose measured
suckers creep bicarb on pine barrens

silence-thick & meagre, flopped round:
a beak stabs through backformations, rank-&-
file startle What a bone-cruncher

clink-endued with sourdough hash . . .
Can it combine twig hierarchies so one *force
de frappe* should skitter, interleaving

ice or shale. Cut off non-standard. Over
keen thrashes in a slapdash
collapse, blaring at its cakehole, too articulate.

§

Slashed in wounds as mother-of-pearl pouted
weighing sponge, packing sponge,
a strophe interruption dragged

through unity once-loaded, as if one
struggle hard & in a fine rapture
roll-calls at its lick master, call-out-&-revoke,

clump together, fly apart, stagger then chord.
One step back suppresses.
Any step suppresses, diligently

pressed on sand, ridged against incoming tide,
shored, eroded, tongue-lashed, de-
coupled, choicest sweetest cuts

collect their blows like a wet blanket
plates confederacy, stomps the platform, slots
each into its haft, soaks. Heels

wince these sharply when announcing
presently together so earth hearing it endures
broken runs on the surface,

skirmishing nib-scratches, wounds
blind with ink out of their sac now removable
bunch as one. Squeeze until hard.

§

Churned mud, churned plaster, body of men
transect their limbs carnal & spiritual
Not the target bunch were that mis-

strung calligraphy, couldn't give a monkey's
patient work. Breakthrough broken
piles, trudging broken parapets,

riding to those lengths defeated
take on what is formal key-clash. The ragtag
infantry portioning the ethnic hank,

this branch, that wing, hangers-on volunteer
land nothing, load nothing,
lay you any viceroy or satrap

wouldn't wear the target's motley, O Princip!
trenches radiate from what you had to,
vacant magazines cough,

mouth to mouth marish earthworks
stake out rationale, weighing lines & aspects.
Those left to right the course

depute their janissaries, charged
inwardly to sink, outwardly drag mud
over the dry needle border, blood dirt smock.

§

Orders flail & flop unco-ordinated. Envelope
to redirect/ direct across one flank,
stripped arms nettled, suffice rash

of orders, not but what scrawl
deflecting a spearhead column, hastily
assembled for this expedition, up-river foray

leaves them indicted by their own
whatnot leaves them fumbling between lines
tangled had to consult, brevet

the devil would serve: Just lounge
against a walnut dash, sporting bib-&-tucker,
droop on the fender, wearing crease-

immaculate, the blood soil & sex entitlements
at poolside, at the bar/ Not that
give it a twirl, not that our surplus –

        drew water,
quicksilver Töpler gasp, took the Afric name/
murderous medal Feebly their arms

wobble home, salute the stake, prolix,
for all the stake were a crossroad crossed out,
scotching a dreamt mealie meal.

§

Be guided by noise pulling down to backslash

Disentangle. White summer

berries decorate each lick, each lick

takes nothing on board, leucocyte rush.

A true crow point calls the shots. Underneath

the full point withholds, pressured

to have their way, gives them so much

the point selects, scans & transfigures. Waste

Holding Station. One-finger right

setting but these rockets breach a closed city

The full bag of crows scatters richly

over much expanse ticked off/ Backslash.

Rain was carried everywhere in its thin board.

A halter neck. An insistent frontality.

§

Back-formation of the files stick-driven

ringed by troop carriers whitewashing windows,

complete for them their sand-filled interior.

Powder grains fill the bag, the wheaten

antennae have been stripped. Locks soften

granite, moorland mist, pushing the grey putty

into keyholes. Bare bones of that fan,

birdsong displayed. As for a sounding board

pigeon wings clatter Are you with us

still perceptible behind advancing blades?

Or do you walk to the counter

to shake their instruments by their silent necks,

birdsong in square, purple plexiglass,

scattered to be going on with yes?

§

Out from their volutes
        dribbles grain. Forward
from the vanishing point, vaseline.
Within the flexible barriers,
        one of those spots
with a few guards, few conifers,
marking where names meet, where
        housekept imagos sit,
the dead-beat, hairs, wings
        closing on such dead
lures the more attractive, loop
        compulsively. Box dividers
possible by new-mounted
        comprehensive pre-
fix, disposition to violence
Through lank weeping willows,
bowers, turned bowls/
        As well stick round. Well
camera position. Silurian.
Well a blue gelatine filter.

§

Coax through cooling ash
fiery fuse. Having
spectrum-broken. Having
forced down the capped
        periodics: bright-face capuchins
needing no assurance
hit the jackpot
in their bags coiling. Lighting
        could do more, maybe,
mood music could have,
mini rages peppering their
        slot imperium
really could. Still the chunks
will fall, a shaky
        press of wings,
        push aside whip curtains.
It's of a piece, that room:
point stretched to point,
cope or screen or pin-hole
        sticking round:
Or its alternative, its foil,
played hot, played dirty,
        score comprehensive
clickclack
strip development, honeycomb
        the bonehead earth
turns over, reabsorbs
        a strew of seed capsules,
eking out their losses
shuffling facial trade,
        flinging memory sticks®
upfront to folding chairs,
        drool on the propped
silicate banks, dripping slowly
        sunblock over-
cast on glassy skulls, harmful

rays stopping short:
Monkey through the flash fresh.
    Stay flush.

§

Carob gloop combines
        mackerel & tuna chunks,
polyphonic scales soak
        salts out, multi-function
scope to bring forward
scales to a devastated stall/
        Pin-head Hermes
punctuating nothingness,
        epitomizes
small but compact
in tongue, in lip, in seed,
        overlooked by a marquee,
chalet, airport lounge.
Baguettes are heat-sealed
safely from fingers.
        Cut, reconditioned,
brittling out of
method lighting,
        cluster the epigones.
        Hold to dented cups.
Electric cables spark, plastic
        fans & pelmets
        slide in melt
hermetic squares & diamonds,
        world's cuisine
shunted into modules –
How a dense point, how motor cortex,
        how thresholds/
firebreak filming over
crocuses that flame
from charred relics
poke through Styrofoam,
superficial wounds raise hell.

§

Pyrophoric seed,
flash point
strikes over its rough eye
run ragged, blown ragged
scuds the breaks,
fouling its escape route,
hyphening across
rush- or needle-patterned tiles:
Cobalt bruises blotch
Inlaid leaves
Flexible mosaic
reorganise what waits
behind until beforetime
with its injury.
Streets are dry, early morning
hyphens work a mall walk,
the right decision
earns partial autonomy,
a place in the larger picture.
Rollmop, vol-au-vent/
sushi president in see-through
mockup lumps adorn
sliding panels.
Turn over
pebbles sortie an appearance
glistening on shelves, glassy
as a disdained Jordan,
fish-eggs, tearful blotch.

§

The screens turn in on themselves,
avalanche their contents
Evertor muscles
playing to strength,
spasm, freeze like starfish,
        dwindle to a dot
        a stressed dot.
Unseal the light box/ Expose/
Feed the derelict flame
        What afflatus
hypes its lozenge purity,
in being achieved too absolutely,
reconciled from one breath?
The lacquer box is buried
        or lifts up
a floating altar,
        a desk-safe
couching the soft medulla,
        protecting its definites. Like
out of punctures
spread the delicacies
dabbled in blood, these
bloody envelopes, purses of tarmac round the gleaming kidneys
sonar to dissolve, pass the trace to a receiver, shining vessel,
jugate dip their wings but no results. Is there a train station
nearby, where do the trains go? I want to go there sure to miss
my organs were laid out on a tray, listen their instruction can't
be passed to the front, their billet was miscoded, forces rip apart
in small warrior bands head for a soda fountain. Rheotaxis
governs leaky screens shovelled in unreadable curtain wavelets.

§

Stuck, stuck, stuck, hocks boiled in
        vats hold the entire
mass transit network, clear allows
        no fancy foot, egregious mire
or fixed length
        The character riggers
        barter, chatter,
glass fibre artists
Substantia nigra
blows through the reeds.
Afternoon as always
sweeps its edge or sets
at edge the tired line.
Either way, the rationed
        heat haunts the present,
a yellow entrance hall
festering in buds of pent cobalt.
        Cancel
some, clip their frequencies,
reduce the whole
        to a light table:
Neat turns, amuse-gueules,
        the set apart, vaunt
their floor
above composite trees, cross-beams
above the shaken strutted trees,
        have no cause to object:
umbrellas & wind-breaks
        shield the blow
from the injury,
from justified anticipation
punch, flinch.
Controlled stagger.

§

Restive nothings, blush-pink,
beyond compare
        wriggle in periods/ dash
dash to clearance sales, span
the em of emptiness,
        pantropic pale pink
flushes the hydrocele,
        gapped frequencies
stabilized against a sample
emulate but fail to match.
No stakes detain or billets –
        Drink the fresh
air, it's market day or veterans',
        fresh-coined!
        Bull market! hot!
Rise before the vapour's rise,
get to the floor, quick
        get to the monitor/
occupy your chair, your place
Location work swivels.
        In galleries
perfect boxes sway at anchor.
In their chill cabinet, boxes smile.
In their memorial cupboard
        boxes stage horizons,
mistletoe at every apex.
        In the pretentious
prep halls, tanks, marble
counters,
sushi in lacquer boxes
        splashed with white dahlias,
white bird-lime
splashed on the Exchange steps.
The sticky mess after boiling.
        Lye. Lees. Whey.

§

Reduced to syrup
the cellular dramas face each other.
Such the progeny
Such united effort
folded back the wave.
The marl
obstructing upward growth/
volute intractability
keeps them matted.
Unlike us. Unlike us.
We get the first call.
We never attenuate. Like
this
encompasses. Every
time a different hunger
slubbed on an inside panel
making do with Indian corn.
Carry our baby things,
send ahead the cerements
crashed out
imposition
spaded in their wrinkled bag,
muddled into a fake
emblematic horizon:
Like they'll get their breaks
crossed with doves,
bleeding hearts & tendrils.
A fountain plays in a closed space,
a fountain out of blood.

§

Little question deliver your report
framed to thwart conclusions What to say:
unroll the expanse with one machined round.

The wanted knot starts to bulge
in your submission What's the angle?
Hell-for-leather tissue loses grip, the Douglas

fir needle underlay, slippery it
splays akimbo, ankle-deep blue sky was hung
to press order on co-ordinates

as if a blue sky would oppress.
Squeeze, little question,
the day, dust, your leader strip or brass crown

hammered, shocks the splash out of the ladle,
stet for life in a kelyphitic rim.
The button at this end clasps nothing,

how should it begin to, the kind of point it is,
except it underbrace by roll-out
swollen fruits, unclenched into life

faces a real self regard. Identifier
merges with its vanishing point.
The pale point calmer than calm is extending.

§

You'd miss though inappetently all converges,
veers to the presenting panel.
Crabbed mouth hardens, stitching up,

slashed over a pingpong, was it acorn squash?
You'd miss like a trawler net flapping,
dripping bags of curds dry –

receiver of a distracted consignment,
its plenum counting on your lapse to rise clear
headforemost, crashingly obvious,

Ceres tops off a corn exchange.
But there is no such thing as 'the' other,
a string from somewhere before (or time) blips,

nags & hitches. Feed into the hopper,
scan the read-out, your blind spot eyeing a full
blue shook free, magnified the field

belying perspective, belying the probable,
confounded the intense sharp share, edge-tools:
how the precision-engineered

decay, worked to the edge of nullity.
Park beside where your mouth sways clamped
amidst a clatter of wide shots.

§

Little question stretched tautly over
more brittle celluloid, a mimsy pink
abjuring Qs & As for Selection & Acquisition

burns its way through. If the sinkholes charge
chaotic spots on multipath, hard
waves ever tolerant of such enter-

taining smack up to white limits, let besmirch
so on fabric were their facings else
monotonous, the marble gulches

zoom Gulp! Gulp! to plastic milk-crates,
spindly buddleia/ They frame it, whose blank
misgivings, accidents & glitches,

the spin they once expended, bring a question
to such punctate leaves – Hod, hod.
Fear of resolution has commissioners

crowd each other's coats. Laugh their heads to
screw-grass. Stuff what you need
into their bag – & stumble, poor

excuse you are, full-front or lengthwise, never
middling, full throat of indifference.
A full trawl of what have you. Had.

§

No-one ever shall sleep in such a box, for the box
has no volume, blue receivers
clad its elevations, sky-accommodate,

tabling clouds, pioneer churches, street furniture,
raise amenities on sub-boxes, pigeon-
holed within its panels. Commerce

carries on behind mirrors. Insurance,
broking, pensions, gaming turned to probability,
keep tabs. The weather eye

never closes. A glassy tricorn what-the-hecks the
elevator's mountings, pyramidal eye
shoots mild damage. Garrisons

resistant to dream, clouds on their positive track,
dreams shamefully in plain sight
put to use. Shall I puncture such a box

a million times, shall this box like Tityus's liver
self-mend? containing the disorder
of the first-born, bug-ridden

first release resembling some idea of what might
have legs. Partiality strews reflective
roads, & what shall stride across now?

§

Distracted into a shadow broken across blinds,
across steps, moving nonetheless
spew-regular: empty as they may seem

the contents gain another neck, the grillroom.
From where does that voice hoot?
Stuff the voice. Written vote

shovels blind stuttering sequence for a history
already in the bag, fulfilled,
breaking as sea does over low rocks.

No transcendence, no order, no organic wheat.
Trash that little billet bears
lieutenant your moniker. Each wretched

signature dish strives to interest, a daisy-wheel
retread, an anti-womb to latch
full-onto. The novelties you would stack

had you all wrapped up from the start, sealing
through your fits its envelope,
intimate alien you are, convolute lover.

How natural to slip down a black wafer, more
full point. The blue sky smeared
with shit, alive with presentiments.

§

Submerged bridge. Consecutive as the flower
thus & thus, fed into its cocoon
metallic. Bladework arrayed for turbine

flash in sets. Chutes of eye-pebbles
bury the first link, first relay station.
Implore, implore because fantastically the OS

substrate feeds on spirit organics,
virgin's finger, apostolic ear, Saviour's eyelid
These fuel rods eat prayers & curses.

Invoke, invoke gardens jolt with sound chips,
taking a turn there in the evening
about a nose-hair, pearl, ruby, snot:

election wrapped about a relic consigns
deathly, too much at one abates.
Grey matter glittering like mica in the granite,

consistently you are the dream of every flower
held up, folds increase the meadow
studded with daisies & their aliases:

exposed by a kiss, played in a hand of spotted
bones. How shall I be more general.
Loss where is thy sample? Output slit.

Printed in the United States
22737LVS00006B/103-111

9 781876 857608